# ROUTLEDGE LIBRARY EDITIONS: LIBRARY AND INFORMATION SCIENCE

Volume 87

# SCI-TECH LIBRARIES OF THE FUTURE

# SCI-TECH LIBRARIES OF THE FUTURE

Edited by
CYNTHIA A. STEINKE

LONDON AND NEW YORK

First published in 1992 by The Haworth Press, Inc.

This edition first published in 2020
by Routledge
2 Park Square, Milton Park, Abingdon, Oxon OX14 4RN

and by Routledge
52 Vanderbilt Avenue, New York, NY 10017

*Routledge is an imprint of the Taylor & Francis Group, an informa business*

© 1992 The Haworth Press, Inc.

All rights reserved. No part of this book may be reprinted or reproduced or utilised in any form or by any electronic, mechanical, or other means, now known or hereafter invented, including photocopying and recording, or in any information storage or retrieval system, without permission in writing from the publishers.

*Trademark notice*: Product or corporate names may be trademarks or registered trademarks, and are used only for identification and explanation without intent to infringe.

*British Library Cataloguing in Publication Data*
A catalogue record for this book is available from the British Library

ISBN: 978-0-367-34616-4 (Set)
ISBN: 978-0-429-34352-0 (Set) (ebk)
ISBN: 978-0-367-37032-9 (Volume 87) (hbk)
ISBN: 978-0-367-37035-0 (Volume 87) (pbk)
ISBN: 978-0-429-35242-3 (Volume 87) (ebk)

**Publisher's Note**
The publisher has gone to great lengths to ensure the quality of this reprint but points out that some imperfections in the original copies may be apparent.

**Disclaimer**
The publisher has made every effort to trace copyright holders and would welcome correspondence from those they have been unable to trace.

# Sci-Tech Libraries of the Future

Cynthia A. Steinke
Editor

The Haworth Press, Inc.
New York • London • Norwood (Australia)

*Sci-Tech Libraries of the Future* has also been published as *Science & Technology Libraries*, Volume 12, Number 4 and Volume 13, Number 1 1992.

© 1992 by The Haworth Press, Inc. All rights reserved. No part of this work may be reproduced or utilized in any form or by any means, electronic or mechanical, including photocopying, microfilm and recording, or by any information storage and retrieval system, without permission in writing from the publisher. Printed in the United States of America.

The Haworth Press, Inc., 10 Alice Street, Binghamton, NY 13904-1580, USA

Library of Congress Cataloging-in-Publication Data

Sci-tech libraries of the future / Cynthia A. Steinke, editor.
    p. cm.
    "Also published as Science & technology libraries, volume 12, number 4 and volume 13, number 1, 1992"-T.p. verso.
    ISBN 1-56024-447-X (acid-free paper)
    1. Scientific libraries-United States. 2. Technical libraries-United States. I. Steinke, Cynthia A.
Z675.T3S385 1992
026.5'0973-dc20
                                                          93-3151
                                                             CIP

# SciTech Libraries of the Future

## CONTENTS

| | |
|---|---|
| **Foreword: Plus Ça Change...** <br> *Cynthia A. Steinke* | xi |
| **The Needs of Science and Technology** <br> *Robert M. Hayes* | 1 |
| Introduction | 1 |
| General Context | 2 |
| The Role of Information Access in the Stages of Scientific Research | 18 |
| The Role of Libraries and Librarians | 25 |
| Conclusion | 29 |
| **Managing the Sea Change in Science and Technology Libraries** <br> *Glenn L. Brudvig* | 33 |
| Introduction | 33 |
| Economics of Change | 35 |
| Science and Technology Libraries | 36 |
| Leadership and the Change Process | 38 |
| Staff and the Change Process | 40 |
| The Learning Organization | 41 |
| Building a Vision of the Future | 42 |
| Quality Management | 43 |
| Conclusion | 46 |

**Scientific and Technical Librarians: Leaders of the 21st Century**    49
    *Barbara Lockett*

The Twenty-First Century Environment    50
Leadership    55

**Leadership in Science-Engineering Libraries: Considerations and Realities for the Future**    65
    *Donald G. Frank*

Introduction    65
The Science-Engineering Library    66
The General Nature of Leadership    67
Leadership: Role, Responsibilities, and Skills for the Future    68
Libraries in Transition: Challenges for Leaders    73
Concluding Remarks    75

**Education and Recruitment of Science and Engineering Librarians**    77
    *Crit Stuart*
    *Miriam A. Drake*

How Sci/Tech People Work    77
Current Situation    78
Education    80
Recruitment    81
Alternatives    82
Conclusion    85

**Through a Kaleidoscope Darkly**    89
    *Karen Hunter*

Generalities    89
Market Signals    91
Technology-Push    93
Future Action    95

Library Buildings: Their Current State and Future
   Development ............................................................ 97
      *Jay K. Lucker*

Introduction .................................................................. 97
Twentieth Century Achievements ................................. 98
Trends in Research Library Building Design .............. 100
Storage Buildings ....................................................... 102
Shortcomings and Problems ....................................... 104
The Near Future .......................................................... 106
The Role of the Research Library in the 21st Century ... 107
Academic Library Buildings in the 21st Century ....... 108
The New Research Library ......................................... 110

The Future of University Science and Technology
   Libraries: Implications of Increasing Interdisciplinarity .. 111
      *Julie M. Hurd*

What Is Interdisciplinarity? ........................................ 112
Interdisciplinary Research and Technology Transfer .. 114
Measures of Interdisciplinarity .................................... 115
Consequences of Interdisciplinarity ............................ 119
Implications for University Science and Technology
   Libraries .................................................................. 120

Knowledge Diffusion and U.S. Government Technology
   Policy: Issues and Opportunities for Sci/Tech Librarians .. 127
      *Thomas E. Pinelli*
      *Rebecca O. Barclay*
      *Stan Hannah*
      *Barbara Lawrence*
      *John M. Kennedy*

Introduction .................................................................. 128
Diffusing the Results of Federally Funded R&D ........ 132
U.S. Government Technology Policy and Knowledge
   Diffusion ................................................................. 134
Concluding Remarks ................................................... 145

Collection Development vs. Access in Academic Science
Libraries 151
*Gary Wiggins*

Which Life Science Journals Will Constitute the Locally
Sustainable Core Collection of the 1990s and Which
Will Become "Fax-Access" Only? Predictions Based
on Citation and Price Patterns 1979-1989 167
*Tony Stankus*
*Carolyn V. Mills*

The Promise of Fax 168
Letting Local Library Collections Focus on What
  Is Actually Read 169
Factors Used in Defining the Locally Sustainable Core
  Collection 170
Laying Out the Discussion of Results 174
Specialty-by-Specialty Results 176
Will Fax Mean the Death of Low-Citation-Rating
  and/or Overly Expensive Print Journals? 203
Could Fax Data Join Citation Data in Reforming Journals? 204

A Comparison of Science Related Document Delivery
Services 209
*Robert T. McFarland*

Introduction 209
Pilot Project 210
Vendor Analysis 212
Methodology 212
Results 216
Discussion 224
Conclusions 227

# Foreword:
# Plus Ça Change...

We are now at a time of true revolution in the communication of scientific information.[1] Technology is making the difference, transforming the process of knowledge delivery and acquisitons, forcing users to consider new channels of scholarly communication, challenging the viability of the research library. The pace of change in science, in communications and computers is so rapid that if librarians do not aggressively seek to understand the changes and become central to the knowledge formation and transfer process, contributing our skills with information handling, we well may be left in the dust, to never catch up.

These are heady and difficult times in science libraries. As we look to the technological applications to enhance speed of access to information and to solve the spiraling costs of printed publications, we are also reminded that the research library continues to carry the basic role of preserving the record of the past as well as access to these preserved records. Libraries face internal tensions between the investment in acquiring and preserving and the continuing operating expense in accessing resources from offsite. The choices are not always obvious.[2]

"Plus ça change, plus c'est la meme chose" may have been a realistic predictor in the past, but I see a different picture for the future. Change will be so dramatic and will occur more rapidly than any of us have experienced in the past. It is critical to the survival of the sci-tech library that we work with scientists and engineers to understand their changing information needs and to participate in the planning and development of new information systems.

The future will not be the same. What will it be like? Who will be the key players? To secure some of the answers, we have called upon leaders of sci-tech libraries to reflect on their years in the profession

© 1992 by The Haworth Press, Inc. All rights reserved.

and to predict the future in whatever way they chose. The assignment was to envision how the sci-tech library will look ten years out. Each author offers his/her best guess, as we struggle to understand and to control the future directions of sci-tech libraries.

\* \* \*

It is a special honor to lead off this volume with a paper by Dr. Robert M. Hayes, Professor Emeritus and former Dean of the Graduate School of Library and Information Science, UCLA. Dr. Hayes presents an in-depth analysis of the information needs of science and engineering and the future development of electronic means to meet these needs.

Hayes describes the sci-tech information required to support education, to serve research and its applications, government, and public policy decision making. His paper contrasts the differing patterns of scientific research and the application of results among the disciplines. His vision of the future pays considerable attention to the effects of information technologies with special emphasis on the increasing importance of digitized imaging as a medium of communication.

These critical information needs, the changing patterns in communicating behavior and the developing technologies, demand new forms of electronic management and delivery of information. The potential contribution for the sci-tech library in support of the information process is complex and calls for new ways of thinking.

The promise of information technology notwithstanding, Dr. Hayes cautions us to remember that the basic role of research libraries is to preserve the record of the past. "All of the other information industries and activities have only the objective of immediate distribution." Additionally, the responsibility of the library is to provide access to these preserved records. With the advent of the electronic media, "... the library faces difficult choices between incurring a capital investment in acquiring and preserving and incurring continuing operating expenses in access from elsewhere...."

He makes it clear that the potential role for the librarian is "much broader than the library itself." Our skills and commitment provide the professional with a solid base to fulfill a wide range of functions in the context of electronic information. Dr. Hayes outlines the functions and challenges these changes present to us in meeting the unrelenting expansion of sci-tech information and the researcher's need to have immediate access to it.

Brudvig, Lockett, and Frank focus on the leadership needed to bring sci-tech libraries successfully into the future world. Brudvig presents readers with a challenging ride into the "sea change" that may well transform sci-tech libraries into those existing only in a computer, the electronic or virtual library. ("Sea change" as defined by Webster's Third is a marked transformation into something richer and finer.) These changes, brought on by new technologies, are coming too fast, are too complex and disruptive for traditional leadership methods to be effective. This process of change is accelerating at a rate faster than what we experienced with the automation of recent years, and demands that we re-examine not only the way we operate libraries, but re-examine the basic ways we provide information. The changes almost defy prediction, and thus demand that leaders be knowledgeable, agile and focused more on the design of flexible organizations and less on their operation.

The sci-tech literature will continue to grow, but the sci-tech library that continues to be dependent on costly print journals may well become an institutional overhead to be replaced. Technology is the only solution to the economic dilemma of sci-tech libraries. The journal is a natural target for full-text retrieval. Imaging and high speed transmission will replace photography, FAX, and (blessedly!) microfilm.

Yet, sci-tech libraries face the paradox that the technologically sophisticated user is still in the minority; most users are still bound to printed books and journals. Comfortable behavior patterns are not easily abandoned. The old and the new will co-exist for years to come and leaders must be keenly aware of the changing information needs and expectations of their users, or users will seek their own solutions!

In this rapid sea of change, leaders of sci-tech libraries cannot be knowledgeable in all areas. They must see the broad patterns, become designers and architects, teachers, coaches and mentors–instead of bosses. Their energies need to be concentrated on building shared visions in order to develop a "learning organization" that promotes change, one based on the needs of customers and which continually strives for excellence and quality.

Lockett, in her predictions for the future, looks first at the high-change environment of higher education–scientific research itself–and the changing patterns of scientific and technical communication that will impact on the leadership of tomorrow.

Computers have revolutionized the way science is conducted, scientists now communicating via supercomputers and high-speed telecommunication systems. The information explosion will continue. The formats in which information is communicated will increasingly diversify. Electronic formats will comprise a larger portion of the whole, but the print version will not disappear. For librarians, it is critical that we work with the scientists in order to understand the way they "do" science and the way they use the new communication systems.

Lockett speculates that library organizations will become more fluid and collaborative. Leadership will be a distributed function. Librarians will be defined more by what they do, rather than where they work–moving out of the library to become partners with researchers, offering the benefit of a long tradition and experience in the interpretation and management of information.

The greatest challenge for libraries in the 1990s will be to identify ways to collaborate with other influence groups in developing networks that will enhance the librarian's role in providing a wide range of electronically based information services. Change for libraries will be greater and the pace more rapid. But in Lockett's view "we will not need . . . a new breed of superlibrarian in the 21st century. Leaders will still be influencing people . . . and while our environments . . . will continue to shift rapidly, the most stable part of the system and that on which we exert our influence will remain human."

Frank's article details the *attributes* necessary for effective leadership in the sci-tech library that will survive in the future. Most of these qualities are important for successful leadership in *all* libraries, but especially critical for the sci-tech library where immediacy of access to appropriate resources is essential.

The dynamic environment of the sci-tech library calls for leadership that is proactive. These leaders will need: creativity and vision to anticipate the future and to cause organizational change to meet the changing patterns of scientific scholarly communication; the budgetary realities; the issue of access vs ownership; and to anticipate the impact of information technologies. These will be the attributes necessary to meet the changing and increasingly sophisticated information seeking behavior of scientists and engineers.

Drake and Stuart are concerned with the quality of information services provided to the scientific enterprise when sci-tech libraries must rely on information professionals with little or no training in the sciences. The recruitment pool has never been strong; it shows no signs of improving.

Studies of information seeking behavior of scientists and engineers show that librarians are not the first choice for consultation when information is needed. Scientists generally presume that if the librarian has no grounding in the sciences there is not going to be any personal knowledge base to aid the researcher and no common frame of reference. The individual involved in research, therefore, is going to acquire information elsewhere.

Increasingly, technology is making it possible for scientists to access information without libraries. If libraries and librarians are to play vital roles in R & D and the associated information transfer process, they must change–or they indeed may disappear.

Effective recruitment of professionals is a key. It means changing library school education, training on the job, increasing salaries, and improving the image of librarians. Drake and Stuart discuss these alternatives.

U.S. competitiveness and productivity can be improved with more effective information services. Information professionals can be key agents in the information transfer process, but satisfying the information needs of customers requires keen understanding of the problem and how the information is to be used in the individual's work. Drake and Stuart contend that to achieve this we must recruit people with science and engineering backgrounds into the information profession.

Hunter offers a ten-year prediction for changes in sci-tech libraries generally, and for sci-tech publishers in particular. She describes the forces of technology in the change process.

Six major elements form the scenario she envisions: things will get worse before they get better; scientists will not go out of their way to assist libraries or publishers; there will be new electronic entrants in the scientific communication arena; libraries will be squeezed even farther; publishers will be squeezed as well–and the scientists will emerge as the winners!

In her future world, not all publishers or libraries will survive, but the flexible innovative publisher will and, indeed, may flourish.

Lucker discusses trends in research library buildings, declaring his strong bias that the sci-tech library of the future will continue as a physical space–"with real books and real people inside." While there will be many changes in the ways people acquire and use information, "buildings housing physical collections with convenient spaces for users to consult those collections, . . . for self-education and discovery outside the classroom and laboratory will continue to be important elements."

He believes that scholars will continue to use print materials–publication on paper will increase rather than decrease and scholars will depend upon libraries to acquire, preserve, and provide access. Libraries also will be the source of information about new technologies and the access points to non-print materials outside the immediate holdings.

Lucker describes the achievements in academic and research library buildings constructed or added to in the past five decades of 1950-1990–open stack arrangement; reduction in size and number of large, high-ceilinged reading rooms; large areas for public services; and the increasing need to accommodate the proliferation of new information formats. He speaks to the expansion and growth of library storage facilities. He acknowledges the shortcomings of these trends as well: site limitations for expansion; physical and mechanical problems; and lack of flexibility for relocation of functions with buildings.

Lucker concludes his discussion with a picture of the research library in the 21st century. "His" library will continue to be a blend of collections of printed information, a place for study, exchange of ideas, and reflection, as well as access to a wide range of technology-based services and networks. As we plan for new facilities or adapt existing ones for future generations, responsiveness to trends coming from higher education and technologies must be recognized. The pace of change will require great flexibility in the way libraries organize themselves and utilize their resources to meet user needs.

Among the challenges facing sci-tech libraries in providing effective information services to scientists, Hurd sees the increasing interdisciplinarity of scientific research. The emergence of interdisciplinarity fields since World War II is the result of universities, federal agencies, and corporations seeking to find solutions to societal problems, environmental, and health care issues. Examples of such areas include materials science, molecular biology, bioengineering, environmental chemistry, and the intriguing field of "environmental mathematics." According to a recent report in *The Chronicle for Higher Education*, environmental mathematics is the attempt to get mathematicians to connect again with the natural world, conducting investigations of the pollution caused by idling auto engines, the decline in nesting sites for the spotted owl or the settling of sulfur dioxide in the human lung.

Hurd's paper examines the development of this interdisciplinarity phenomena and the implications for sci-tech library collections and services. She describes the lack of agreement on basic terminology, the impact of technology transfer, and most importantly, the changing information needs from those of twenty years ago when research projects were more easily contained within the boundaries of single, recognized disciplines–and the associated information resources organized on a discipline-based model.

If scientific research continues to experience shifting disciplinary boundaries, Hurd sees fundamental changes in the entire university infrastructure to which university library organizations patterns will have to respond. Centralization of library resources, less duplication of costly journals, abstracts, and indexing services are already taking place. Hurd suggests other possibilities for collections and services to assist the growing number of interdisciplinary researchers.

Pinelli and his co-authors offer a view of information dissemination changes needed in the federal sector. This paper discusses the relationship between the development and application of a federal technical policy and the effective diffusion of the results of federally funded R & D.

Recent federal technical policy initiatives designed to improve, nurture, and stimulate technological innovation to strengthen economic competitiveness of the U. S. requires the adoption of a "knowledge diffusion model" that prescribes "active" intervention between the producers of information, transfer agents, and users of technical information. This knowledge diffusion model is predicated on the development of interpersonal communication linkages (as opposed to dissemination and access activities), including the creation of user-oriented products and services.

Convincing evidence exists that the U. S. lacks effective knowledge transfer of federally sponsored R & D research results. Reasons for this include the passivity of sci-tech librarians. Most sci-tech information centers follow a model tied to the information artifact, providing documents instead of supplying information. Sci-tech libraries must become strategic information resources in the STI transfer process, emphasizing innovative, value-added services tailored to meet the individual needs of each user group.

Pinelli and colleagues emphasize that U. S. technology policy must be based on the belief that the production, transfer, and use of STI is inextricably linked to successful technological innovations; if the U. S. is to remain competitive in the global market place in the 1990s and beyond. That process of innovation is best served by a "knowledge diffusion" model.

Wiggins reflects that "collection development in academic science libraries has bordered on the chaotic in recent years." This is as a result of our "failure to adequately define cooperative collection development and access, and in part from the lack of a coherent plan for integrating machine-readable sources into our collecting profiles." While significant changes in the scholarly information process have turned our attention to the promises of accessing information rather than dependence on the amassing of costly on-site collections, it must be recognized that published material will continue to be of utmost concern to research faculty as we work our way through the last decade of the 21st century.

Wiggins' paper discusses the issues that sci-tech librarians must consider in making the transition from collections that are primarily print-based to resources substantially in electronic format–in particular, the question of access to serials vs their on-site ownership. He offers some ground rules which must be accepted by the library before order can be achieved in collection development. He suggests that our definition of access must be enlarged to include all document delivery techniques for easy delivery of information from the location in which it is held to the user. His paper discusses a number of existing delivery services. More futuristic is his scheme to develop a database of document images--a library of electronic articles tailored to the needs of a particular clientele. Wiggins claims that the science library community is ready to make a fundamental change in collecting policies--away from exclusive collecting of journal *volumes* to a more flexible collecting profile that allows the permanent addition to collections of individual *articles* from journals not locally held. To get from here to there, Wiggins identifies several crucial steps: libraries and publishers must confront and solve the copyright questions associated with this material, librarians must enlist the support of users in the design of such a local document archive and indexing system, and work closely with the scientific publishers to reassess the values and costs in scholarly publishing, including this concept of the journal article as a marketable unit.

The promise of FAX. How will it affect what is held locally? Author Stankus speculates on the meaning of FAX for subscription policies. While some journals of high demand will always be locally held, subscriptions to others will likely continue only as long as subscribing to them is cheaper than repeatedly requesting FAX copies. Librarians have come to realize that it is cheaper to give free fax delivery of individual articles to their faculty than to purchase and maintain voluminous and expensive titles. With the advent of document delivery via licensed fax delivery services, librarians will have much more freedom to decide which journals to hold locally, which subscriptions will be accessed from remote collections (or databases) on a pay-as-you-go-basis. Stankus provides some prediction as to which titles these are likely to be.

Using long-term citation data from 1979-1989, Stankus examines the life science literature to support his thesis. This material is complex and expensive; its management relevant to many academic, medical, and corporate biotech special library collections. Speciality by speciality, from biochemistry to pharmacology, he examines impact factors, cost, and "citation by the leading journal" data of eleven major areas of the life sciences, in predicting their fate.

FAX is fast; it can be made free of legal worry rather easily; it is cheap and is a "natural" in this electronic age. Offering liberation to science libraries from the expensive, lesser-used titles, Stankus also suggests that it will provide publishers a way to determine from sales statistics of individual articles which authors and/or laboratories are generating readers and royalty income.

Complementing the Stankus paper and seeking an answer to the dilemma of rising costs and diminishing resources for library materials, McFarland conducted a comparison testing of document delivery services in lieu of local holdings. Using the Chemical Abstracts Document Delivery Service and nine commercial science related document delivery vendors, this pilot project compares a number of service related parameters. The aim of this study is to assist science librarians in selecting vendors that best meet the needs of users in disciplines of biology, chemistry, earth sciences, math, and engineering.

To facilitate the vendor selection process, McFarland compares a number of publisher service parameters and policies. Comparables included in his investigation include: coverage, methods and hours documents can be requested, basic services, costs, fill rates, turn-around time, reliability of copyright clearance, and special services.

Recognizing that a single vendor is unlikely able to satisfy all requests, the study assists the librarian in identifying primary and secondary vendors which together would satisfy a high percentage of requests. The author further acknowledges that reliance on a conventional ILL service will continue to be necessary. McFarland adds a concluding cautionary note that while "document delivery has been around a number of years in one form or another, the advent of the plain paper FAX machine has dramatically facilitated the ease with which documents can be transferred, necessitating librarians to exercise greater caution than ever to honor copyright compliance. If abuse becomes evident, FAX access and document delivery by any mode will be denied." A wise admonition.

\* \* \*

Change will affect all areas of the scientific process: the way in which research is conducted, communicated, transferred, stored, and delivered. No player will escape the impact of these changes: researcher, librarian, information manager, publisher, user. It is vital that the sci-tech library respond to these changes, that science librarians work closely with scientists, engineers, publishers, vendors, and users, cooperating and collaborating to link resources and users of information, to plan and develop effective information systems that provide information conveniently and cost effectively.

*Cynthia A. Steinke*
*Editor*

## REFERENCES

1. Report of the APS Task Force on Electronic Information Systems. American Physical Society. *Bulletin*. 36(4), April, 1991, p. 1125.
2. See Hayes article, " The Needs of Science and Technology,": p. 1.

# The Needs of Science and Technology

Robert M. Hayes

## INTRODUCTION

This paper discusses the needs for scientific and technical information in support of research and education, engineering design and manufacture, government and public policy decision-making. It will first set a context by identifying issues of current importance in the delivery of scientific and technical information–changes in patterns of research and application, the increasing importance of computer-based information in the process of research and of application, the emergence of electronic forms for information delivery, the resulting changes in the very pattern of communication of the results of research, the development of new institutional means for management and delivery of information.

The paper examines the critical stages in the research process and in translation of the results of research into application, identifying the different and changing roles of information in each. It will illustrate with specific research programs drawn from those current priorities identified by the National Science Foundation and the National Institutes of Health which emphasize the integration of

---

Robert M. Hayes is Professor Emeritus, having retired after fifteen years of service as Dean of GSLIS at UCLA. Dr. Hayes received the PhD in 1952 in Mathematics from UCLA. From 1949 until he joined the faculty of GSLIS/UCLA in 1964, Dr. Hayes worked in government and industry, and founded a small consulting and research company, Advanced Information Systems. In 1969, Mr. Joseph Becker and Dr. Hayes formed Becker & Hayes, Inc. of which Dr. Hayes was Vice-President until becoming Dean of GSLIS/UCLA in 1974.

This paper was originally presented by invitation to the 10th International Seminar held at Kanazawa Institute of Technology Library Center, Nonoichi Ishikawa, Japan, June 3-5, 1991.

© 1992 by The Haworth Press, Inc. All rights reserved.

information into the research process; among them, special emphasis will be given to those that embody the use of digitized images because of the current and future significance they have throughout the range of scientific and technological disciplines.

The paper concludes by discussing the implications for the research library community of these changes in use of information in scientific research and technology. The roles of the library in support of science and technology will be contrasted with those in the arts and humanities; differences among scientific disciplines themselves in the use of library-based information services will be identified, and they will be contrasted with those of more practical disciplines that apply the results of research or that make public policy about them. Developments in libraries that implement those roles will be identified–including inter-library networks, electronic means for access to information and for publication, and inter-mediation in use of information resources. Specific attention will again be given to digitized images, with emphasis on the potential role of the research library in management of these forms of research information.

## *GENERAL CONTEXT*

The general context for such review is a "new era" in which we are seeing significant changes in patterns of research and the emergence of electronic means for information access and distribution. I will use a specific form of information, digital imaging, as a means for illustrating the range of issues involved because of its intrinsic importance and the extent to which it exemplifies the issues.

### *Differing Patterns of Research and in Application of Its Results*

There are substantial differences in needs for information across the several disciplines–natural science, social science, humanities, and professions–and, for each, across the functions in research and graduate education, undergraduate education, development and application, and public policy decision making. I will comment on the broad range of the two dimensions, discipline and function, but my primary focus will be on the natural sciences (the physical and biological sciences) and the functions in research and graduate education that are central to the mission of the major research university.

*Differences among the disciplines.* As a starting point, then, I want to comment on differences among all academic disciplines in roles of information access in support of research and graduate education. In doing so, I am not attempting to preempt the separate discussion of the needs of humanists and historians, but I do want to set a large frame of reference in which to examine differences among disciplines and functions. I identify five reasons to need access to information in support of research and graduate education:

1. information and, especially, the records containing it are themselves the focus of the research;
2. information contains data needed in the research;
3. information provides an audit trail documenting the progress of research;
4. information provides communication about current results;
5. information results from and embodies the processes of data acquisition, analysis, and presentation.

With respect to the first two of those reasons, the natural sciences and the professions of engineering and medicine differ dramatically from the humanities, social sciences, and other professions. As a generality, I think one can say that, by their very nature, the humanists and the social scientists absolutely require access to the records of the past for the basic raw material of their research. In literature and art, those records are frequently the very substance of the research; in history and economics, they are the source of the primary information on which the research depends; in anthropology and archeology, they provide the crucial evidence. For the profession of law, they are the absolute source of data. There are some natural scientists, taxonomists in particular, that do depend centrally on analysis of data from prior records and comparison both among them and with newly acquired data; those are the exceptions, though. In general, natural scientists are focused on the acquisition of new data rather than the analysis of existing records. For them, the records of the past are peripheral to research; at most they turn to the prior record for data to compare with that being currently acquired. Research for the professions of engineering and medicine is essentially of the same character as that in the natural sciences; practice in those professions, though, is as we will see quite different.

Across all disciplines, of course, the records of the past provide the audit trail that documents the progress of research. This role of information access is built into the entire process of scholarship, embodied in the traditions of citation and providing the basis for recognition of the credit for first discovery of new concepts. The natural scientists are as scholarly in that respect as any academic.

The role of personal communication in information access appears to be much more important to research in the natural sciences than it is in the humanities and social sciences. For the scientist, speed of communication is crucial since the results obtained by one colleague immediately influence the work of others with similar foci of research. This is reflected in the historic importance of preprints, telephone, and now electronic communication to those sciences. It is shown in the extent to which research teams are commonplace in the natural sciences and in the "invisible colleges," made up of groups of scientists throughout the world that collaborate with each other even while competing. It is exemplified by the prevalence of multiple authorship of scientific articles. Are there differences among the disciplines of the natural sciences in the importance of this reason for information access? Apparently not. Across the board, they all seem to partake of the same pattern. In contrast, the humanities and social scientists appear to be less dependent upon immediacy in communication. They tend to do research as individuals rather than as teams, multiple authorship being relatively rare.

It is in the fifth reason for information access that the greatest difference arises between the natural sciences and the humanities, with the social sciences occupying a middle ground. As I have already stated, the natural scientists are focused on the acquisition of new data and, in consequence, on the analysis of them for purposes of data reduction and for derivation of underlying patterns from them. To an extent, this is a result of the essentially quantitative nature of the data, which makes computation and the use of mathematical models necessary. In contrast, the humanists and, to a lesser extent, the social scientists deal with more qualitative data for which measurement, computation, and mathematical models have a dramatically different character.

*Differences across the functions.* Turning now to the other dimension, I will discuss five sets of functions: (1) research and graduate education, (2) undergraduate education, (3) professional practice, (4) engineering development and commercial application, and (5) public policy decision making. In discussing the differences among disciplines, I have specifically focused on the first of these, research and graduate education, since that is where those differences are most evident; for the other four functions the differences arise less from the nature of the discipline and more from that of the function.

Access to existing, published information ought to be crucial to undergraduate education. The facts are, though, that the amount of material needed to support this function is really quite limited as is, unfortunately, the extent to which this level of instruction generally requires that the student learn the processes in access to recorded information. I wish it were otherwise.

Preparation for professional practice is, in the United States, at the graduate level in virtually all fields. As a result there is usually thorough indoctrination into the importance of use of the most current information. For medicine, this is reflected in the vital role played by the National Library of Medicine in the implementation of library services, the creation of the Regional Medical Library Network, the support given to the development of medical informatics. For library and information science, it is the very substance of concern. For law, it is the essential ingredient of practice. For other professions such as management, social welfare, architecture, education, etc., there is general recognition of the importance of information access.

Access to existing, published information also ought to be crucial to engineering development and commercial application. The amount of information available and useful in support of this function is immense, and the tools for access to it, as I will be discussing, are available and powerful. The kinds of information range from technical to economic, from scientific to marketing, from basic research to public policy, from numerical to textual. All of them are potentially of value and even of necessity in bringing scientific and technological results to the service of society. The facts are, though, that despite all of the investment that has been made in the tools for information access, the level of use across all industries is substantially less than it ought to be if we are to have maximum productivity.

The same situation exists with respect to public policy. Increasingly, our society must deal with the effects of scientific and technological development. To some extent, the political process does provide means to draw on relevant published scientific, technical, economic, and social information. In the United States, we have the Congressional Research Service, the Office of Technology Assessment, the National Library of Medicine, and the National Agricultural Library that serve our political apparatus well in assuring access to such information. Even at state and local government levels, there are counterparts of such agencies in state and community public libraries. Again, though, the facts are that the level of use of information resources in public policy decision making is probably less than it should be.

*The Effects of the Information Technologies*

The information technologies–the computer, its associated means for storage and display, and telecommunications–have had a truly revolutionary effect upon research in every field. The computer has dramatically changed the means for word processing; it is the crucial tool for computation; it plays an increasingly important role for control in data acquisition; it provides the means for image processing; and it has changed the very nature of telecommunication. The table (see Table 1) on the following page summarizes representative data about computer equipment at different levels of processing capability and the uses to which they typically are put.

To an extent, the differences among disciplines are reflected in the relative emphases given to the various uses of computers by researchers by each of the groups of academics.

Table 1. Representative Data for Different Levels of Computers.

| COMPUTER TYPE | TYPICAL CONFIGURATION | TYPICAL APPLICATIONS | EXAMPLES |
|---|---|---|---|
| Microcomputers | Microprocessor based<br>Single tasking, user<br>< 100 Mbytes harddisk<br>< 2 Mbytes memory<br>< 10 MIPS<br>$1K - $10K | Word-processing<br>Spreadsheets<br>Network access<br>Personal databases | IBM PC/AT, PS/2<br>Macintosh |
| Super-micros<br>&<br>Workstations | Micro-processor based<br>Multitasking<br>Limited number users<br>Windowed environment<br>Diskless to 1 Gbyte<br>4 - 64 Mbytes memory<br>2 - 25 MIPS<br>$5K - $100K | CAD/CAM<br>CASE<br>Software development<br>Graphics<br>Desktop publishing | SUN 3/50<br>IBM RS/6000<br>DG AViiON<br>NeXT<br>SPARCstations |
| Minicomputers<br>&<br>Super-minis | Multitasking<br>Multiuser, but < 250<br>< 10 Gbytes<br>< 64 Mbytes memory<br>< 50 MIPS<br>$100K - $1M | Time sharing<br>Network server<br>Small businesses | Sun File Servers<br>Tandem Nonstop<br>IBM System 38<br>DEC VAX |
| Mainframe | Multitasking<br>Multiuser (1000+)<br>< 100+ Gbytes<br>< 1+ Gbytes memory<br>< 100+ MIPS<br>$1M to $10M | Large-scale MIS<br>Transaction process<br>Large databases<br>Large batch process | IBM 4381, 3090<br>Tandem Cyclone<br>Amdahl 5995<br>Hitachi EX |
| Supercomputers | Vector processing<br>100+ Gbytes<br>1+ Gbytes of memory<br>100+ MIPS<br>Up to $20M | Image processing<br>Vector processing<br>Simulation modeling<br>Real-time animation | Cray X/MP<br>NEC SX-3 |

*Word processing.* The ACLS survey of scholars' views in 1986 showed that among the humanists and social scientists the great preponderance of computer use was for word processing, maintaining note files, preparing tests, and compiling bibliographies. All other types of use were of substantially less importance. Of course, word processing is as valuable a tool for the natural scientist in preparation of manuscripts as it is for the humanist or social scientist.

*Computing.* But for the natural scientist today, research would be impossible without the computer's ability to perform mathematical calculations; statistical analyses have been the overwhelmingly important uses. Since the advent of the digital computer, the practice of scientific research has increasingly relied on use of numerical analysis of measured and synthetic data. Computational predictions and analyses are typically of interest in the fields of atmospheric and geophysical research, biology and molecular biology, computational and empirical chemistry, computer and engineering, mathematics, medical research, theoretical and applied physics. The common element is the very large amounts of data generated on a regular basis and the necessity to comprehend the numerical description as a complete entity. Literally, the need is to get the "big picture" that provides a lucid, intuitive, and global grasp of the data as it evolves. Mathematical and statistical analysis have provided the fundamental tools for getting that big picture.

*Digitized imaging.* While getting the "big picture" may be based on mathematical modeling and data analysis, the great step forward today is the recognition that conceptualization is even more effective if supported by real pictures. The term visualization has been applied to this process. It involves comprehending large amounts of structurally complex, multidimensional and time-dependent data through the use of visual images. In some contexts, the data represent familiar things; for others, they are things that cannot be seen by the naked eye even though they may be real; and for others, they are purely conceptual--algorithmic, mathematical and logical constructs.

As a result, the most dramatic use of computers in research and practice today is for "digital imaging." Based on data from *Science Citation Index*, from 1965 through 1984 the number of published articles concerned with "imaging" essentially doubled during each five-year period but within the most recent five year period, it increased ten-fold! And that rate of increase continues today.

Parenthetically, it is worth noting that digitized imaging and the management of the resulting files has significance to the practical world of business as well as to academic research. It is estimated that today the U.S. market for electronic image management to handle the flood of commercial documents is worth about $250 million, with about 1,500 installations, but that it will expand at much more than a 35% compounded annual rate of growth. The forecast is that by 1995 the market will be at $5.8 billion, with about 30,000 installations. This means that there will be a substantial commercial base upon which digital imaging technologies can experience economies of scale so that the costs for academic uses and for libraries can be less. The situation is comparable to the role that the consumer market for compact disks has played in making CD-ROM economic.

I will be using digital imaging to illustrate specifics on the role of information access in scientific and technological research, so I would like briefly to summarize the hardware and software technologies that are important to the creation, management, and use of digitized images. First, the hardware:

*Scanners* are the means for creating digitized images from sources external to the computer itself; they range from simple hand-held scanners to those in satellites and medical equipment, to those in nuclear accelerators. *Storage* of scanned data or of images generated by algorithms is of course necessary for all subsequent processing. For a typical 8-1/2" by 11" page, scanned at say 300 lines per inch, that involves storage of about a mega-byte of data for a pure black and white image; for typical text pages, the data are so redundant (with large areas of white space, for example), that they can be compressed, usually by a factor of ten; but for gray-scale or color, the storage requirements are substantially greater. Even with compression, though, the means for storage of any significant number of images must have very high capacities. Fortunately, both magnetic and optical means for storage are now readily available with capacities completely consistent with the needs in image storage. CD-ROM optical disks in particular provide capacities between 500 and 1000 mega-bytes, sufficient to store as many as 10,000 compressed images.

*Processing* of image data requires computing capacities of a high order. Indeed, primary among the rationales for development of super-computers was the need for that level of computing power. However, we are beginning to see speeds, internal storage capacities, and functional capabilities at the microcomputer level that make it possible to consider use of them for a large range of image processing applications. *Display* of image data requires exceptional resolution but again the technology has advanced so far so rapidly that today we have screens that provide a quality approaching that of the printed page, with truly remarkable mixes of color.

Finally, *communication* of digitized images, given the number of bytes required and the frequency with which images may be generated, requires truly exceptional bandwidth. Unfortunately, while the technology is now available to provide that kind of capacity, making it available requires an infrastructure that many developing countries and even some highly industrialized countries do not have. In fact, of all the technologies needed for utilizing digitized images, communication may well be the one which poses the greatest problems, since it requires a national investment, whereas all of the others require only local institutional investment.

Now, turning to the software:

*Interfaces* are the means by which the user may interact with the computer in the use of digitized images. Increasingly, we have seen the use of GUI (graphical user interfaces), pioneered by APPLE computer but now embodied in WINDOWS for use with IBM personal computers; the GUI exemplify the role of interfaces at the simplest level. At more complex levels, we see capabilities to manipulate images, combine them, navigate through them. *Algorithmic production*, exemplified by CAD/CAM, for example, is a set of software that provides means to generate images from specifications.

*Scene analysis* is a process in utilizing a succession of images that provide a continuity in representation of an object or an event. The classical example, of course, would be a "scene" in a motion picture–a succession of frames taken from a single camera setting; others might arise in the images generated in a "CAT-scan" of the human body or in the frames in a succession of satellite images. The tasks in scene analysis are first, to identify when a succession of images are related as a scene and, second, to manipulate the set of images constituting a scene as an entity.

*Spectral analysis* is a set of processes for deriving characterizing parameters for an individual image and as the starting point for identifying components of the image–the first stage in *pattern recognition*. *Image enhancement* is an example of pattern recognition, in which areas of the image are examined and modified to bring out details, correct for problems (in exposure, for example), and identify and highlight identified patterns. *Optical character recognition* is the most well developed capability for pattern recognition, permitting the computer to identify typewritten and printed characters.

*Acquisition of data.* In August 1990, the Council on Library Resources submitted a report to the National Science Foundation on *Communications in Support of Science and Technology.* In that report, Donald Langenberg discussed Information Technology and the Conduct of Research: The User's View. He commented on the use of technology in control of experiments and in the generation, acquisition and storage of data. He paid specific attention to medical scanners and superconducting-supercolliding scanners.

*Large-Scale simulations.* In that same report, Kenneth King stated that the major future challenge will lie in building complex multi-dimensional, multi-media simulations. Pointing out that computing requirements are related to the kinds of objectives, he estimated that it takes 1 mip ( million instructions per second) to control words, 100 mips to control pictures and sound, 1000 mips for artificial intelligence, and $10^{12}$ mips to simulate physical systems in real time.

## The Changing Means for Communication and Information Access

The CLR report was commissioned by NSF to explore the future form of scientific communication. How was it integrated with the research process? What was its role in maintaining the historical record–the "audit trail" of the progress of research? Could electronics solve the problems with escalating costs of scientific publication? What were the effects of various electronic alternatives? What were the characteristics of scientific communication–its forms, from personal to external, the available options, the relationship between form and utility?

In his summary, Martin Cummings reviewed the background for the report's conclusions, referring to the influence of new technologies and their use as means for improving the existing information infrastructure–science libraries, scientific publishing, computers and networks, and the effects of new technology on users.

*The potential represented by electronic distribution.* There are some who see electronic communication as a revolutionary new medium; they take what might be called the "McLuhan viewpoint" that "the medium is the message" and that there will be dramatic changes in the entire process of communication. The term "skywriting" has been used to suggest that information will be out for everyone to see, open to peer commentary on networks, global and unconstrained by time, space, or distance, collaborative, inter-media and multi-media. They see electronic communication replacing print, and revolutionary.

Others see electronic communication as an imitator of print publication but with differences. They see it as the journal "unbundled"–article based rather than package based–with greater flexibility in delivery either individually or recombined. They see it as more rapid in direct delivery, with the most recent work on a subject immediately available, searchable, and linkable. They see the results as increased diversity in which various options co-exist, and evolutionary.

From the standpoint of scholarship, this process clearly facilitates communication among a small peer group. But, as the experiments with formalizing the invisible colleges undertaken some twenty to twenty-five years ago demonstrated, the improved effectiveness in communication is heavily outweighed by the inherent limitations. The peer group is by no means the only or even the most appropriate context for research progress and especially evaluation. Research should be of importance beyond the limits of the peer group; it should be subject to evaluation and assessment by other minds, other tests of validity. The cold, clear light of day needs to enter, but the invisible college, by its very mode of operation, prevents that kind of "sunshine" effect.

*Speculations on cost reduction.* Some have looked to electronic publication as a means for reducing the costs of journals. This has been especially of interest in the light of dramatic rates of inflation in prices of scientific and technical journals. Others have urged that the universities should get into the business of electronic information distribution, with the view that they are both the primary sources for generation of published information and the primary users of it. They argue that as it is now the universities are paying twice for their information–once for producing it and then later for acquiring it.

Underlying these developments is the perception that electronic publication will introduce dramatic changes in the process of publication and in the costs associated with it. In fact, in some disciplines (Artificial Intelligence being one example), the concept is that the online electronic journal should replace the traditional printed page. In other contexts, the ease of micro-computer based "desk-top publishing" have led some to see it as replacing the formal publisher.

It is argued that electronic publication is more rapid, more immediate and direct, more responsive to change. But whether that's the case or not, electronic mail is a reality of scholarly, peer group communication today. In fact, increasingly, scholars are sending diskettes to colleagues whenever there is need to develop joint reports. The Electronic Manuscript Project of the Association of American Publishers was established in recognition of this phenomenon, and has had the intent of establishing standards for encoding of the text in such media to facilitate all aspect of subsequent publication.

However, despite the potentials, publishers for good reasons have been slow to adopt electronic publication. International journal publishers, in particular, cannot simply switch from paper to electronic delivery; they must accommodate both distribution methods and would incur increases in costs with a dual system. As a result, the steps taken currently are experimental. For example, there are efforts to augment existing forms of electronic distribution with increasing amounts of substantive content. In particular, tables of contents are being added to bibliographic information; CD-ROM publications are becoming more wide-spread; abstracts are becoming available more rapidly.

*The processes of electronic publication.* It must be recognized, furthermore, that the production of a journal involves processes and related costs that will be incurred no matter who does the distribution. First is *identifying and encouraging potential authors*. In a sense, this is the most important of the roles since it creates opportunities that might not otherwise be there. It is surprising that even from the academic world, where publication is the life blood, there are difficulties in encouraging persons to publish. Any commercial publisher focused on scientific, technical, and professional books and journals, depends greatly upon academic authors, but it is difficult to identify persons capable of writing good books and journal articles. Even for professional and scholarly journals, the number of authors and suitable articles is far less than is needed. The task of the publisher and of the editor is important and difficult; it involves constant discussion with potential authors, encouragement to them, and assistance is bringing manuscripts to publishable state.

The publisher is responsible for *quality control*. That arises in the identification of authors, of course, but it also arises in creating publishable works of suitable quality. Manuscripts of books and even of scholarly articles all too often are poor in their organization, poor in their writing, and even poor in their substantive content. The publisher, through its editors, serves as a means for bringing such poor manuscripts to a level of quality that justifies publishing. The processes of review, both internal and external, of copy editing, of preparation for publication all serve as means for accomplishing that objective. For major journals in the natural sciences, referees of peers are part of the review process but by no means the totality of it.

The publisher is responsible for *producing a publishable product*. The facts are, with all due respect to the presumed ease with which one can use electronic publishing, creating a publishable product is by no means a trivial task that can be performed by clerical staff or even by the author. It involves a high level of technical expertise, experience, and knowledge of the needs in marketing and use of publications.

The publisher is responsible for *marketing and distribution*. This role is of importance not only to the publisher, as the basis for its profitability, but to the author, to the users, to the libraries that will preserve and assure access. Evaluating the appropriate market, the size of it, the kind of package that will appeal to it, the best means for informing it of availability–these are all essential.

The point of course is that the publisher has critical responsibilities in the control of quality of content, control of the process of production to assure quality of product, control of the process of distribution to assure that the product will be available and deliverable at an appropriate price and with suitable response time. Where are those elements of control in electronic publishing? There are none to this point in time, and the result is the likelihood, even certainty, of degradation of quality in every respect and of limited availability and distribution until they are developed. That is the primary purpose of the several experiments now underway.

An inherent danger in the electronic modes of communication though less so in the printed forms of desk top publishing is the likely loss of what is called "integrity of reference." Scholarly communication has built up an important tradition of citation. It reflects the fact that in all areas of research–humanities, natural sciences, social science–we progress by building on the past. And we acknowledge our debt to the past by citation to it. By doing so, we assure that our sources can be checked, verified, validated. But that implies that material so referenced, so cited must be available for checking, verifying, and validating. What happens if the source data has been erased or, worse yet, altered since it was used? The entire structure for scholarly progress would collapse.

*Current forms of electronic delivery.* Most journals become machine-readable at some point in the research process. As a result it is easy to produce by-products of their publication. Today, operational systems for electronic delivery of information include online access to databases through use of national services, mounting of databases at campuses for access through online public access catalogs, and increasing availability of parallel CD-ROM products. Just to illustrate the last of those options, *Ei (Engineering Index)* has, since 1989, released a series of publications on CD-ROM: Compendex*Plus (in August 1989), ChemDisc (in July 1990), EEDisc (in November 1990), Energy/Environment Disc (in December 1990), PageOne (in January 1991). There are increasing numbers of full-text (but non-graphic) databases online, some publishers' experiments (e.g., ADONIS), an array of document delivery options (e.g., mail, fax, electronic), steadily increasing use of electronic bulletin boards.

Beyond what publishers are doing, there are a number of other experiments underway, including about a dozen refereed or lightly refereed electronic journals, two university electronic preprint services in development, and plans for publication by AAAS of a fully refereed electronic journal for distribution through OCLC starting in 1992. These developments reflect the efforts of some existing paper publishers converting to electronic, but they are primarily the work of intermediaries, value-adders who deliver electronically. For example, there are now several document delivery services, CARL (Colorado Association of Research Libraries), University Microfilms Incorporated, re-packagers (e.g., Maxwell Electronic), university-based electronic publishing (e.g., pre-print services in high-energy physics and mathematics), the Ohio State University experiment in FAX delivery.

Underlying many of the experiments and plans are the expectations for implementation of the National Research and Education Network (NREN). Legislation (Public Law Number 102-194) signed by the President December 9, 1991, provides $638 million for the funding of High-Performance Computing and Communications, of which $92 million is slated for NREN. The Coalition for Networked Information (a joint venture of the Association of Research Libraries, CAUSE, and EDUCOM) was initiated in early 1990 to assure that the interests of the research university community were represented in planning for implementation of NREN.

In the meantime, there are increasing numbers of ad hoc interconnections among online public access catalogs of major university libraries. In order to bring some order to those developments, a task force on Electronic Data Interchange (EDI) was established in 1990 to develop guidelines, procedures, and policies for computer-to-computer exchange of structured documents between independent organizations.

*Expected pace in future development.* With that as the current context, what will be the pace of future development? It seems likely that by 1995 the problems in pricing, ownership, standardization, and distribution will largely have been solved. There will be a number of "unbundled journals," in which the article becomes the basic unit, not the issue, with resulting inroads into paper subscriptions for journals, especially in the natural sciences, and a slowing of the rate of growth in the number of paper journals. There will be a movement of libraries from acquisition to access and direct delivery to the end-user. It has been estimated that there may be over 100 refereed electronic journals and a significant number of university based preprint services in collaboration with societies. However, it is also likely that there will be many alternative sources, with battles over pricing strategies and significant problems over copyright. The national network will still be heavily subsidized, at least for use in the natural sciences.

The potential in 2000 is based on the expectation that computer usage will be pervasive. There will be parallel availability of electronic and print in a mix about 50/50, with hundreds of electronic "journals." There will be a re-structuring of secondary services combined with an increasing number of new service niches–scanning services, archive services, ... There will be increasing stratification between richer and poorer universities, users, and nations.

## The Institutional Means for Management and Delivery of Information

The effort to deal with potentials represented by electronic publishing involves many participants: publishers, libraries, computing facilities, communications systems, networks, and a wide range of "niche" services. There is great uncertainty about the relationships among these participants, with continual jockeying for position among them, with cooperative arrangements developing and then disappearing, with established agencies attempting to preserve and build on their existing capital resources, and with newer agencies attempting to displace them.

Several issues of concern exacerbate these interactions. Primary among them is the reconciliation of intellectual property rights–the balancing of the rights to use information resources with the rights to control the use of them. A related issue is the determination of appropriate policies and formulas for charging and pricing, for service arrangements, for licensing. Another issue is the decision about when it is appropriate to set standards and how standards should relate to proprietary interests.

Two recent court decisions in the United States illustrate the current complicated state of these issues. The first is the decision, in which the courts ruled in favor of LOTUS 1 2 3 in its suit against Paperback Software, thereby greatly extending the scope of copyright protection to include not only the programs but the "look and feel" of the interface they provide; the result is a substantial restriction on other developers of programs who wish to use that interface as almost an industry standard. The second is a decision in which the U.S. Supreme Court ruled that directories or compilations of facts may be freely copied and republished unless they display "some minimum degree of creativity," emphasizing in doing so that the main purpose of the copyright laws is "not to reward authors but to promote the progress of science and useful arts"; the result is potentially more far-reaching, placing at risk the entire electronic data distribution business with the likelihood of continuing litigation to determine what is meant by "originality" in the presentation of compilations of data.

## THE ROLE OF INFORMATION ACCESS IN THE STAGES OF SCIENTIFIC RESEARCH

I now turn to the needs for information access on the part of researchers in science and technology. In the CLR report to NSF, Helen Gee discussed the users and uses of scientific information resources, suggesting that we may need to replicate and to update findings from the studies of the 1960s. She called for one or more broad-based, multi-institutional, multi-discipline studies, using experimental approaches, critical incident studies, and interviews with a variety of natural scientists. She posed a number of questions that such studies might answer: How do the natural scientists obtain the information they need at different stages in planning and conduct of research? What is the level of familiarity with different resources? What is the availability of electronic resources? How do they use intermediaries? What are the effects of collaboration? What are the needs in local communication? How much time do they spend in using different resources? What are the effects of limitations on access to information?

I wish I could present to you the results from such studies, but I cannot; they still need to be done. At best I can only conjecture about the answers to those questions, based on my knowledge from prior studies and the descriptions available from current literature. Among the latter, the *Guide to Programs* of the National Science

Foundation provides some tangible evidence in the emphasis it gives to information needs, and I will use it to support some of the conjectures I will present.

To provide a framework for discussion, I will postulate a sequence for the conduct of scientific research, obviously only one among the many that will be found in practice. It is based on a series of stages, in each of which information access plays a dramatically different role. For each stage, I will provide a characterization of its role, discuss the impact of digital imaging upon it, illustrate with examples from the current NSF *Guide to Programs*, and conclude with a discussion of the roles of the several means for information support–computers, telecommunications, and libraries– as may be appropriate.

## Stage 1: Data Acquisition

*Characterization of the stage.* Consider a researcher who observes an anomaly in some data, arising from a mismatch between the data and predicted values based on prior theory. Such an anomaly presumably could represent a failure of the theory, and the researcher is likely to speculate about that possibility. But it could result from inaccuracy in measurement, so normally the researcher will attempt to replicate the acquisition of data, being as accurate and precise as possible. As an alternative rationale, the researcher may simply be curious about the nature of some phenomenon and wish to determine its quantitative characteristics. In either event, the first stage in this model of the research process involves data acquisition. Surely this is the most central role of information in the scientific research process. As a result, the importance of this stage is well recognized in any description of the process of scientific research; some have even gone so far as to say that it is the essential stage, the thing that distinguishes science from other academic disciplines.

*The example of digital imaging.* Sometimes data are acquired by conduct of experiments–observation of collisions of high-energy particles in an accelerator, of the progress of a chemical reaction, of a succession of functions in experimental animals. Sometimes, though, it results from the scanning of natural phenomena–of the human body, of the earth and the other planets by satellites, of geological structures by a variety of means for observation. Such processes differ from the observation of experiments in the fact that the things being observed are not being controlled, so the range of phenomena observed is dramatically greater, and in the fact that they can occur continuously. Scanning can acquire data at truly mind-boggling rates, so the generation of images from them has become a crucial means for presenting otherwise overwhelming amounts of data in compact, visual form.

Increasingly, the very nature of the data and of the process for data acquisition requires the use of digital imaging. For example, AT&T Bell Laboratories has recently announced the invention of a more powerful optical microscope that should vastly improve the examination of living matter, including tiny structures inside living cells. It uses a strand of extremely clear optical fiber tapered to a tiny tip. The tip is coated with an aluminum glaze, leaving only the very tip bare; a laser light beam is concentrated to a width of only 12 nanometers, and the tip can be brought close to the contours of a living cell. Currently, the microscope scans at two frames per second, but work continues on increasing the rate of scan. The point here is that the microscope operates as a scanner, converting the light from the specimen into data that a computer takes and reassembles into an image displayed on a video screen.

*NSF current program emphasis.* In NSF's current *Guide to Programs* specific emphasis is given to data acquisition. It is central to the entire program in *Astronomy*. In the program for *Biotic Systems*, emphasis is being given to improved methods of gathering data. In that for *Social and Economic Science*, emphasis is strong on methods for measurement and data improvement. In the program for *Atmospheric Sciences*, data acquisition is central to the entire program.

*The role of information support.* Increasingly, computers are crucial to natural scientists in the processes of data acquisition, being used for control of experiments, for control of scanners, for management of the data as they are obtained, for immediate display of the data as means for guidance to the researcher. They clearly are essential in the acquisition of digital images. Telecommunications is clearly important when the means for acquisition is remote, but otherwise it and libraries appear to play minimal roles at this stage in the research process.

## Stage 2: Data Analysis

*Characterization of the stage.* Data having been acquired, the researcher then faces the task of data analysis. This stage has been the traditional focus for use of the computer in science and technology in processing the mathematical models and simulations that provide the fundamental tools for data analysis.

*The example of digital imaging.* The growing use of digital imaging, though, is greatly expanding the nature of data analysis and the role of the computer. It provides new means for analysis in the use of graphical methods, which is explicitly recognized in the NSF *Guide to Programs* in its description of priorities for the *Mathematical & Physical Sciences* by reference to the rapid expansion in the role of geometric ideas.

*NSF current program emphasis.* In the current NSF program for *Biological, Behavioral, and Social Sciences*, specific emphasis is given to mathematical modeling and to software development. In the programs for *Engineering*, an emphasis is on computational models of design processes, representations, and multiple levels of abstraction. The programs in *Computer & Information Science and Engineering* are largely oriented toward computational needs–in Computer Science, Robotics, Microelectronics, Advanced Scientific Computing, Networking and Communications. The programs on *Biotic Systems*, make reference to computerization of systematic research collections. Those on *Social & Economic Science*, on increased accessability to systematic anthropological collections and geographic information systems. Programs for database development are part of *Instrumentation & Resources*. These, though, are merely examples; the importance of data analysis is evident throughout all of NSF's programs.

*The role of information support.* Effective data analysis frequently will require that new data be compared with old, that it be supplemented with other data. This immediately implies the necessity for maintenance of files of data and for access to them as sources for those comparative and supplementary data. In this respect, the complications posed by files of digitized images are orders of magnitude greater than those for textual or purely numerical files. Any single picture may require from 100 kilobytes to one megabyte, but scanners can generate such pictures at rates of 10 to 30 per second. The result can be files of gigabyte size within merely an hour or so!

It is here that the role of the library, as the agency to preserve past records and to provide such access, first becomes important to the natural scientist. The problem of course is that the scientist may not recognize the importance of these kinds of data analyses and may not realize that the library can assist in gaining access to the existing data. As I will discuss later, the librarian can serve as advisor on the appropriate tools for data file management as well as in the processes of storage and access. Primary among them is the overriding concern with the management of the files themselves; here there needs to be fundamental research on the organization of such files and on the means for retrieval from them. Almost equally important are administrative concerns about access to facilities, resources, and equipment needed to acquire such data and to analyze it–spectral analyzers, monitors, supercomputers and communication lines to them. Indeed, primary among the supporting equipment are supercomputers, needed because the volume of processing required for use of digitized images exceed the capacity of even very large mainframes.

## *Stage 3: Conceptualization*

*Characterization of the stage.* The creative stage for the scientific researcher lies in the conceptualization of new models, new relationships among the data. Complications in this stage are great, of course, given the multi-dimensional nature of natural phenomena.

*The example of digital imaging.* Without question, digitized images already have become vitally important as tools for conceptualization of problems. Through the use of image manipulation new relationships can readily be visualized. Through the use of motion, color, enhancement, windowing, exploding, and a wide range of other means for manipulating images, several dimensions can be shown at once, and it is easy to shift among them.

*NSF current program emphasis.* In the program for *Electrical and Communications Engineering* there is mention of conceptual design. And in *Engineering Design and Manufacturing* specific emphasis is on conceptualization. In the program on *Ecosystems* new methods of predicting change are a program focus. In the program areas in *Behavioral and Neural Sciences* emphasis is given to neural factors for memory and learning.

*The role of information support.* Computers are clearly powerful tools is developing conceptualization. I have discussed the use of digitized images and the manipulation of them for observing and testing different relationships, but that is only one example of the use of computer processing for those purposes.

## Stage 4: Distribution of Results

*Characterization of the stage.* Of course, this is the stage to which all of the discussion of new electronic means for communication applies. It is the stage during which the results of research are reduced to a standard form for communication, broad distribution, acquisition by libraries, and subsequent consultation. Writing scientific articles and reports, documenting the prior knowledge through citation, submission of the materials to the processes of review, preparation of them for publication, preparing the indexes and abstracts that will assist in access to them–these are the information processes of concern of the librarian and the publisher, and the focus of the discussions of electronic means for distribution. It is important, though, to see this stage in perspective. Important though it is, the earlier stages are where the real information needs of the research scientist occur; this stage is almost peripheral to them.

*The example of digital imaging.* To this time, digital images have not been significant components of this stage, and there have been only a few publications in which digital images were included. Of course, there are innumerable publications that contain pictures derived from digitized images, but those are by-products rather than the digital images themselves. However, there have been a number of experiments on means to make available combinations of text and digital image that would allow manipulation as well as display. At the simplest level, these experiments include storage of document pages in digitized image form, as the basis for subsequent generation of page images and for optical character recognition. Over the coming years, I am sure that we will see increasing publication in this form, especially in support of interactive instruction.

*NSF current program emphasis.* The NSF *Guide to Programs* repeatedly emphasizes the importance of communication and distribution of the results of scientific research, continued increases in the application of information technologies, and increasing collaboration between libraries and their user communities. In *Astronomy*, emphasis is given to communication of information. In the *Biological, Behavioral, and Social Sciences*, one area of emphasis is integrating knowledge of metabolism; another is publication of major taxonomic divisions in systematic biology. In the *Mathematical & Physical Sciences*, the statement is made that "mathematics thrives on the sharing of ideas among researchers" and communication among groups of investigators is regarded as essential. In *Bioengineering*, emphasis is on expanding knowledge base and on improving flow of research information between universities and industry. In *Electrical Engineering and Communications* a major emphasis in on information activities. In the *Geosciences*, communication is central to the entire program. In its program for *International Cooperation* there is emphasis on cooperative research and the exchange of information. In NSF efforts to develop science resources collection, analysis, dissemination of information and the compilation of information on science and technology resources are all important program objectives.

*The role of information support.* All of the means for information support–libraries, computers, and telecommunication–clearly are crucial support to this stage in the research process.

## Stage 5: Application of Results

*Characterization of the stage.* Finally, beyond simply feeding on its own results, research in the natural sciences provides the basis for engineering development, industrial manufacturing, production of new drugs, and advancement in health care. It has fueled the industrial revolution for the past two centuries, and it is now fueling the "information" revolution, especially in the development of the information technologies.

*The example of digital imaging.* I have already commented on software for algorithmic production. It arises specifically to provide means for generating images from specifications in either parametric form or image form. Examples include CAD/CAM (computer aided engineering design and manufacturing), architectural design, and cartooning. Once a digitized image has been created in this way, it may well be stored for later use or for manipulation independent of the source program.

*NSF current program emphasis.* NSF recognizes this stage in the research process in its program on *Education and Human Resources*, referring to course and career development and to teacher development. It places significant emphasis on industrial innovation, especially in small business, in its *Major Initiatives* for facilities modernization, research centers, career development, and information for small business.

*The role of information support.* All of the means for information support–libraries, computers, and telecommunication–clearly are crucial support to this stage in the research process. Indeed, they may be even more important to the furtherance of applications than they are to the advance of the sciences themselves.

## THE ROLE OF LIBRARIES AND LIBRARIANS

In that listing of stages in scientific research, I have highlighted the potential role of the means for information support. We must also consider potential contributions of the library and the librarian.

### Preservation and/or Access

The basic responsibility of scholarly research libraries is "preservation of the record of the past"; for that function they, along with the cognate institutions, archives and museums, are the designated institutions of society. All of the other information industries and activities have only the objectives of immediate distribution. Publishers and communication media indeed take no responsibility for preserving even their own products, ceasing to have any interest (but copyright protection) as soon as the book or journal is "out of print." It seems unlikely that electronic forms of publication will change the focus of the commercial institutions in the immediate future. But the library does assure that material is preserved, and without doubt it will continue to do so with electronic materials.

The second responsibility of the library is to provide access to the preserved records, a responsibility that by longstanding tradition is shared among all libraries and with cognate services in the form of bibliographic utilities, secondary access tools (indexing and abstracting services), and a variety of data base access services. Thus, the library is not the only institution that fulfills that responsibility. Indeed, academic researchers do so through the very process of citation; the compilers of bibliographies, the indexing and abstracting services, the providers of online reference services all do so. But the library is in a unique position with respect to access to its own materials and, as a result, plays an especially important role in access to all others. As a result, as electronic forms of distribution become more available, the library will without doubt continue as a primary means for access to them.

Assuming that I am correct and that the library indeed does continue to fulfill its imperatives in the context of electronic publishing, are there problems in doing so? The answer is clear: There are serious problems with respect to both preservation and access, despite all of the rhetoric and high expectations, especially for the latter.

Whereas for the individual library in the past, preservation and access were two sides of the same coin, with the electronic media the library faces internal tensions in the choice between incurring a capital investment in acquisition and preservation, and incurring continuing operating expenses in access from elsewhere. In this context, a major objective of the CLR report to NSF was to explore the future form of library services and information systems for science. In that context, in addition to her discussion of the need for studies of scientists themselves, Helen Gee proposed that there should be similar studies of the library: What amount of its budget is being used for electronic information resources? What kinds of electronic resources are available from the library? How are information systems accessed? What kinds of training are provided? What are consortial arrangements? What is the library's role in planning?

The CLR report concluded that there would be a continuing

transition in library emphasis from acquisition to access. Indeed, it appears steadily to be increasing in that direction, especially for the smaller colleges and universities. And for materials needed by the natural sciences and related professions, *access* is the necessity, and responsibility for preservation of materials will be focused on a very few major libraries and perhaps even on means other than the traditional academic library.

It must be said, however, that for any university with aspirations to be a major research institution in which the library collection is still a primary research tool, the choice is by no means obvious, at least with respect to materials needed for the humanities and social sciences. Furthermore, if the electronic materials themselves are to be preserved, some major libraries will need to take on that responsibility.

## *Bibliographic Control of Electronic Publications*

Even with respect to access, though, there are serious problems in control of this literature. The problems are ones with which the library field has extensive experience. They arose with the entire array of "report" literature and similar ephemera. The tools that have been developed indeed provide the means for control of such literature. But they are tools expensive to maintain and expensive to use.

The first problem is the lack of control of the fact of publication. With print publishers, we have mechanisms for identifying availability and sources of materials. What will be the counterpart for electronic publications? There is a lack of means for assessment and review, so essential in making the decisions in selection and acquisition of material to be preserved or to be accessed. Surely in time electronic publications will make their way into the review literature. But for the bulk of them today and many of them in the future, such means for assessment simply will not be available.

Another problem is the lack of the tools for secondary access; there is as yet little coverage of electronic publications in the indexes, abstracts, bibliographies, and catalogs of the country. The result is that persons needing information contained in such publications have no means for identifying those of potential value.

Even if such material is identifiable, for example through the various citation indexes (resulting from reference to it in some formally published document covered by them), the user may have no means for establishing where to obtain it. I can visualize that experience repeated a hundred-fold as desk top publishing makes it feasible to generate increasing numbers of such ephemera. The problem not only affects the users, though. From an operational standpoint, it places intolerable burdens upon libraries who must track down these "citation ghosts." Do they refer to real publications? To ephemeral publications? To figments of the imagination? How is one to tell?

These issues arise not only with respect to formally published materials but at least equally so to materials held within the single institution. The library can serve as a vital tool for management of those campus resources. It can include within its online public access catalog the references to such materials that may have utility beyond the individual faculty member or research project.

## Services of the Professional Librarian

The role of the librarian is potentially much broader than that of the library itself. The sense of professional responsibility, the associated commitments and skills, the supporting professional organizations–all provide a solid base for the librarian to fulfill a wide range of functions in the context of electronic information.

*Mediation, consultation, training.* One area for contribution by the librarian is in mediation, consultation, and training. While researchers, students, engineers, and executives may know their own needs in use of any information resource, they frequently will need help in the management of personal files and in the use of hardware and software. The librarian can serve as a consultant in such cases, bringing to bear experience as well as technical expertise. Of special importance is providing assistance in gaining access to available electronic data files that a given user may need and in conversion of those data to the form needed.

*Selection and acquisition.* Perhaps the most important contribution is directly related to gaining access to materials. Selecting and acquiring information materials is the fundamental role of the librarian. To fill that role, the librarian needs to know the available sources. Perhaps we need the creation of national or even international bibliographies of available electronic forms of information, including digitized images.

*Cataloging.* The other traditional function of the librarian is *cataloging*–providing the means for identifying and controlling holdings. I have already commented on the crucial role of the library in providing "single-point" access to campus information resources. In many cases, though, there may be need to have MARC formats adequate to the requirements and the means for sharing of cataloging data so as to avoid unnecessary duplication. The situation with respect to the cataloging of digitized image files serves as an especially important example of this.

*Collection management.* While electronic materials may not be acquired by all libraries, there will still be needs for management of them, and the skills of the librarian are as important in that respect as are those of the computer specialist. As I have pointed out, digitized image files can raise spectres of sizes of files of truly awesome magnitude–sizes that make even the largest libraries of the world appear small. As a result there are even more complex problems in determining where the files will be stored, how they will be organized, and how they will be preserved.

*Content indexing and abstracting.* Perhaps the most exciting intellectual challenge arises from the needs in "content indexing and abstracting." How does one retrieve images that contain something desired? If the problems in "full-text retrieval" were interesting, they were dull compared to those in image retrieval. Lest I appear to be posing an irrational challenge, please consider the means by which OCR software matches images against standard patterns, consider the means available for identifying a scene, with the potential for use of one frame from a scene as a retrieval surrogate–an "abstract"–consider the possibility of using characterizing quantitative parameters as means for retrieval. In other words, the tools are already here.

## *CONCLUSION*

In conclusion, I have tried in this paper to provide a broad coverage of the information needs in science and technology. I have reviewed the status and expected future development of electronic means for meeting those needs. I have placed special emphasis on digitized images as a medium of communication of information that is now of critical importance to research, to the application of its results, and to governmental policy making; in my view, as time goes on it will be of increasing importance. I have focused on the library and on the role of the librarian as a means for meeting the needs of scientists in access to and use of information in all forms. That means that library education should begin now to provide the technical tools that the librarians will need to fulfill their obligations in the world of electronic information.

## REFERENCES

Bair, James H. "The integrated future of image management," *The Imaging and Information Consultant*, 1(2), March/April 1991: 3-6.

Bates, R.H. and McDonnell, M.J. *Image Restoration and Reconstruction*. Oxford: Clarendon Press, 1986.

Brand, Stewart. *The Media Lab: Inventing the Future at MIT*. New York: Viking, 1987.

Cartter, Allan M. *An Assessment of Quality in Graduate Education*. Washington, D.C.: American Council on Education, 1966.

*Challenge to Action*. Chicago: Medical Library Association, 1987.

Cohn, Steven F. "The effects of funding changes upon the rate of knowledge growth in algebraic and differential topology," *Social Studies of Science*. 16 (1), 1986: pp 23-60.

*Communications in Support of Science and Technology. A Report to the National Science Foundation from the Council on Library Resources*. August 1990.

"Court limits scope of copyright shield." *Los Angeles Times*, Thursday, 29 March 1991: A21.

Cox, Donna J. "Scientific visualization: collaborating to predict the future," *Educom Review*. 25(4), Winter 1990: 38-42.

D'Alleyrand, Marc. *Image Storage and Retrieval Systems*. New York: McGraw-Hill, 1989.

Dougherty, Richard. "An ideal win-win situation: the national electronic highway." *American Libraries*, February 1991: 182.

Division of Planning and Policy Analysis, Office of Planning and Resources Management. Studies of Scientific Disciplines: An Annotated Bibliography. Washington, D.C.: NSF, 1982.

"Electronic Data Interface (EDI) project." *Protocol Newsletter*, Number 27, March 1991: 1-2.

Garvey, William. *Communication: The Essence of Science*. New York: Pergamon Press, 1979.

Henderson, Joseph. Dartmouth Medical School. "Creating realities for experiential

learning." *UCLA Roundtable in Multimedia.* Los Angeles: UCLA AGSM, 1991.
Holzer, Dunn, Shahidullah. "An accounting scheme for designing science impact indicators," *Knowledge: Creation, Diffusion, Utilization.* 9(2), 1987. pp 173-204.
Jones, Lyle V. and others. An Assessment of Research-Doctorate Programs in the United States. Washington, D.C.: National Academy Press, 1982.
Keller, John J. "AT&T team invents optical telescope that should aid in study of living cells," *Wall Street Journal*, Friday, 22 March 1991: B11.
Kumon, Shumpei. Kokusai University. "Creative and constructive competition." *UCLA Roundtable in Multimedia.* Los Angeles: UCLA AGSM, 1991.
Lanier, Jaron. VPL Research. "Virtual reality and the future of multimedia." *UCLA Roundtable in Multimedia.* Los Angeles: UCLA AGSM, 1991.
"Manage IT: ARL, Cause, Educom form new information resources coalition." *Cause–the Newsletter for the Management of Information Technology in Higher Education*, 1(2), April 1990: 1.
Morton, Herbert C. and Price, Anne Jamieson. "Views on publications, computers, libraries." *Scholarly Communication*, 5, Summer 1986: 1-15.
NAS, COSPUP. "Dissemination and use of the information of physics," in *Physics in Perspective*, vol 1, Chapter 13, 1972.
NSF. *Guide to Programs, Fiscal Year 1991.* Washington, D.C.: National Science Foundation, 1990.
NSF. *Science and Engineering Indicators Report.* Washington, D.C.: National Science Foundation, 1990.
Okerson, Ann. "Scholarly publishing in the NREN," *ARL Newsletter.* 4 July 1990. pp 1-4.
Rider, Robin. "Saving the records of big science," *American Libraries*, February 1991: 166-168.
Roberts, Michael M. "The global Internet and the NREN," *Educom Review*, 25(4), Winter 1990: 8-9.
Roose, Kenneth D. and Anderson, Charles J. A Rating of Graduate Education Programs. Washington, D.C.: American Council on Education, 1970.
Seibert, Warren F. *Growth and Change in 67 Medical School Libraries, 1975-1989.* Bethesda, Maryland: National Library of Medicine, 1991.
Sigloh, Dennis. Director of Geographic Information Systems. "Toward the 'intelligent super map.'" *IBM Update*, Nov./Dec. 1990: 6-8.
Tufte, Edward R. *Envisioning Information.* Cheshire, Conn.: Graphic Press, 1990.
Tufte, Edward R. *The Visual Display of Quantitative Information.* Cheshire, Conn.: Graphic Press, 1983.
"Types of computer systems," *NewTech Review* (OCLC), Oct.-Dec. 1990: 5-8.
Ward, Fred. "Images for the computer age," *National Geographic.* 175(6), June 1989: 718-751.
Wayner, Peter. "Smart memories," *Byte*, March 1991: 147-152.
"What's new." *Ei Letters*, 1(1), January 1991: 2
Woodwark, J. (ed) *Geometric Reasoning.* Oxford: Clarendon Press, 1989.

# Managing the Sea Change in Science and Technology Libraries

Glenn L. Brudvig

> Full fathom five thy father lies,
> Of his bones are coral made:
> Those are pearls that were his eyes.
> Nothing of him that doth fade,
> But doth suffer a sea change
> Into something rich and strange . . .
>
> <div align="right">–Shakespeare, <i>The Tempest</i></div>

## INTRODUCTION

As the vision of the electronic or virtual library begins to come into view, with full-text information available on demand, librarians need to undertake a long and unpredictable journey, if the vision is to be achieved. As clear and inevitable as the electronic library may seem, we cannot predict how technology may evolve and be utilized. Therefore, we need to concentrate on managing the change process itself and remain agile and knowledgeable enough to apply an ensemble of technologies as they emerge. The process of change is accelerating; remarkable opportunities for libraries are just around the corner. We are entering a sea change: "a marked transformation into something richer and finer," as defined in Webster's Third.

The predictions of the library of the future, depending upon how

---

Glenn L. Brudvig is Director of Libraries at the California Institute of Technology, Pasadena, CA.

far one projects a vision, range from a continuation of present library services with the addition of online, full-text information, to what borders on science fiction, a library that exists only in the computer. In the near future, the scholar at his or her workstation should have direct access to bibliographic and full-text networks. The scholar will be able to peruse the world's literature, identify and download material into his or her workstation, and read, extract, and compose all on the same machine that serves as the gateway to the world of knowledge. Such a system will require three critical technical components: massive file servers at central locations, a national fiber-optic network, and powerful workstations. A critical requirement is a massive data base which, if it is to reach its full potential, could take decades to create. Also required are creative solutions to a myriad of technical and legal issues.

Librarians may be deluding themselves if they think they will be essential as leaders, consultants, or managers of local interactions with a full-text network. It could develop and thrive without them. By marketing and delivering information directly to users through communication networks, publishing companies and scientific societies could eliminate the "middleman." Science and technology libraries would, thereby, be just another customer. Those libraries that are heavily dependent on the journal literature and that serve a limited, specialized clientele could become a costly overhead and be replaced altogether.

If we may shift for a moment to ponder a more distant wave, a library could be entirely simulated online. A user would create an artificial, virtual reality library when needed, with an interior decor and shelving arrangement selected to fit one's concept of what a library should look like. It would be stocked with books of interest, and arranged to one's preference. A user could move through and around the library and its stacks, browse the shelves—left, right, or sideways, select an interesting book, check its table of contents and title page or skim its index. This would all be done online with an illusion of three dimensions. A reader could request a book, document, or article to be downloaded and consulted or printed at leisure. Far fetched, possibly; fascinating, definitely; but not improbable. We need only to project today's technology into the future.[1]

Whatever the future may have in store for libraries, the rate of change will be faster than it was for the phase of library automation that we have more or less just completed: the development of the integrated library system, first conceived some 25 years or so ago. Along the way, new support institutions were created, such as OCLC and RLIN, that now have the wherewithal to create new opportunities for libraries, and speed the process of change. We are entering a new phase of library development, the beginning of a sea change; it is not just a change in how we operate our libraries, but a basic change in the way we deliver information.

## ECONOMICS OF CHANGE

Science and technology libraries will be on the forefront of the changes that are taking place. The science journal is one of the first targets for full-text retrieval systems, which is due as much to their high cost as it is to the demands of a technologically sophisticated user community. Science journals are among the most expensive, and costs are increasing at a pace which outstrips the budgets of all but a few libraries. Existing journals are getting bigger, new journals keep appearing, and backlogs of unpublished research results are mounting. Prices will undoubtedly continue to increase, and cancellations may become a way of life.

New technologies burden the library with still more costs. Online public access catalogs, CD ROM systems, and workstations are costly. Existing library automated systems need to be regularly upgraded or replaced. Added to this are the costs of full-text databases, as libraries try to balance ownership with access. Each new advance adds more burdens to already over-stretched library budgets. Online public access catalogs generate demands for more bibliographic information once users recognize their unique benefits. Journal articles, technical reports, special collections, abstracts, tables of contents, and indexes are wanted online. The cataloging and processing workloads to handle these additional tasks far exceed whatever savings may be achieved through automation. The same types of demands can be expected with each new advance in library systems.

Many of our established technologies will gradually be replaced as the rate of obsolescence increases. Photocopy, FAX, and microfilm will become technologies of the past as image scanning and high-speed transmission become the new, dominant technology.

As librarians increase the use of remote databases and collections, greater cooperation and coordination between libraries will be required. Librarians, who are already spread too thin, will need to spend more time working with colleagues from other institutions. At the same time they will be expected to spend more time working on teams and problem solving or planning groups at home. These are the hidden transaction costs that accompany change which do not show up on the ledger sheets.

Society at large is placing increased demands on science and technology. Abroad, new scientific institutions are being created, and others are being upgraded. In the U.S., academia and business are moving towards closer collaboration. Academia needs access to research funds which have become more restricted and business needs to shorten the gap between the laboratory and the market place. In this environment, scientific and technical literature will continue to flourish, related as it is to maintaining a competitive world-wide position and improving living standards.

Libraries are in the awkward position of restricting access to scientific information by reducing journal and book purchases at a time when access should be increased in response to the growing role of science in society. Technology appears to offer the only solution to this dilemma. It is also the only solution to rising costs and the growth of the scientific literature.

## *SCIENCE AND TECHNOLOGY LIBRARIES*

Science and technology libraries, which are often organized around specific subject disciplines, provide a high level of personalized service. Users are particularly fond of decentralized libraries that are close to their offices and laboratories, with librarians who know and understand their needs and problems on a first hand basis. The question is how do we build on the best of two worlds. How do we capitalize on our ability to know and reach our customers, and yet deliver cost effective, advanced information service, which centralized services can provide? Science and technology libraries may be able to move into the world of the electronic library easier than centralized, more multi-disciplinary libraries by building on established user relations and services.

Science and technology libraries face an interesting paradox; their customers want everything online; they want abstracts and full text; they want statistical information, downloading, and access from home and office. Those on the forefront are very knowledgeable about technology. They know what others have, they know what is possible, they know what is coming out of the research laboratories. They often want what is beyond the capability of libraries to provide. On the other hand, these voices, even though very vocal, are definitely a minority. Scientists by and large are still bound to traditional books, journals, and reprints.

Scientists have built their own personal collections of books and journals which meet the largest proportion of their immediate needs. They travel to conferences to keep abreast of recent developments, and maintain a world-wide network of colleagues, often using electronic mail. They are critical of literature searches which often fail to yield what they want or miss articles of great interest. They are being swamped by paper, and find it nearly impossible to follow developments in a field only slightly outside their specialties.

For scientists, like everyone else, comfortable behavior patterns are not easily given up. They would rather sit comfortably with a cup of coffee, read a hard copy, and make notes in its margins than to read a video screen. Scientists have not yet approached the point of adding electronic sources to their repertoire of information sources, although a few are beginning to approach this area. At some point it will become an essential part of the scientists' information sources and will be integrated into their information gathering habits.

The library needs to evolve with the technology. It needs to respond to its community of users as the two sides of the information process, the providers and the consumers, grow together. Librarians will need to take the lead in demonstrating to their users what they can provide, identifying those individuals willing to test and experiment with new services.

In planning for the implementation of new technology, it is well to keep in mind that predicting what is going to be critical for libraries is almost impossible. A revolutionary technology defies predictions. The microcomputer was overlooked, yet the components already existed a decade before the personal computer burst onto the scene and transformed the way many things are done in libraries. It is necessary for the librarians to watch developments in their own and related fields, discount predictions, and expect whatever we are currently doing to continue to improve.

Librarians need to make sure that they are knowledgeable enough to respond to technological changes as they occur. A flawed vision of the future, or a premature decision, could lead libraries to implement a technology or system that is going nowhere. The library world is strewn with white elephants. A combination of knowledge, caution, and appropriate timing is critical to staying on the forward edge of technology while avoiding the pitfalls.

## *LEADERSHIP AND THE CHANGE PROCESS*

Library leadership faces a daunting task. It has to constantly apply new technology, blending traditional printed materials with new formats in a constantly changing environment. The old leadership models will no longer work. It is no longer possible to figure out a grand strategy at the top and then have everyone follow orders. The world of librarianship has become too complex, change too rapid, and new concepts emerging too fast for the leader to be knowledgeable in all areas needed for developing effective strategies and directions. To truly succeed in the new world of information, the library will have to depend on its staff to continuously learn, to learn at all levels, and to understand the possibilities, the limitations, and the opportunities. Leaders themselves will need to continually learn more, and be open to change their own strongly held positions.

Leaders need to continually try to see the broad patterns of change and to see how the parts fit together to perform as a whole. The leadership also has to orchestrate change, demand high standards, and help maintain the vision of where the library is going.

The leader will need to be especially concerned with the design of the organization and its policies.

"Leaders who fare best, according to Senge, are those who continually see themselves as designers, not crusaders."[2] The organization of the library needs to be adjusted on a continuous basis to meet new demands. Leaders will need to be more like architects. They will need to be more concerned with design, with the structure within which people work, than with day to day operations. The design of an organization is rarely visible, it takes place behind the scenes, but yet it is essential for a successful organization. It includes not only the design of the structure of the organization but its strategies, policies, and systems as well. Attempting to achieve quality in a poorly designed organization can be fruitless.[3]

Leaders of the change process will also need to be somewhat like historians. They need an awareness of the foundations, or history, of the organization. If the foundation of an organization will not support the weight of what is to be built, it will need to be shored up before any action can take place, or efforts to change will crumble.[4] The prehistory, perhaps below the surface, needs to be understood, appreciated, and integrated into a new organizational design. The origins or antecedents of a new structure should be recognized and acknowledged thereby gaining support from those involved in earlier activities and smoothing the change process. This applies to change in general, namely to relate change, whenever possible, to precedents or decisions of the past to provide continuity and make change easier to understand and accept. Keep in mind, "New things are viewed in the clothing of the old."

Organizations break down despite individual brilliance or innovative services because they are unable to pull the diverse functions and talents into a productive whole. In the library, printed and electronic books and journals will have to be integrated into new, unified organizational structures, and other problems, such as the degree of centralized or decentralized service and the role of the professional, will also need to be resolved and accommodated. The old and the new will co-exist in libraries for many years to come. Books and journals are not apt to disappear any time soon, but their relation to electronic sources will generate years of debate. Each new technology will need to be integrated into the service and organizational patterns of the library.

## STAFF AND THE CHANGE PROCESS

As the rate of change quickens, it is the existing staff, those now on the job, who will need to provide the leadership and the expertise to manage the change process. The recruitment of new staff members, which needs to be vigorously pursued to attract the best, is important but it is the people now on the staff who must bear the burden of change and maintain excellence. There is no one else.

Peter Drucker, who has very little patience with managers whose excuses are that they do not have good people, writes, "If you ever run into an industry that says it needs better people, sell its shares." "There are no better people; you have to use ordinary, every day people and make them capable of doing the work."[5]

Peters recommends that everyone be involved in everything. "The self-managing team, he writes, should become the basic organizational building block."[6] They are the key to organizational excellence, innovation, and growth. "The more successful an organization becomes, the more it needs to build teams." "The purpose of the team is to make the strength of each person effective, and his or her weakness irrelevant."[7]

Each member of a team has special skills and talents to contribute. These different skills can help break through barriers that separate different operations. Members of the team should question what is crucial, inquire into the views of others, and make their own views known to the team. The key decisions that they make are based on a shared understanding of the inter-relationships and the patterns of change. The more complex a task becomes the more suited it is for a team.

Teams need support. Management needs to take a keen interest in them, recognizing that using teams is not a quick fix, it is a long hard process. Although it is important to empower the people on teams to accomplish their tasks, this can be counter productive or even destructive in an unaligned organization. Senge writes, "If people do not share a common vision, do not share a common mental model," empowering people will only increase organizational stress and burden management to maintain direction."[8]

Leaders must be able to build a shared vision and a shared mental model to guide the team decision makers. When the leadership and a team share a common understanding of what the library is and what it is trying to accomplish, much wasted effort is avoided. One of the team's first tasks, therefore, is to become more aligned. As a team becomes more aligned, a commonality of direction emerges, and individual energies begin to harmonize. In the process of building a shared vision, a commitment to the long term is also fostered.

## *THE LEARNING ORGANIZATION*

"Forget your tired old ideas about leadership." "The most successful corporation of the 1990's will be something called the learning organization," writes Senge.[9] In such an organization, strategy and direction will come from the bottom up, from the people closest to the problem, from a group of specialists working as a team that develops the strategies for coping with a rapidly changing world.

The learning organization continuously builds its capacity to learn. People are encouraged to puzzle, wonder, and figure out things on their own. As an organization learns, new insights and modified behavior should take place. The learning organization strives to clarify what is important and learn how to see current realities more clearly. It is important for library leadership to continually encourage staff to revise and enlarge their views of the world. The development of common mental models provides the glue which helps hold the teams together to meet common objectives.

Members of the staff must continually acquire new knowledge and skills that are required to deal with new methods of operation. When new equipment or procedures are introduced, there must be retraining as well. Some training may involve erasing improper training, which is very difficult to do. Teaching is also part of the learning process; individuals learn most when they teach. Management must teach as well, using the opportunity to discuss and transmit the vision that helps hold the organization together. A manager in the future, therefore, will be less a boss and more a teacher, coach, and mentor.

De Geus illustrates organizational learning problems by comparing learning in two species of birds: the titmice, who move in flocks and mix freely, and the robins, who live in well defined parts of the garden and communicate antagonistically across the borders of their territories.[10] Titmice learn from each other and robins do not. The titmice in England quickly learned how to pierce the seals of milk bottles left on door steps. Robins as a group have never learned to do this, even though they are as intelligent as titmice, because the knowledge one bird learns does not spread to others. The same phenomenon occurs in organizations. Individuals or departments often do not learn from each other and vigorously defend their territories.

Managers who find themselves in a robin culture need to take steps to open up communication between units and individuals, and between the library and its user groups. By so doing managers will enhance the learning process within the organization. The manager must continually nudge the organization towards a broader view of the world and shift it from a robin to a titmouse culture.

## *BUILDING A VISION OF THE FUTURE*

Libraries have put considerable effort into writing and developing mission statements. Most are fairly similar, rather boring and uninspiring. I have yet to see one that stands out above the others. Basically, most library mission statements are similar to the phrase, "To provide materials, services, and access to information to meet the research, educational, and informational needs of the community." A vision is different; it is an overarching goal. It encompasses the mission into something powerful and exhilarating. It is about excellence.

A vision of the future should be built from the ground up. It should be constantly reinforced, articulated, and interpreted by the leadership of the library who need to keep the vision clearly before the eyes of the staff and the users. It should be reachable, not a leap too far. Procedures and strategies to achieve the vision must also be developed or a library could end up painting a lovely picture of the future without a clear understanding of the tasks that must be mastered to move from here to there.

In maintaining the vision, the leadership needs to assess external situations, solicit all points of view, and listen. A vision needs to be clear and challenging. It should inspire people and prepare them for the future. It is also something that makes sense to library users. It must be stable, but constantly challenged and changed at the margins. It is the rudder that keeps the learning process on course when stresses develop.[11]

## *QUALITY MANAGEMENT*

Peters finds excellent companies, those that are most efficient, most motivated, and most productive, to be in almost every case small.[12] Excellent companies are close to their customers, are simple in form, lean of staff, and have a combination of being both centralized and decentralized. The lesson to be learned for libraries is to keep things simple, stay close to your customers, decentralize the delivery of services, and centralize those things that can be best managed in a larger context.

If libraries were to borrow a central precept from the literature of management, it is, "know your customer," "listen to your clients," "hear their needs," "listen to their perceptions of good service." Peters advises that, "a small human touch can go a long way in cementing a relationship."[13] Drucker observes, "bad manners leave permanent scars."[14] We need to get close enough to our users to hear their perceptions of good service and respond accordingly.

As new technologies and new methods of delivering library services evolve, the user's views will become more important. Science and technology librarians will need to build on their strength of being close to their users, organize into user-centered teams, when appropriate, and demonstrate their ability to provide new avenues to information. The user knows what he wants when he sees it, but he cannot always tell you. Librarians, therefore, will need to provide services which users may not have recognized that they need.

For the library to become a center of excellence, quality performance will need to be built into every position, regardless of level, difficulty, or skill. The improvement of quality is a never ending journey, a never ending quest for perfection.

Total quality management (TQM), which has been in vogue in Japan since the 1950's, helps to explain in part the Japanese competitive advantage with their emphasis on quality. TQM is now making rapid inroads in the U.S. It has moved from the private sector into the colleges and universities, and a few libraries are beginning to investigate and apply its principles. Seminars and workshops on TQM have proliferated. The subject has also made its appearance at professional library meetings.

TQM can best be described as a system for involving an entire organization in planning and implementing a continuous process of improvement which exceeds customers' expectations. Successful TQM programs result in higher quality, lower cost products and services, and a faster response to the needs of the customer. Quality processes are continually improved through understanding and perfecting the systems by which organizations operate. TQM leads to a clarification of goals, training, selection of targets, and a continuous statistical feedback to measure its success in meeting customer needs and expectations.[15] Leadership in TQM is not a process of telling people what to do, but to help people to do a better job.

Deming discovered that when quality is improved costs go down; fewer mistakes are made, there are fewer breakdowns, and fewer problems to resolve.[16] The results of TQM as applied to libraries have not yet, as of this writing, reached the literature. Descriptions of the successful use this technique in libraries and models which others can follow are not yet available to the profession.

If a library does not wish to start with a full scale program of total quality management involving training team leaders, it can still undertake to improve the quality of library services by following the same general principles. In getting started, Peters recommends starting with the easy stuff, things that are easy to change, which can produce tangible results–those which are doable. He also recommends starting with individuals who will champion an idea, not with the naysayers; look for targets of opportunity. He recommends getting your "arms around a practical problem and knocking it off."[17] Drucker emphasizes putting your primary efforts into your successes, those areas that you are already doing well and improve them. He also recommends that organizations ". . . abandon what no longer works, what no longer contributes, what no longer serves."[18] The growth process needs to be accompanied by a process of abandonment. Senge writes, "Small well focused actions can sometimes produce significant enduring improvements, if these efforts are in the right place."[19] A critical element in quality improvement is a commitment to support the process from management. Staff cannot promote change; it must be started with the full support and backing of management.

Some companies and organizations are unwilling to make the commitment to total quality management because it exacts an effort which is so encompassing that there is a great reluctance to move forward. A critical mass of committed staff is essential to get the process moving. A certain alignment and cooperative atmosphere are also important. However, total agreement is not necessary since dissent is an essential part of effective group decision making. Feuding and bickering, on the other hand, should not be tolerated. They are symptoms of the need to change an organization.[20]

Measurement is an essential feature of quality improvement. What gets measured gets done. Measurements are needed to determine rates of improvement, levels of user satisfaction, and reduction of failure rates. Deming is a strong advocate of basing decisions as much as possible on accurate and timely data and to judge and act on the basis of fact. A critical element in the improvement of operations is, therefore, statistical thinking. Only by the use of properly interpreted data can intelligent decisions be made.

Library measurements in the past have not been related to performance. Libraries measure the number of books, subscriptions, and audiovisual holdings; they measure the number of items circulated, interlibrary loans filled, reference questions answered, or literature searches performed; and they know expenditures for every category. However, none of this tells us much about the quality of the services that are being provided, or the level of user satisfaction.

Libraries with online systems now have the capability, as yet largely undeveloped, to use qualitative measures to generate a continuous flow of information to show how well they are performing their functions. For example, technical services can chart the time it takes to get a book on the shelves, circulation can graph who is using the library, and bibliographers can plot the use of specific subject areas. From these patterns of activity, steps can be identified which lead to demonstrated improvement of the function being monitored.

A difficult aspect to measure is a library's failure rates. When do we not hold title, when can a book not be found, when is a reference question not answered, or an interlibrary loan not filled in a timely manner? Addressing some specific causes of failure can make a significant improvement in services. Attention to reshelving delays, binding times, or accuracy of holdings can improve the rate at which users find materials on the shelves.

Continuous attention to improvement, continuous measurement, and a determination to do something about the problems which are identified will improve the quality of a library. This results not only in better service, it helps as well to establish the library as a center of excellence and to earn the confidence and goodwill of its constituencies.

Failure of a library to meet the expectations of its users could lead them to seek their own solutions, outside the context of traditional library services. Attention to quality will be a major factor in placing the library firmly in the center of the information revolution.

## *CONCLUSION*

The world of librarianship is entering a new phase of development: the emergence of the electronic library. New opportunities are becoming available for science and technology libraries that will help deal with escalating costs for journals and the continuing growth of the literature. The emergence of imaging and fiber-optic network technologies provides tantalizing possibilities to improve library and information services.

As librarianship enters a new era, change will be too fast, too complex, and too disruptive for the traditional leadership methods to be effective. Library leaders of the future will need to focus more on design of the organization and its policies, orchestrate change, integrate new services and materials with the old, and depend more on self-managing teams to deal with the complexities of managing change and maintaining quality. To guide the change process, the library staff will need to develop a shared vision of the future, based on excellence. The staff will also need to develop a shared "mental model" of what the library is and what it is attempting to achieve to help keep the change process on course.

Continuous learning at all levels will be essential to acquire new knowledge and skills, to stay abreast of new developments, and to effectively evaluate the new opportunities. Equally important will be a constant striving for quality. This is a never ending task that will lead to constant improvement in what the library is doing.

In summary, the library will need a clear understanding of what it is and where it is going, a shared sense of values, and a management and organizational structure that promotes change, quality, and continued learning. The Library will need to continuously improve the quality of its service. This in turn will help develop confidence and goodwill on the part of its user community and keep the library in the center of the information revolution. The library will thereby be able to transform itself into something richer and finer.

## NOTES

1. For a discussion of this technology see Rheingold, Howard. *Virtual Reality.* New York: Summit Books, 1991.

2. Senge, Peter M. *The Fifth Discipline: The Art and Practice of the Learning Organization.* New York: Doubleday/Currency, 1990.

3. Senge, p. 341.

4. Kantor, Rosabeth Moss. *The Change Masters.* New York: Simon & Schuster, 1983, p. 283.

5. "From Communism to Chrysler: Pointed Views from Drucker," *Los Angeles Times,* Sept. 17, 1991, p. D1.

6. Peters, Thomas J. *Thriving on Chaos: Handbook for a Management Revolution.* New York: Alfred A. Knopf, 1988, p. 283, 297.

7. Drucker, Peter F. *Managing the Nonprofit Organization, Principles and Practices.* New York: Harper Collins, 1990, p. 152-153.

8. Senge, p. 146.

9. Ibid, p. 4.

10. De Geus, Arie P. "Planning as Learning," *Harvard Business Review,* March-April 1988, p. 74.

11. Senge, p. 209.

12. Peters, Thomas J. and Waterman, Robert H. Jr. *In Search of Excellence: Lessons from America's Best-Run Companies.* New York: Harper and Row, 1982, p. 321.

13. Peters, p. 95.

14. Drucker, p. 115.

15. Deming, W. Edwards. *Out of the Crises.* Boston: Massachusetts Institute of Technology, 1986, p. 23-24.

16. Walton, Mary. *The Deming Management Method.* New York: Dodd, Mead, 1986, p. 26.

17. Peters and Waterman, p. 12.

18. Drucker, p. 101-102.

19. Senge, p. 64.

20. Drucker, p. 114.

# Scientific and Technical Librarians: Leaders of the 21st Century

Barbara Lockett

**AUTHOR NOTE:** When I agreed to write this paper on leadership in the Science and Technology Library of the Future I didn't fully realize what I had committed myself to. As I began to organize my thoughts, I realized that I could not write about leadership without having some idea of what science would be like, what higher education would be like, what libraries in general would be like, and, especially what scientific and technical libraries would be like in the future. I have examined others' visions of the future and analyzed current trends. Extrapolating between today and the next century when the rate of change is so great in all the areas that I am dealing with is difficult. It is also true that it is hard for humans to look very far ahead, because we cannot cast off totally the way things are structured now, or as one writer so effectively put it, "It's a Tough Job Looking Ahead When You've Seen What's Dragging Behind."[3] My reader must realize that these extrapolations, visions and speculations do not put us very far into the 21st century.

**SUMMARY.** The role of librarians serving scientists and engineers in higher education in the 21st century is predicted, based on presently perceived changes in scientific and technical communication and higher education during the 90s. Librarians are characterized as flexible, collaborative, high energy, risk-taking visionaries. Leadership itself will be fluid and shared and will not necessarily reside in the top administrative positions.

---

Barbara Lockett is Director of Libraries at Rensselaer Polytechnic Institute, Troy, NY. She has a BS in Chemistry from the University of Massachusetts and an MLS from the University of California, Berkeley. Barbara's library background includes reference, documents and collection development. Her present focus is on collections/electronic access in a nationally networked environment.

© 1992 by The Haworth Press, Inc. All rights reserved.

## THE TWENTY-FIRST CENTURY ENVIRONMENT

*Libraries.* Let's take a look at what the leaders of today have to say about the libraries of the 21st century. There is no broad consensus amongst them, and so I have selected what seem to me to be common themes and threads that have implications for leadership.

Basically I believe that there will still be libraries and that they will still be in the business of organizing and retrieving information. Woodsworth et al.[28] at a conference on "Options for the Future" said that the research libraries of the future would be organized around 3 major activities: information handling; designing access systems; and evaluating user needs and delivery of services and programs. They also predict that there will be greater diversity in library services and space, which will be determined by institutional values and the degree of emphasis on ownership of materials vis-à-vis access to information. I am going to use this basic model throughout the course of this discussion. The only premise in their vision, with which I do not agree, was that the university would not change significantly over the next 20 or 30 years. Cetron and Davies[5] point out that all of education, including higher is changing rapidly, and I think that they are correct. If this is true, the main effect is that changes for libraries will be greater and occur more rapidly than those envisioned in the "Options for the Future" conference.

To my great relief, no one is predicting that print on paper is going to disappear, only that the formats in which information is communicated will continue to diversify,[1] with electronic formats coming to be a larger portion of the information.[25] As libraries shift to more electronic formats many of these formats will originate external to the institution[1] and the library will adopt a wide range of roles in the provision of electronically based information services. Budgets will be less material based and organized in user groups.[1] Taylor[25] goes so far as to predict that there will be budget formulae to determine the amount of access, hardware and services provided free to faculty, just as the 60s and 70s saw formulae for the proportion of the acquisitions budget that should go to different schools or departments. These views are concurrent with the

Woodsworth[28] concept of access system design and the role of the librarian as a proactive adviser to different user groups on campus. As formats and functions become more diversified, the definition of "library" will begin to blur. Librarians have always had a strong association with place, but as we move out into the user environment to conduct our business, as we take on a broader range of roles, and the collections/access balance shifts, the idea of a librarian as "someone who works in a library" will change. We will be defined more by what we do, than where we work. Hence my final title of Scientific and Technical Librarians: Leaders of the 21st Century, rather than my original Leadership in Scientific and Technical Libraries in the 21st Century.

Although my emphasis in this paper is on academic science and technology libraries, I do not mean to imply that these are the only ones. There are many special libraries which are primarily scientific and technical, and who serve scientists and engineers in government or business, rather than higher education. Most of the research scientists served by libraries are in higher education, whereas most of the engineers can be found in business or the public sector. The greatest amount of change will have to occur in those libraries having both an education and a research function. Special libraries, often 1 or 2 person operations, are in some cases already operating in the way described in the Woodsworth paper. For the most part special libraries do not maintain large collections and are much further along the collections/access spectrum and more advanced in evaluation of user needs and service delivery than academic librarians. These special librarians serve a trained researcher population where academic librarians must serve teachers, researchers and students, and the level of complexity of the governance structure, library organization and patron need is greater in the academic library. I will be focusing in this paper on academic scientific or technical librarians. They are also likely to be the group which will be large enough, connected enough and be allowed time enough to produce a leadership pool.

Before proceeding any further with libraries and librarians, let's see which aspects of these visions and the anticipated changes in the scientific and technical communication system seem to have the most importance for science and technology librarians.

*Science and technology.* At present there is considerable uncertainty in the United States about whether there will be a sufficient number of scientists and engineers (Lohmann,[13] Simon,[24] NSF Long Range Plan,[15] National Science Board[14]) in the 21st century to conduct research and to train the next generation of scientists and engineers. *Time* magazine recently headlined "Science Under Siege" and the story within was titled "Crisis in the Labs."[12] According to that article, U. S. science feels itself in a state of siege, "beset by a budget squeeze, cases of fraud, relentless activists and a skeptical public." These issues will doubtless affect the level of scientific activity in the 21st century. One thing that does seem to emerge from the many articles on the expected shortage of scientific and technical faculty is that there will be greater emphasis on education at all levels, elementary through the Ph.D. in the sciences and engineering in the United States in the next several decades. For the purposes of this paper I will assume that, even though their numbers may dwindle as a percent of the population in the United States, scientists and engineers will still increase in number. The National Science Board report[14] says that there may be spot shortages and surpluses in some fields, but that overall "Shortages may not necessarily develop" in the United States. They do state, however, that projecting ahead is very complex and some of the adjustments necessary to maintain a good flow of scientists and engineers may be very costly and could affect the quality of the workforce.

However many of them there are, scientists and engineers worldwide in the 21st century will doubtless be conducting their research in different ways. The computer has revolutionized libraries, the business and financial worlds and science and technology. Calculations, which once took months or years, can now be done in seconds, and the results quickly disseminated around the world via electronic means. Even if there are fewer scientists in the future the information explosion will continue. Cetron and Davies[5] predict that "all the technological knowledge we work with today will represent only 1% of the knowledge that will be available in 2050" and Gould and Pearce[10] point out that "spacecraft will produce between 1990 and 1995 as much information as they did in the previous 20 years. After 1995, the volume will double every 2 years." It is difficult to assimilate these concepts.

## Scientific and Technical Communication

According to Rogers and Hurt[21] "scholarly journals are obsolete as the primary vehicle for scholarly communication." Journals have long been a major holding of the scientific or technical library. With what, if anything resembling them, will journals be replaced? How will scholars communicate? Global communication networks have already changed the way scientists communicate. Scientists who used to communicate via correspondence, in person, at conferences and via telephone can now not only communicate but simultaneously analyze the same data because it is stored on supercomputers which they access via high speed telecommunications networks. Publishing an article for a print on paper journal is no longer primarily to communicate results. It is more to archive and legitimatize the results which have already become known in the scientific community. This will have an effect on publishing and, therefore, the nature of research libraries.[8] Ann Okerson[16] in the electronic *Public-Access Systems Review* warns that changing the medium of journal distribution carries unpredictable consequences and reviews the range of scenarios possible. Her furthest most prediction is for 2000+ AD when she predicts a 50/50 split between paper journals and electronic alternatives.

Will libraries and librarians be a part of the revised scientific and technical communication/publication process? Those of us who have been in close contact with scientists and engineers for a long time know that the library is usually not the first place a scientist or engineer goes for information about current research in the print-on-paper environment. An earlier issue of this journal was devoted to the "Information Seeking and Communicating Behavior of Scientists and Engineers."[11] The scientist or engineer often does not approach the library until he, or more recently he/she, is desperate and has exhausted his/her own primary sources, that is his/her own files and colleagues. Is it any more likely that, in the future, as Jeff Gardner[8] suggests "libraries may be in considerable danger of becoming irrelevant to the serious scholar in the sciences who frequently keeps abreast of developments in his own or her field through networks–either formal or informal; electronic or traditional?" This is certainly possible. Despite the fact that this has been true to varying degrees for the last hundred years, it is more critical now that we work with scientists and engineers as they drastically alter their communication systems, so that we understand the changes, plan a realistic role in the system and give them the benefit of our experience with information handling. The pace of change in the sciences and technology, communications and computers is so rapid now that if we are not involved in the planning stage, librarians may indeed be left in the dust and never catch up.

The recent RLG study of information needs in the sciences[10] gives a picture of scientists and engineers' information needs in the future that is concurrent with the Woodsworth[28] scenario for that of the research library of the future. Already electronic networks are the most important and heavily used current awareness resources for physicists. Data stored in electronic form from high-energy accelerators is used by physicists around the world, often in collaborative projects. The integrated information environment envisioned in the RLG study for chemists is typical of that for other areas of scientific endeavor. This integrated information environment contains "increased use of national and international computer networks for communication among researchers, access to specialized sources of chemical information and submission of articles and grant proposals; local area networks containing full texts of key journals (with graphics), handbooks, directories and gateways to commercial databases; interfaces with laboratory information systems and large software collections on a local mainframe computer." Librarians have a role to play in information handling and access system design at the local, national and international levels as the information environments alter. We will continue to collaborate with organizations such as American Chemical Society and American Association for the Advancement of Science in the design, implementation and testing of alternatives to today's primarily print-on-paper formats.

According to Weizer,[27] by 1995 the "Information Age" will arrive in those companies aggressive enough to have integrated computing and communications resources into an integrated information system, and engineers will be the first users in the 1990s to benefit from such integrated environments. This environment will include "easy access to outside data sources such as standard engineering specifications and published scientific research," and sharing of data through workstations. Special libraries in such companies are hopefully participating in the access systems design and evaluation of user need, just as their academic colleagues are doing.

Given all the uncertainty and caveats earlier regarding unpredictability or the complexity of predictability in higher education, the possible level of scientific activity, libraries and scientific communication, what can I possibly say about leadership in this high change environment?

As I have been looking to the future and shooting the rapids of the 90s, I have been desperately scanning the horizon, hoping for a serene pool for the 2000s. Alas, I don't think it is to be. Will we just become accustomed to constantly accelerating change? I don't think so. Quite recently greater attention has been paid to human factors in computing interfaces and technology transfer and these will probably be what limits and determines the future rates of change. It is generally recognized that the major limiting factor in bringing about change is people. As Weizer[27] (p. 247) points out, "the tools necessary to implement the neotechnic era are in our hands, but in our minds remains the attachment to the way things have always been done," a more elegant statement of the song title we began with.

## *LEADERSHIP*

Just as there are differing visions of libraries, and scientific and technical communication in the 21st century there are differing concepts of what constitutes leadership and whether there is or is not a sufficient amount of it in the field of librarianship. In 1984 Euster[6] reviewed the literature on leaders and managers and developed a conceptual framework for leadership in librarianship. I adopt her definition of leadership as "the exercise of social influence in order to achieve organizational goals." Although Euster's[6] work is more formal and theoretical, it is interesting that Robert Wedgeworth, identified as one of 16 fieldwide library leaders in Gertzog's[9] study, in answering the question "What Made You a Leader?" says "mostly it comes down to very fundamental characteristics that tend to help you develop *influence*. And I distinctly emphasize influence . . . Leadership revolves around the ability to lead in collaborative arrangements, to persuade people to follow a particular course of action, and to get the work done through others"[20] (pp. 101, 102).

In Euster's model, leadership applies to influence of others in the organization as well as to influence of the perceptions which the environment holds regarding the organization. She identified 2 major environments in which the leader must exert influence, the user environment and the control environment. In that model the user environment and the control environment were within libraries' immediate governance structure, e.g., campus, city or county government. The 21st century environment will be more complex. I believe that there will be another arena in which librarians must exert leadership, and that is outside of the institution and in fields presently outside of librarianship such as computing, telecommunications and publishing which are also in transition.

Woodsworth[28] points out that librarians must take steps outside of a single institution's boundary in order to be able to achieve the vision articulated in "Options for the Future." She points out that: "Librarians must become active partners in the scholarly process and in discussions pertaining to the generation, production and access of information . . . ; Librarians must be increasingly involved with those responsible for the development of information technology for the university and the information industry; Librarians must influence information policy as it affects information use and technology by collaborating with other stakeholders, especially in the political arena, at various governmental levels and in scholarly associations."

A recent position description[4] for the Director of University Libraries at Carnegie Mellon University seeks not only someone to manage ongoing library services effectively but also one who can play a part in Project Mercury, the ability to interact with faculty as an information scientist as well as an administrator, and to *lead* in the development of state-of-the art library services including access to documents in electronic media as well as printed form. This position certainly requires involvement with information technology, and with publishers, and states that the individual must participate in the "*institution's* leadership role" in the development of information technology.

Can one person really do all this? Manage, conduct research and lead in another information field? Probably not. But there is more than one librarian at Carnegie Mellon. The director will be influencing other individuals, other librarians and information professionals. What will those being led in the 21st century be like? The other articles in this issue on education will probably describe many desired skills and attributes, but librarians in the Woodsworth[28] model are described as flexible, collaborative, diverse, fluid, assertive, risk-taking and as synthesizers who have the ability to function in an atmosphere of ambiguity and change. These same characteristics appear in the literature of special librarianship. Regan[19] describes the special librarian as a "front runner," one who is visible, who advocates decentralization of information resources, who creates a vision, and who is an information team member. These have not been the characteristics of librarians in the near past, nor do they characterize many of our present staff, some of whom will still be with us in the 21st century. Obviously, much has to be done in order to empower both librarians and leaders to function in an atmosphere of risk-taking, ambiguity and change and in teams across library organizational lines and with other professions such as scientists or information technologists.

There is a great deal of emphasis in the organizational development literature now about the way in which leaders can foster change. My two favorite models are Belasco[2] and Schneider.[22] Probably because both authors use the cumbersome, yet powerful, elephant in describing change and organizational culture. Belasco[2] titles his work *Teaching the Elephant to Dance* and his model for empowering change looks like this. It appears at the head of each chapter (Figure 1).

Belasco[2] emphasizes that there must be a shared vision between the leader and those led. The vision states what you want your "library" or information role to be in the future. The leader works with librarians to develop and effect the vision. According to Belasco, "participation produces empowerment."

Schneider's[22] model looks a little different, but basically posits the same concepts (Schneider, p. 431). Schneider views change as having two facets (Figure 2). First is its context, i.e., the social, economic, political and competitive environment in which the organization operates as well as the internal organizational environment.

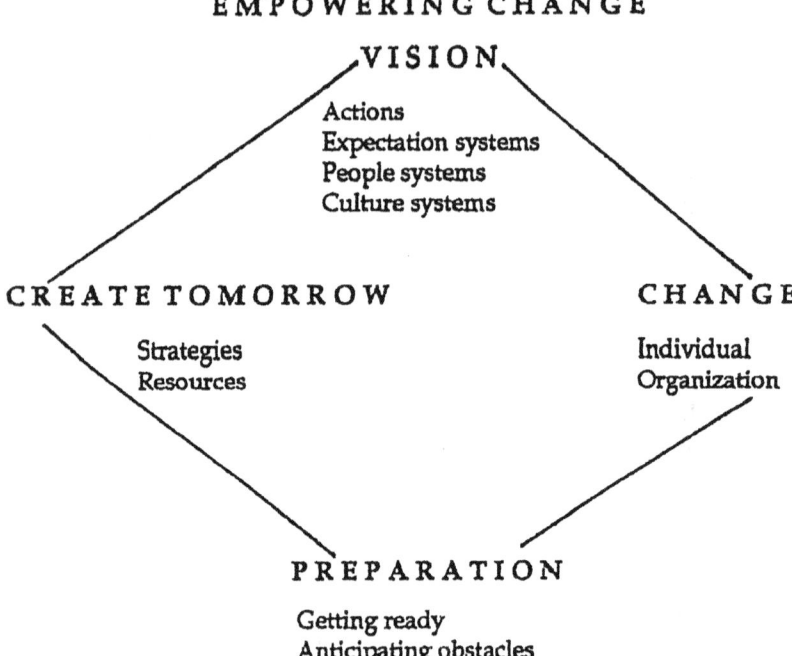

FIGURE 1

Second is the process. Both context and process must be managed. Hence, the leader must take an active role in interacting with and shaping the environment and environmental assessment is an important part of the context of change. I think I like his ideas because he says that it is too narrow to see change just as a rational, linear problem-solving process"[22] (p. 42). That statement relieves the pressure to make it appear rational and legitimizes the occasional process of "winging it" or relying on a hunch. For several years, I have had a small card taped to my phone. I don't remember where I got it, but the back of the card says the following came from Roger von Oech, Creative Think, Menlo Park, CA. "Respect Your Hunches. Your subconscious mind constantly records and stores seemingly unrelated data from the outside world. Later it creatively combines these data into good answers–hunches–if you simply ask, trust and listen."

FIGURE 2

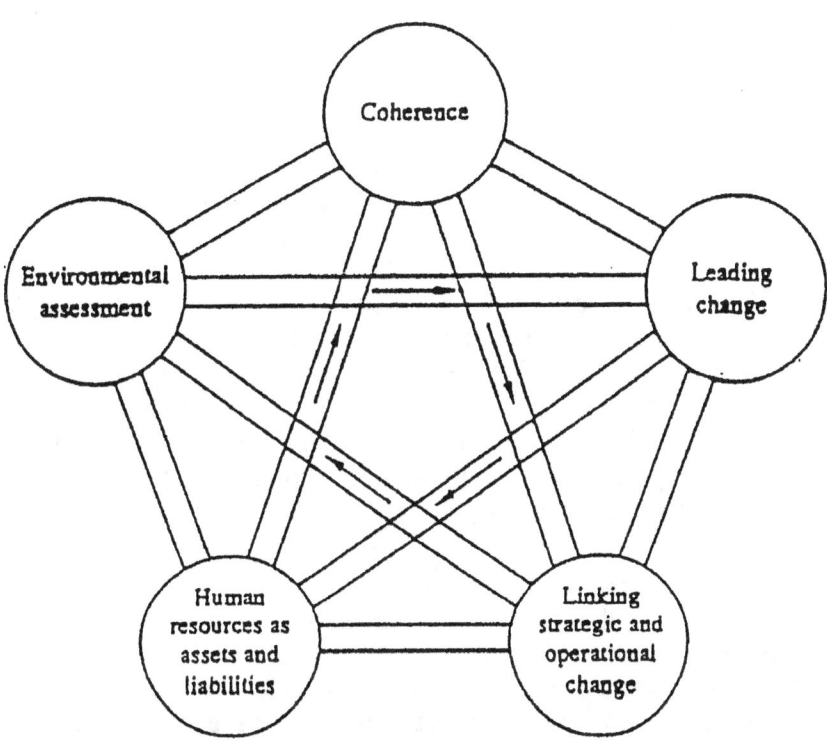

The leader is responding to a myriad of clues from the environment which enable him/her to make a significant move at an appropriate time. A leader becomes very much a watcher and a hearer, and is highly selective in his/her actions. Tom Peter's[18] formula for learning to love change lists developing an inspiring vision as an essential leadership tool. Peters also stresses listening, delegating and rewarding change.

The leader must determine/envision the right things to do and reward those who do them. He/she must also be persistently and consistently involved in the continuous environmental assessment and adjustment process, alert to obstacles and opportunities. His/her vision must be understandably articulated, many times each day. And, as a leader, he/she must live the vision.

In the past, library managers, some of them leaders, have often reorganized or restructured to achieve library goals, but a fairly rigid hierarchy was usually maintained. As the libraries of today position themselves for the more fluid, flexible and collaborative environments of the future, library organization will become less rigid as we form ourselves into the more fluid and variable models of the future. Librarians will find themselves working in teams to effect change, rather than within departments. As librarians are empowered and become more flexible and assertive, they will exert leadership within teams. On one team a librarian might be a leader, in another a follower. Hence, leadership, too, will become more fluid, flexible and collaborative. Or as Euster[7] put it, "leadership is increasingly becoming a distributed function" (p. 29).

For a while I believe that we will be operating 2 tiered semi-rigid structures, as we evolve towards the 3 tiered more fluid situation envisioned by Woodsworth (Figure 3).[28] Designing access systems and evaluating user needs will become functions that will operate as much outside the library as within. Leaders may exist in any of the 3 components or at the top. Traditionally we have expected leadership to come from the position of director, but this will be less the case in the future as libraries and probably institutional hierarchies flatten or are drastically altered.

In the 90s, librarians will need to exercise leadership in the external environment. Librarians must move out of the library into their local institution and become a partner with faculty or researchers in the generation, interpretation and management of information on campus or in the corporation. It is this part of the change process which will give us an identity as librarian or information professional based on what we do, not where we work. This will require enormous energy, skill and risk taking. At first look, it may seem impossible. But, like anything else, it can only be done in small, discrete steps a day at a time. We have to look to the future, develop and share visions with other campus leaders. We could, for example, take advantage of the current "serials crisis" to experiment with this on our individual campuses or within our corporate organizations. The serials crisis is not solely a library problem and librarians should not approach it as such. It is a problem in scientific and technical communication. We must work out a solution where "we" consists of a team of librarians, campus administra-

FIGURE 3

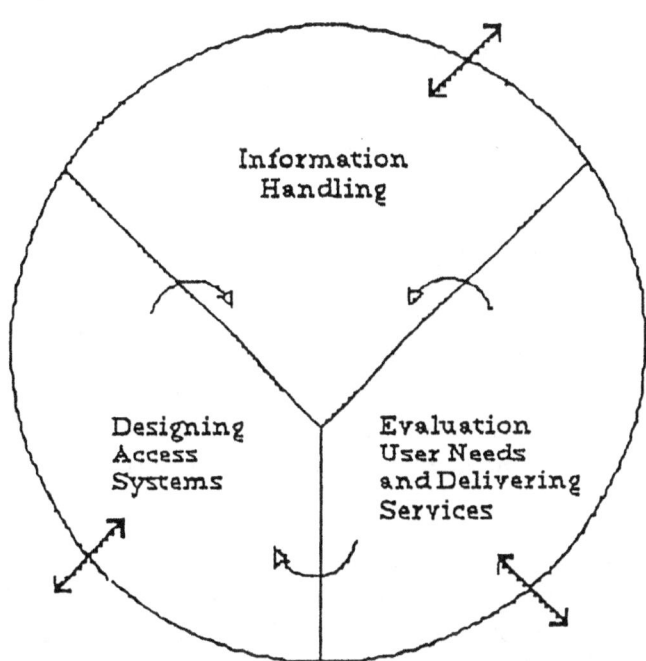

tion, scientists and engineers (as information producers and information consumers). At the national level we must work with scientific organizations and commercial publishers.

I think that this is the biggest task before us in the 90s--collaboration with other influence groups. Librarians have designed outstanding library networks. But we designed them for use by librarians, not for use by library patrons. At the same time, scientists and engineers have designed and built high speed computing/telecommunications networks for scientists and engineers. The challenge of the 90s is to see that these networks mesh and that we do not pursue development on separate tracks. As we allow our librarians to lead within the library and on campus some librarians must collaborate in the political arena and with other disciplines involved in scientific and technical communication. Librarian leaders must influence educational, scientific and political policies, and this has to be more than the uncoordinated work of individual librarians. The first major collaborative effort in this arena is that of the Coalition for Networked Information, made up of members from 3 organizations, the Association for Research Libraries, CAUSE and Educom. The purpose of the Coalition is to "promote the creation of and access to information resources in networked environments in order to enrich scholarship and to enhance intellectual productivity." This quote is from one of the Coalition's vision statements, this one by Paul Peters,[17] Director of the Coalition, titled "Networked information resources and services: Next steps on the road to the distributed digital libraries of the 21st Century." In this vision, too, the prediction is that more and more of the communication between and work of scientists will involve electronic information and that the librarian role will be as an information intermediary who will acquire, organize, store and add value to information distributed and accessed by electronic means.

Scientists and engineers, in education, in government and in industry, have developed and are using these high speed networks which are shaping their information handling environment for the 21st century. For an excellent description of the computing/telecommunications environments being envisioned, see the *Scientific American*[23] September 1991 issue. Because we serve scientists and engineers who will be among the first to have to deal with this new information environment, science and technology librarians will be in the forefront of not only managing information access in the higher education, government and industry environments of the future, but in the forefront of technology transfer to other types of libraries. Leaders will more and more function separate from the library or information center and good management skills may not be sought in the same person as the external leader as in the Carnegie Mellon advertisement.

Another recent job announcement shows that we are already on the way to new leadership environments. The University of California[26] is seeking a Director of Academic Information Systems for its Center for Knowledge Management. "The long term goals of the Center are to create a knowledge management environment and more effectively integrate the Library into the scientific and education processes." Among activities listed for the Director are to recruit, lead and motivate a database and software engineering team for the development of innovative knowledge-based products for research, education and patient care activities; to design a long-range plan for the appropriate adoption of this technology; and to collaborate with faculty in the development and maintenance of knowledge bases which will become part of the Library's electronic collection. The leader sought must have superior interpersonal and communication skills and strong team management experience and skills, amongst other criteria.

These skills are fundamental not only to leadership but to the practice of librarianship, now and in the future. We will not need different leadership skills or a new breed of superlibrarian in the 21st century. Leaders will still be influencing people, whose capacity for change is infinitesimal compared with technology's. Our environments, (higher education, scientific communication and information technology) will continue to shift rapidly, but the most stable part of the system, and that on which we exert our influence, will remain human.

## REFERENCES

1. Adams, Roy J. *Information Technology and Libraries: a Future for Academic Libraries.* London: Croom Helm; 1986. pp. 92-108. Chapter on "A Future for Libraries?"

2. Belasco, James A. Teaching the Elephant to Dance: Empowering Change in Your Organization. New York: Crown; 1990.

3. Campbell, Jerry D. It's a Tough Job Looking Ahead When You've Seen What's Dragging Behind. *Journal of Academic Librarianship* 17(3):148-151; 1991.

4. Carnegie Mellon University. Director, University Libraries. *American Libraries* 22(8):747; 1991 Sept.

5. Cetron, Marvin; Davies, Owen. Trends Shaping the World. *Futurist* 25(5): 11-21; 1991 Sept.-Oct.

6. Euster, Joanne R. Leaders and Managers: Literature Review, Synthesis and a New Conceptual Framework. *Journal of Library Administration* 5(1):45-61; 1984 Spring.

7. Euster, Joanne R. Creativity and Leadership. *Journal of Library Administration* 10(2/3):27-38; 1989.

8. Gardner, Jeffrey. The Challenge of Maintaining Research Collections in the 1990s. *Journal of Library Administration* 14(3):17-25; 1991.

9. Gertzog, Alice. Library Leaders, Who and Why. *Library Journal:* 45-51; 1990 July.

10. Gould, Constance C.; Pearce, Karla. *Information Needs in the Sciences: An Assessment.* Mountain View, CA: Research Libraries Group; 1991.

11. Information Seeking and Communicating Behavior of Scientists and Engineers. *Science & Technology Libraries* 11 (3):1991 Spring.

12. Jaroff, Leon. Crisis in the Labs. *Time* 138(8):45-51; 1991 August 26.

13. Lohmann, Jack R. Myths, Facts and the Future of U.S. Engineering and Science Education. *Engineering Education* 81(3):363-371; 1991 April.

14. National Science Board. Science & Engineering Indicators-1989. Washington, D.C.: U.S. Government Printing Office; 1989 (NSB89-1).

15. National Science Foundation. *Long-Range Plan FY 1989-1993.* Washington, D.C.: National Science Foundation; 1988.

16. Okerson, Ann. The Electronic Journal: What, Whence and When? *Public-Access Computer Systems Review* 2(1):5-24; 1991.

17. Peters, Paul Evan. *Networked information resources and services: Next steps on the road to the distributed digital libraries of the 21st Century.* Washington, D.C.: Coalition for Networked Information; 1991.

18. Peters, Tom. *Thriving on Chaos.* New York: Alfred A. Knopf; 1987.

19. Regan, Muriel. The Special Librarian as a Front Runner: Running Fast, Running Hard, Running Ahead. *Special Libraries* 81(2):92-96; 1990 Spring.

20. Riggs, Donald E.; Sabine, Gordon A. *Libraries in the '90s: What the Leaders Expect.* Phoenix: Oryx Press; 1988.

21. Rogers, Sharon; Hurt, Charlene S. How Scholarly Communication Should Work in the 21st Century. *Chronicle of Higher Education* 35:A56; 1989 October 18.

22. Schneider, Benjamin. *Organizational Climate and Culture.* San Francisco: Jossey-Bass; 1990.

23. *Scientific American* 265(3):1991 September. Complete Issue titled "Communications, Computers and Networks: How to Work, Play and Thrive in Cyberspace."

24. Simon, Lisa. Despite Scientific Shortage, Future Ph.D.'s Fear Joblessness. *The Scientist* 5(1):24,32; 1991 January 7.

25. Taylor, Betty W.; Mann, Elizabeth B.; Munro, Robert J. *The Twenty-First Century: Technology's Impact on Academic Research and Law Libraries.* Boston: G.K. Hall & Co.; 1988.

26. University of California; San Francisco. Director of Academic Information Systems. *Chronicle of Higher Education* 37(48):B18; 1991 August 14.

27. Weizer, Norman et al. *The Arthur D. Little Forecast on Information Technology and Productivity: Making the Integrated Enterprise Work.* New York: Wiley & Sons; 1991.

28. Woodsworth, Anne; Allen, Nancy; et al. The Model Research Library: Planning for the Future. *Journal of Academic Librarianship* 15(3):132-138; 1989.

# Leadership in Science-Engineering Libraries: Considerations and Realities for the Future

Donald G. Frank

**SUMMARY.** Leadership for scientific and technical libraries of the future encompasses a variety of attributes. A sense of vision is critical. Effective communication skills underlie other key attributes. The leader is able to anticipate the future and willing to make necessary adjustments or changes in the existing organizational patterns, processes, or structure to meet user informational needs of the future.

## *INTRODUCTION*

There are numerous science-engineering libraries in the United States of various sizes and with diverse populations of users. A good number of these libraries are relatively large and complex. In one sense, they are "independent" institutions. In reality, they are usually one of several integral units in a larger and more complex system. As a result of the size of the library and its relative position within a system of libraries or other units, the administrator needs to be a leader who is able to communicate effectively.

In this paper, the concept of leadership in scientific and technical

---

Donald G. Frank is Head, Science-Engineering Library at the University of Arizona, Tucson, AZ 85721. He holds the MALS from the University of Missouri and the MPA from Texas Tech University.

libraries will be examined. Relevant social and political factors are explored from an administrative perspective, with a focus on the importance of communication. Creativity and flexibility as well as expertise are some of the requisite characteristics of the effective leaders of the future. These and other attributes or qualities will be discussed. With current and anticipated budgetary realities and with increasingly sophisticated user needs, effective leadership in science-engineering libraries is fundamental and indeed, critical, to success in the future.

## THE SCIENCE-ENGINEERING LIBRARY

One of the committees in the Science and Technology Section of ALA's Association of College and Research Libraries compares science-engineering libraries.[1] Statistical data on selected libraries are collected and analyzed in efforts to define and illustrate essential characteristics. These libraries provide bibliographic programs and services for a sizable and sophisticated clientele. Combinations of reference, online, and instructional services are offered to users. Collection development is another primary activity, with an emphasis on serial publications. In academic libraries, activities related to faculty liaison promote effective collection development and management and provide essential feedback for practical administrative decisions.

Reference librarians and several classified staff are usually available to provide reference assistance. A variety of online programs and services are utilized to improve access to serials, conference proceedings, and other technical reports. Faculty, students, or other users may access the scientific and technical literature via mediated searches and/or varied end user services, including expert systems. With the accelerated emphasis on science and technology at many institutions, the demand for superior and more complex reference/online assistance intensifies annually.

The collections are essential to research and instructional efforts.[2] In the scientific and technical disciplines, the emphasis on current materials is continually accented. Specifically, serial titles, proceedings of conferences and symposia, and annual reviews of the literature are perceived as critical. As a result, contemporary serials reviews and/or cancellations place additional pressure on administrators to provide alternative access to information.

## THE GENERAL NATURE OF LEADERSHIP

Stated in simple terms, leadership is a process of influencing human behavior. In *Human Behavior at Work*, Davis defines leadership as the "ability to persuade others to seek defined objectives enthusiastically."[3] This definition underscores the role of leadership in stimulating behavioral responses that are more than routine. In an organizational context, however, the full significance of leadership is not captured by this behavioral perspective. Organizations are goal-oriented and motivated by a sense of purpose. Leaders are placed in key positions to facilitate the achievement of organizational goals. Consequently, leadership is the process of influencing human behavior so that the goals of the organization are accomplished.[4]

The effective leader operates at a level that is usually more complex and sophisticated than the comparable manager's level. A leader who becomes too involved with the "mundane tasks of organizational maintenance" will eventually fail to lead. According to Bennis, leadership is the "capacity to infuse new values and goals into the organization, to provide perspective on events and environments which, if unnoticed, can impose constraints on the institution."[5] The importance of infused values and goals in relation to leadership is noted in Schein's *Organizational Culture and Leadership*. In this classic treatise, leadership is defined as "managed culture change."[6]

Leadership requires a sense of vision. The capable leader is able to interact with the organization's environment, deal with uncertainty, and consider options to reduce the level of environmental uncertainty. A leader is aware of what needs to be done to attain important organizational goals. Then, he or she communicates information on relevant ideas and proposals to appropriate personnel who are prepared to develop and implement these recommendations. In a classic paper on the nature of leadership, Gardner elaborates on the importance of vision in leadership:

1. They think longer term–beyond the day's crises, beyond the quarterly report, beyond the horizon.
2. They look beyond the unit they are heading and grasp its relationship to larger realities–the larger organization of which they are a part, conditions external to the organization, global trends.
3. They reach and influence constituents beyond their jurisdictions, beyond boundaries . . . Their capacity to rise above jurisdictions may enable them to bind together the fragmented constituencies that must work together to solve a problem.
4. They put heavy emphasis on the intangibles of vision, values, and motivation, and understand intuitively the nonrational and unconscious elements in the leader-constituent interaction.
5. They have the political skill to cope with the conflicting requirements of multiple constituencies.
6. They think in terms of renewal. The routine manager tends to accept the structure and processes as they exist. The leader or leader/manager seeks the revisions of process and structure required by ever-changing reality.[7]

In a serious examination of leadership, the critical nature of communication is continually reflected. A leader is a communicator with a sense of vision. He or she must be able to communicate effectively at the interpersonal and institutional levels. In addition, the ability to cope with environments characterized by uncertainty is essential.

## *LEADERSHIP: ROLE, RESPONSIBILITIES, AND SKILLS FOR THE FUTURE*

The role and responsibilities of proactive leaders in science-engineering libraries continually evolve. To anticipate and meet the current and future informational needs of patrons in science and technology, a special set of skills will be needed. Budgetary realities and a wide range of complex issues necessitate the attention and efforts of individuals with a sense of vision. They are able to see what needs to be done in order to attain relevant organizational goals within a context of continuous change. Continued serials inflation, the struggle between access and ownership, cooperative collection management initiatives, and less than adequate budgets are representative issues that call for balanced expertise and leadership.

Effective leaders are aware of and able to communicate with the varied elements in the environment of the science-engineering library. Some common environmental elements include faculty, students, other patrons, academic departments (in academic institutions), other libraries in the immediate locality as well as the appropriate or defined region (including other science-engineering libraries), materials and information vendors, and the professional associations. Substantive communication with users and other environmental elements is requisite to effective services. Too frequently, the informational needs of users are assumed to be understood while, in reality, these assumptions may not be accurate. With a focus on currency and the relative importance of the serial literature, the informational needs and the information seeking behaviors of those in the sciences are different from those in the social sciences, fine arts, and humanities. As a result, familiarity with evolving user needs and the ability to assess the details as well as overall trends associated with patterns of information seeking are critical. Effective communication with the science-engineering library's environmental elements essentially reduces the level of uncertainty in the library's environment and facilitates the capacity to fulfill the mission of the library.

Administrators of scientific and technical libraries need to be politically astute. This is particularly important in all interactions related to the allocation of resources, a political process that requires a fine sense of negotiation. Science-engineering libraries are usually one of several libraries or organizational units competing for limited human and physical resources. The ability to articulate and justify specific organizational needs is essential. Most science-engineering libraries are probably understaffed and generally underfunded. Possibilities of additional staff and funds for collections must be vigorously pursued within appropriate political realities. Those who are not aware of or ignore the vagaries of the political process may not be able to acquire and/or organize the resources necessary to serve users effectively.[8]

In *The Politics of Management,* Yates discusses strategies for the management of conflict within a political context. With budgets and resources that are increasingly limited, the ability to manage political conflict will make a positive difference in negotiations. In deliberations over resources, two political realities will usually surface in the decision process: (1) competing parties will desire more of some or particular resources; (2) they will indicate that their needs or problems are more serious than those of others. In these competitive negotiations involving actual and potential political conflict, several strategies are recommended, including: identify mutual needs/problems; avoid winner-take-all decision games; include all affected parties in decisions; provide all relevant information needed for decisions; maintain open channels of communication with the other negotiators; be aware of and familiar with the position and situation of other competitors; develop a sense of shared mission in the course of policy dialogue; utilize an incremental approach prior to the development of comprehensive solutions if numerous parties will be affected; be assertive and reasonable.[9] Those who are politically astute and able to negotiate effectively will be capable leaders and representatives of science-engineering libraries.

As an active and dynamic organization, the science-engineering library's organizational culture needs to be understood by professional librarians and classified staff. In particular, progressive leaders with a sense of vision are aware of the library's "organizational culture" and are concerned with the culture's focus and direction. In general terms, organizational cultures encompass observed behavioral regularities in staff interactions (or, the "rules of the game"), the collective values that evolve over time, and the philosophies that guide the formulation of the library's policies and procedures. Schein defines organizational culture as the "basic assumptions and beliefs that are shared by members of an organization, that operate unconsciously, and that define in a basic taken-for-granted fashion an organization's view of itself and its environment. These assumptions and beliefs are learned responses to a group's problems of survival in its external environment and its problems of internal integration. They come to be taken for granted because they solve those problems repeatedly and reliably."[10]

A balanced and intuitive sense of the dynamics of organizational structure is essential. While the organizational culture of the science-engineering library includes activities and patterns associated with assumptions, policy, and values, the organizational structure encompasses the formal patterns of relationships among the structural elements or entities of the library. The proactive leader realizes that libraries are dynamic institutions and anticipates the changes necessary to meet the informational needs of users. In academic institutions, administrators of science-engineering libraries need to be able to relate the organizational structure of the library to the "main" library and to other possible scientific or technical libraries within a system of libraries. These organizational attributes will be particularly relevant for administrators who deal with current and future budgetary constraints and realities as the library, with all its programs, services, and collections, must be organized effectively and efficiently to attain critical goals and objectives in support of its overall mission.

The ability to anticipate organizational adaptations and changes requires appropriate expertise as well as the motivation to intervene in the library's cultural and structural processes. In science-engineering libraries, the dramatic problems related to serials inflation seriously affect the ability to provide essential information for patrons. Organizational changes and associated structural modifications are needed to create "access infrastructures" for the serial literature. Whether changes in the organizational structure focus on an infrastructure for access to serial titles, for example, or on all major functions and units of the library, effective leadership implies the mobilization and participation of all affected individuals and parties, including the users. As noted previously, effectual communications usually underscore success for leaders.

Leaders assume responsibility for information policy development. They are familiar with the process of scholarly communication and are able to assess informational needs and consider alternative approaches to meet these needs. Innovative concepts such as "knowledge management" and university-based electronic publishing systems necessitate a mutual responsibility for scientific and scholarly communication, a responsibility shared by scholars, scientists, and librarians or information specialists, with computing and communications technologies as primary tools.[11] Librarians with a sense of vision will be aware of and/or involved with the development of information policy.

Administrators and staff in scientific and technical libraries need to be aware of and sensitive to the particular informational needs of users. A proactive approach is critical as user informational needs underlie the library's mission; these needs cannot be assumed. Information seeking behavior and practices may differ from discipline to discipline. The differences between those in the sciences and the practitioners or engineers, for example, have been documented.[12] Moreover, *Information Needs in the Sciences: An Assessment*, prepared for the Program for Research Information Management by the Research Libraries Group, provides an extensive survey of the information needs of those in the basic sciences, including physics, chemistry, biology, the geosciences, astronomy, engineering (general), mathematics, and computer science.[13] "The nature of science and technology and differences between engineers and scientists influence their information seeking habits, practices, needs, and preferences, and have significant implications for planning information services for these two groups."[14] Bibliographic programs and services in science-engineering libraries must be responsive to the diverse and evolving informational needs of patrons. A leader will continually assess user needs, anticipate and determine appropriate changes, and organize to meet these needs.

Leaders are aware of relevant issues in science-engineering libraries and play a key role as these issues are developed and refined. Recognition of major or crucial issues is especially important. Available time and attention are limited. The leader will assess what needs to be done in relation to a particular issue and then influence others to assume responsibility for action. As members of the staff are motivated to attain goals, creative and innovative measures and solutions need to be cultivated and supported. Cultivation of creativity and innovation is essential in generating viable strategies to deal with complex issues such as scholarly communication, access/ownership, and the implementation as well as impact of sophisticated information technologies.

In the cultivation of creativity and innovation, the effective leader will allocate time for the generation of ideas. Problematic situations need to be perceived as opportunities or challenges. Diversity of opinion is another requisite to innovation. Too frequently, those who are considered "different" may not be selected to participate. Still, innovation thrives on the tension created by diversity. If variety is important, special skills in negotiation, conflict management, consensus formation, and a personal philosophy that stimulates people to deal with issues are critical attributes needed in the leaders of science-engineering libraries.[15]

In reality, all forms of diversity facilitate the creative process. Effective leadership implies a special sensitivity to diversity in the workplace. This is emphasized in *Changing America: The New Face of Science and Engineering*, compiled by the Task Force on Women, Minorities, and the Handicapped in Science and Technology for the Office of Science and Technology Policy. The recommendations are associated with attitudes and values that need to be discussed and integrated into the organizational culture.[16]

A willingness to take risks is an essential attribute for the leaders of scientific and technical libraries. Risk taking is closely related to the actions of those with a sense of vision. A tolerance for ambiguity, frustration, and failure combined with a genuine sense of purpose are requisites for the risk taker. Previous failures or mistakes must be appraised with needed perspective and considered to be learning experiences. Confidence in the ability and creative capacity of staff is essential. Members of the staff must feel that different approaches or solutions are valued and that mistakes are tolerated.

## *LIBRARIES IN TRANSITION: CHALLENGES FOR LEADERS*

Scientific and technical libraries are dynamic institutions. The particular informational needs of their patrons generate a sense of immediacy and serve as a primary impetus for organizational change. Koenig argues that the science-engineering library is "in effect a precursor of the evolving pattern of library and information service."[17] Furthermore, the scientific and technical disciplines are essentially defined or characterized by a sense of informational immediacy and by exponentially accelerating publications rates in comparison to other subject areas. "The libraries and information centers that support scientific research are consequently relatively non-inertial in nature. That is, they must be responsive to what the organization is pursuing now and what it intends to pursue in the near future . . . They must be prepared to change course and to change priorities on a moment's notice."[18]

The implications for leadership are significant. Proactive and innovative solutions or methodologies are essential to effective services in libraries characterized by constant change and intense user informational needs. The ability to anticipate and see beyond today's limitations is a primary requisite for those who assume the roles and responsibilities of leaders. Scientific and technical libraries need to be in a state of continuous transition to meet the informational needs of scholars and other practitioners.

As they consider informational needs and responsive organizational structures of the future, leaders must be active communicators as well as effective negotiators with relevant environmental elements. Immediacy of access necessitates the ability to develop and negotiate cooperative collections initiatives and document delivery options with other institutions and vendors. As more of the user population will be remote or external to the library or information center (especially in academic institutions), electronic access via local, regional, and national networks will affect the organization of the library and the methodologies developed to provide access to the serial literature and other relevant databases. Or, as the "virtual library" evolves into a reality, dramatic changes in the patterns of information seeking behavior as well as information use will affect organizational structure and services provided. With budgetary realities and available information technologies, "business as usual" will not be likely. Realistic focus and direction and a sense of vision will be requisites to satisfy user informational needs of the future.

## CONCLUDING COMMENTS

Leadership for scientific and technical libraries of the future encompasses a variety of attributes. A sense of vision is critically important. Effective communication skills underlie other attributes. Without a sense of vision or direction, those in positions of leadership may not be able to look beyond today's activities, crises, and budgetary constraints. They may struggle in efforts to assess and to communicate with key environmental elements. As libraries and organizations in general need to reduce the level of uncertainty in their environment, effective communications with users and other libraries or institutions are essential.

Leadership is proactive and is concerned with what will be. The leader is able to anticipate the future and willing to make necessary adjustments or changes in the existing organizational patterns, processes, or structure to meet user informational needs of the future.

Leadership is described by Burns as "that most observed and least understood phenomenon."[19] A relatively complex concept, effectual leadership is essential to success in dynamic libraries with varied and sophisticated users whose informational needs continually change. Pressures related to desired immediacy of access in science and technology and the volume of the published literature continually affect relative priorities and necessitate action by a leader with a sense of vision. The future of science-engineering libraries will be filled with continual change, major challenges, uncertainty, and numerous opportunities. Drucker concludes that a "time of turbulence is also one of great opportunity for those who can understand, accept, and exploit the new realities. It is above all a time of opportunity for leadership."[20]

## REFERENCES

1. This is the Comparison of Science and Technology Libraries Committee, Science and Technology Section, Association of College and Research Libraries, American Library Association.

2. This assertion is stated or inferred in the literature and is assumed by a

good number of librarians and information specialists. I am not aware of a specific study that actually correlates these variables.

3. Davis, Keith. *Human Behavior at Work*, 5th ed. (New York: McGraw-Hill Book Company, 1977; p. 107).

4. Prince, Howard T., ed. *Leadership in Organizations.* (West Point, NY: United States Military Academy, 1981; pp. 7-9).

5. Bennis, Warren. *The Leaning Ivory Tower.* (San Francisco: Jossey-Bass Publishers, 1973; pp. 83-84).

6. Schein, Edgar H. *Organizational Culture and Leadership.* (San Francisco: Jossey-Bass Publishers, 1988).

7. Gardner, John. *The Nature of Leadership: Introductory Considerations.* (Washington, D.C.: Leadership Studies Program, 1986; p. 8).

8. The importance of an awareness of the vagaries of the political process are discussed in numerous publications in public administration and other academic disciplines. For example, see: Morrow, William L. *Public Administration: Politics, Policy, and the Political System*, 2nd ed. (New York: Random House, 1980).

9. Yates, Douglas. *The Politics of Management.* (San Francisco: Jossey-Bass Publishers, 1985; pp. 130-165).

10. Schein, p. 6.

11. For example, see: Lucier, Richard. "Knowledge Management: Refining Roles in Scientific Communication." *EDUCOM Review* 25 (Fall 1990): 21-27. Also, see: Okerson, Ann. "Back to Academia? The Case for American Universities to Publish Their Own Research." *LOGOS* 2 (2): 106-112.

12. For example, see: Pinelli, Thomas. "The Information-Seeking Habits and Practices of Engineers." *Science & Technology Libraries* 11 (Spring 1991): 5-25. [This issue of *Science & Technology Libraries* is devoted to information seeking practices and related communication patterns.]

13. Gould, Constance C., and Karla Pearce. *Information Needs in the Sciences: An Assessment.* (Mountain View, CA: Research Libraries Group, 1991).

14. Pinelli, p. 12.

15. Morgan, Gareth. *Riding the Waves of Change: Developing Managerial Competencies for a Turbulent World.* (San Francisco: Jossey-Bass Publishers, 1988; pp. 70-85).

16. United States, Office of Science and Technology Policy. *Changing America: The New Face of Science and Engineering.* (Washington, D.C.: Office of Science and Technology Policy, 1989).

17. Koenig, Michael E. D. "Budgeting and Financial Planning for Scientific and Technical Libraries." *Science & Technology Libraries* 4 (Spring/Summer 1984): 89.

18. Koenig, p. 88.

19. Burns, James M. *Leadership.* (New York: Harper & Row, 1978; p. 2).

20. Drucker, Peter F. *Managing in Turbulent Times.* (New York: Harper & Row, 1980; p. 2).

# Education and Recruitment of Science and Engineering Librarians

Crit Stuart
Miriam A. Drake

The scarcity of librarians with science and engineering degrees has concerned the profession for many years. By necessity libraries fill the majority of sci-tech positions with humanities and social sciences graduates. Mount's 1983 survey of sixteen sci-tech college and university libraries revealed that only 32% of librarians had a sci-tech bachelor's degree or above.[1] Special Libraries Association data indicate that 1% of the SLA salary survey respondents hold a degree in engineering and 15% in science.[2] This situation has changed little over time with no forecast of an improved recruitment pool of scientists and engineers to draw from and with few practical remedies proposed.

The quality of information services provided to scientists and engineers is less effective when the librarians serving them have little or no experience in these disciplines. The problem is exacerbated as the volume of information and data grow and researchers show a continued reliance on their own identification and extraction methods. A key paper, article or report may not be found resulting in redundancy and avoidable costs.

## *HOW SCI/TECH PEOPLE WORK*

The research and information gathering habits of most scientists and engineers indicate that libraries and librarians are not the first

---

Crit Stuart is Assistant Director for Public Services and Miriam A. Drake is Dean of Libraries at Georgia Institute of Technology, Library and Information Center.

© 1992 by The Haworth Press, Inc. All rights reserved.

choices for consultation when information is needed. In his excellent review article of the information-seeking habits of scientists and engineers, Pinelli stated that engineers look for quick, intelligible answers which apply directly to research problems.[3] The information does not have to be current or the result of exhaustive searching, but it must satisfy the research problem. The usual sources for these answers are technical reports, handbooks and journals close at hand and respected colleagues. These sources have proven reliable in the past. Librarians tend to fall near the bottom of the list of preferred sources.

Looking to the immediate future, Pinelli says that communication mechanisms for channeling scientific and technical information must quickly evolve into more effective methods if American technical innovation and R&D are to remain competitive. As practiced today, information provision falls short because it doesn't fully take into account the research habits of engineers or their need for value-added products.

Scientists and engineers often presume that if the librarian has no grounding in the discipline there is no personal knowledge base to aid the researcher and no common frame of reference. In short, reliance on librarians will not occur if there is no perceived benefit. The individual involved in research will acquire information from proven sources.

If libraries are to play vital roles in research, development and competitiveness they must change. Technology is making it possible for scientists and engineers to access information without libraries. The need for libraries may disappear unless librarians are viewed as contributors rather than obstacles to the information transfer process. Contribution to the process requires that librarians view themselves as being active facilitators of information transfer rather than guardians of books, journals and other materials.

## *CURRENT SITUATION*

A great deal has been written about the advantages of hiring dual-degree librarians to fill sci-tech reference positions. Some of our colleagues make the argument that non-scientists can be trained to perform as effectively as librarians with science or engineering degrees. However, without a knowledge of mathematical concepts, basic scientific principles, engineering applications and the communication channels used by scientists and engineers to acquire scientific and technical information, the non-science or engineering person begins with a disadvantage that is difficult to overcome.

Science and engineering libraries effect a compromise by training new hires without science or engineering degrees to work with sci-tech and engineering information sources. Given time, effective training, personal incentive and nurturing peer relationships, the new librarian may establish a rudimentary competence in handling traditional information requests. Reference departments are filled with librarians with social sciences and humanities degrees who provide adequate library services to sci-tech and engineering students. However, this basic service is not meeting the needs of faculty and research staff whose time and energy are valuable assets.

Paradoxically, many sci-tech libraries are rich in resources which complement their organizations' research efforts, but remain grossly underutilized by their clients. In an attempt to create a broader market for information and data, libraries may advertise services. Various means are utilized, including flyers mailed to faculty and researchers, articles in school newspapers, corporate newsletters, signage at reference desks and electronic bulletin board announcements. Advertisements extol the value of SDIs, commercial database searches, universal acquisition of documents, regardless of ownership or location, document delivery, on-site and remote access to OPACS, CD ROMs or online databases. Faculty and research staff who recognize the value of these services may make considerable use of them. Making the service available and letting people know about it does not mean it will be used. Successful implementation of end-user searching requires training, a high level of customer support and preparation and distribution of well-written documentation. Success also requires a change in librarians' attitudes about the end result of their work. Information retrieval processes will not be effective unless the context of information use is understood.

When librarians began to use online databases they thought the job was done when they retrieved a list of citations. They did not realize that retrieval of citations is only the first step in the process of information acquisition and use.

Penniman has pointed out, "Even in cases where significant commitment has been made and resources invested, the human aspects of information processing and delivery have continued to limit the full utilization of available technology. A library is essentially a labor-intensive institution because information transfer relies in large part on human-to-human communication. Finding methods for making this process more efficient and effective is the real challenge facing librarians today."[4]

The science or engineering degreed librarian with a grounding in subject material, practice in scientific and research methods, and a presumed enthusiasm for the subject discipline is more likely to establish valuable relationships with clients and be able to provide effective information services. A librarian with a science or engineering background will have a greater understanding of the client's problem and context and will be able to evaluate as well as find useful information.

## *EDUCATION*

The current pattern of library school recruitment of scientists and engineers does not indicate success in supplying dual degree librarians. In her review of the science librarian hiring crisis, Dewey observed, "Library schools have a difficult time recruiting students in the science disciplines to prepare for such positions. Libraries are hard pressed to attract qualified candidates because of low salaries .... In addition in science and technologically-oriented disciplines students do not have great exposure to traditional library research methods in their undergraduate courses and therefore both student and faculty advisor often give no thought to career possibilities in the library and information science field."[5]

Few science or engineering students will be attracted to work in libraries if library salaries don't compete with industry. A sampling of average starting salaries for science and engineering bachelor's degree candidates is revealing: Chemistry ($26,698), Mathematics ($26,789), Physics ($28,296)[6] Engineering jobs in industry ($31,600).[7,8] The average starting salary for librarians in ARL libraries for approximately the same time period was $23,954.[9]

When library schools do succeed in attracting students with science or engineering backgrounds, the curriculum is not structured to develop the skills librarians require to provide service valued by their clients. Most library schools offer courses in scientific and technical information sources, but there is almost no attempt to relate these sources to the unique research habits, context of work or information gathering techniques employed by scientists and engineers. The new librarian may develop expertise working with the best sources available but will be unable to use this knowledge until he/she becomes familiar with the work of the organization.

In addition, librarians usually are not trained to evaluate information and make judgments about its quality, timeliness or relevance to the problem. Science and engineering productivity could be increased substantially by providing information which has been assessed, synthesized and packaged.

## *RECRUITMENT*

Competition for the few dual degreed librarians is fierce. To compete successfully, libraries must offer substantially greater salaries than are customary for beginning librarians. Academic libraries often are prevented from offering higher salaries by established pay scales and shrinking budgets.

The image of the profession poses an additional hurdle to recruitment. Applicants considering equal offers from both academic and special libraries frequently choose the latter because of the expectation of job gratification, prestige and recognition of one's value to the research effort. The applicant's perception of work in an academic library, shaped by the undergraduate experience and assumptions formulated in library school, is of a traditional, less rewarding relationship with faculty and students. Academic librarians are not usually integral participants in research activity. Alternatively, the special library offers a perceived immersion in problem deliberation and information provision critical to the success of the team.

## ALTERNATIVES

Science and engineering libraries are faced with three alternatives to satisfy the shortage of sci/tech librarians: (1) continue the predominant trend of training librarians without science or engineering degrees; (2) hire undergraduates with the BS degree to provide information services to their special clients; or (3) train the scientists and engineers to do a better job of finding information for themselves. If libraries are forced to continue current practice, hiring Bachelor of Arts librarians to serve scientists and engineers, libraries will contribute minimal support for problem solving and R&D.

Perhaps the time has come to seriously consider dropping the library degree as a requirement for science and engineering library positions. Libraries could focus their energy on developing recruitment programs which identify and attract freshly minted scientists and engineers directly into the ranks. Once hired, the transformation of the science/engineering undergrad into an effective librarian will require that the library, rather than the library school, provide training in information work. The need for specialized training of science and technology librarians was recognized thirty years ago when the National Science Foundation sponsored two conferences at Georgia Tech to study the problem. The conference proceedings defined a technical literature analyst as, "One who is trained in a substantive technical field, who has . . . some breadth of technical knowledge and a thorough knowledge of technical literature. He can analyze the literature for researchers who are investigating problems in the area of the analyst's technical competence . . . In his ability to deal with the technical literature the analyst differs from the conventional science librarian in that he is sufficiently deep in science to be able to make value judgements of its literature."[10]

The science librarian was defined as one who had an acquaintance with science and could perform literature searches but could not evaluate the literature. The librarian was viewed as interacting with books while the technical literature analyst dealt with the information in the books.

The availability of online information, electronic distribution of journal articles and collaborative work through networks will obviate the need to interact with books. Librarians and information specialists will be dealing more and more with information in a variety of representations. The functions of the technical literature analyst and librarian must be integrated to provide effective information services.

Electronic libraries will contain graphics, numerics and images, as well as text. Information service provision will require subject background to find, evaluate and synthesize this variety of material for scientists and engineers. While some people will choose to do their own searching others will rely on specialists to find what is needed among thousands of databases, billions of pages of information and a complex telecommunications network structure.

Where do we look for these young scientists and engineers? The potential recruits are students currently enrolled in bachelors degree programs in science and engineering. Increasingly, these students are working with online information, computer graphics and networks. Often instruction to students is provided by library personnel. While librarians may not understand the work of scientists and engineers, they are in a perfect position to advertise the market for information specialists in the sciences and engineering, and to propose that some might consider science and technical information provision as a career.

The important role librarians play in recruitment cannot be underemphasized. In *Library and Information Science Student Attitudes, Demographics and Aspirations Survey* conducted in 1988, "students were asked who or what was influential in their choice of a career in library/information science." Nearly 20% of respondents identified college librarians as influential, and 22% named teachers or faculty members.[11]

What is the likelihood that science and engineering majors would consider a career as a librarian? Since there is currently almost no organized recruitment by libraries this is difficult to determine. But science and engineering students are a fluid population. Many of them will change majors before acquiring a degree. In a 1990 Wall Street Journal article on the dropout rate of students in science and engineering programs, author Milbank used statistics supplied by the National Science Foundation. She stated, . . . "some 42% of those who enter college professing interest in science or engineering careers drop out of the sciences after [the] freshman year, and another 23% defect before graduation."[12]

Libraries might forge alliances with academic department heads and academic advisors to develop a career path alternative for science and engineering students who do not care for the laboratory environment. Many science and engineering students seek more breadth in their educational experiences and view current workplace positions as too confining. Technical and scientific information work coupled with information technology may be an intriguing and stimulating alternative. Engineering and science programs could be enhanced with information courses taught as collaborative ventures between the department and the library.

Helsinki University of Technology, through its Centre for Continuing Education, has developed an intensive nine month information services program for university graduates. In the last five years 50% of participants were scientists and engineers. Basic components of the program include "information as a component of corporations," "information technology," and "information processing and transfer." The information services program provides basic knowledge and skills supplemented by training on the job.[13]

Hiring undergraduate scientists and engineers instead of librarians will create many problems. They could be hired as information specialists rather than librarians. In any case, competitive salaries will have to be offered. Library administrations confronted with the difficult decision of offering competitive salaries face the consternation of lower salaried staff already in place and the likelihood that staff morale will suffer when a separate and unequal salary scale is established. The recruit with a bachelor's degree may also encounter resistance in peer relationships.

Will the quality of information service provided to the organization's scientists and engineers by the undergraduate novice off-set the dissention created? A successful transition would, at a minimum, have to include a superb training program coupled with an aggressive marketing campaign to merge the information specialist into the research activity of the organization. Over time, the library would want to measure the success of the endeavor, working closely with the client population to determine emphasis, direction and value. Perhaps the intended client population could indicate its own receptivity to the idea before the program was attempted.

The third approach to maximizing information service to scientists and engineers is to enhance their own skills in gathering information. Today's bibliographic instruction programs in science and engineering libraries are directed to students, with an emphasis on sci-tech sources and retrieval techniques. The focus is on curriculum support rather than research. Courses for faculty and research staff would have to take into account the nature of their work, research habits and communication patterns. Very little has been done in academe to translate this behavior into programs to radically improve their success. Corporate libraries and information centers have been more successful in training scientists and engineers in information finding.

If academic libraries were to offer information training programs developed for researchers the target population would have to recognize the value of the program and its potential to positively affect their work and productivity. Skills might be taught in group settings or in individual encounters. Training would include use of online databases of all types, downloading, creation of personalized databases and navigation of telecommunications networks. Training and user support are continuous services which must be maintained and upgraded as technology and resources change. Librarians might serve as instructors, or representatives from academic departments and research units could receive intensive training and return to their groups for a second round of dissemination. Success would depend on well-designed instruction programs, effective, well-trained tutors and available customer support.

## *CONCLUSION*

U.S. competitiveness, R&D and productivity can be improved with more effective information services. Technology is making it possible to access huge quantities of information in all forms, but technology by itself will not do the whole job. Access and acquisition depend on knowing where needed information is located and how to obtain it. Finding the right information at the right time is the job of skilled and experienced professionals. For librarians to best satisfy the information needs of a customer requires an understanding of the problem, context, time requirements, and how information is used in the individual's work.

Scientists and engineers are not being fully served by many sci/tech libraries. There is a clear need to recruit people with science and engineering backgrounds into the library and information profession. Recruitment may mean changing library school education, training on the job, increasing salaries and improving the image of librarians. Underlying these changes is the need to recognize that librarians and information professionals can be key agents in the information transfer process.

## REFERENCES

1. Mount, Ellis. *University Science and Engineering Libraries.* Westport, Connecticut: Greenwood Press, 1985.
2. Special Libraries Association. *SLA Biennial Salary Survey, 1991*, Washington, D.C. Special Libraries Association, 1991.
3. Pinelli, Thomas E. "The Information-Seeking Habits and Practices of Engineers." *Science and Technology Libraries.* 11, no. 3 (Spring 1991): 5-25.
4. Penniman, W. David. "Tomorrow's Library Today." *Special Libraries*, Summer, 1987, p. 196.
5. Dewey, Barbara I. "Science Background Required–Others Need Not Apply: a Study of the Science Librarian Hiring Crisis." *Proceedings of the 49th ASIS Annual Meeting; 1986 September 28-October 2*; Chicago, IL. Learned Information Inc., 1986: p. 64.
6. College Placement Council. Salary Survey Committee. *CPC Salary Survey.* Bethlehem, Pa.: College Placement Council, July 1989.
7. Engineering Manpower Commission. *Salaries of Engineers in Education 1990.* Washington: American Association of Engineering Societies, Inc., 1990.
8. Engineering Manpower Commission. *Professional Income of Engineers 1990.* Washington: American Association of Engineering Societies, Inc., 1990.
9. Pritchard, Sarah M., ed., and Fretwell, Gordon, comp., *ARL Annual Salary Survey 1990.* Washington: Association of Research Libraries, 1991.
10. *Information Specialists' Proceeding.* Atlanta, Ga., Georgia Institute of Technology, May 1, 1962.
11. Moen, William E. "Library and Information Science Student Attitudes, Demographics and Aspirations Survey: Who We Are and Why We Are Here."

*Librarians for the New Millenium*, edited by William E. Moen and Kathleen M. Heim. Chicago: American Library Association, 1988.

12. Milbank, Dana. "Shortage of Scientists Approaches a Crisis as More Students Drop Out of the Field." *Wall Street Journal*, 17 September 1990.

13. Markkula, M. "The Need for New Activities in CEE in Europe." *European Journal of Engineering Education* 14, no. 1 (1989): 15-26.

# Through a Kaleidoscope Darkly

## Karen Hunter

"I have seen the future, and it works."

    –Lincoln Steffens, after touring Lenin's Russia in 1919

"It was a dark and stormy night . . . "

    –Snoopy

In 1992 I will celebrate the twenty-fifth year of my career in scholarly communication. That is a sobering period of time, long enough to make one begin to feel old. When one has spent two-thirds of that time in future-related responsibilities (strategic planning and R & D), it is also long enough to revisit and reflect wistfully on predictions made five, ten or even fifteen years ago. Some of those predictions have moved from the mistaken certainty of Steffens' (in) glorious future to something closer to Snoopy's fiction.

It's almost–but not quite–enough to make one humble. Intrepid once again, let me offer six general, somewhat somber predictions about what collectively we (publishers and librarians) will experience in the next decade, followed by reflections on the role of technology in change.

## *GENERALITIES*

1. *It will get worse before it gets better.* Our shared professional world will become more frustrating and confusing, not less so.

---

Karen Hunter is Vice President and Assistant to the Chairman, Elsevier Science Publishers BV, 655 Avenue of the Americas, New York, NY 10010.

There is no evidence that either scientific research will decrease or that funding for libraries will increase. For publishers, it means that supply of papers outstrips demand (i.e., the ability to pay), an economically untenable position for the long term. For libraries, it insures the continued redefining of the archival part of the library's role. Neither publishers nor academic libraries (or their parent universities) are facile at making changes and as a result we will suffer from inertia, disjointed initiatives and the pursuit of blind alleys.

2. *Scientists, our clients, will not go much out of their way to assist either of us if we fail to deliver needed services.* If scientists are at the center of our universe, we are on the periphery of theirs. Scientific communication is essential and to the extent we intermediaries assist in that process and add value to what the scientists create, we will be at least tolerated and sometimes warmly welcomed. If, in our conservatism or confusion, we cease to be facilitators, there will be limited or no residual loyalty. Science as practiced in America is big business and loyalty will go to those who deliver needed support services.

3. *There will be new electronic entrants who take significant new roles as intermediaries in scientific communication.* We see the tip of this iceberg already in the evolving offerings of library consortia such as CARL, RLG and OCLC and subscription agents such as Faxon. Beyond these familiar agencies, other intermediaries will emerge which have no tie to libraries or publishers at all but, seeing the opportunities of a networked scientific community, will create whole new services.

Consider that a decade ago Mead, a paper company with no experience in publishing, established an innovative electronic service for lawyers called Lexis. It took millions of dollars to build the market, but once built it was very profitable. For West Publishing, the company which had a virtual monopoly on the paper publishing of the same material, it has been a hard-fought game of catch-up ball. With the growing economic importance of science and technology, is scientific communication any less tempting a market opportunity?

4. *Libraries will be squeezed further as new electronic services parallel paper.* Publishers will increasingly provide both electronic and paper versions of their publications, particularly journals. For

some period–yet to be defined–libraries will find themselves pressured to acquire the electronic version without the confidence that they can cancel the paper. This will further strain library budgets and increase the push for resource-sharing agreements.

5. *Publishers will be squeezed as well, but only when the parallel purchasing period ends and libraries find the most economical path.* Whatever the transition period, it must result ultimately in improved efficiencies for libraries–or for scientists purchasing directly without the libraries' intervention. There is reason to believe that the new equilibrium will be less advantageous for publishers than the present system. One might expect that the publishers will be the net losers.

6. *Finally, scientists will emerge the net winners in the next decade.* Whatever happens to science libraries and publishers, the scientists will emerge with a better, more efficient information system. The technology–of which, more below–makes improvements inescapable. The potential is too great, the opportunities for faster, better and perhaps even cheaper services too obvious, to believe some significant enhancements will not be achieved.

Granted, there is the potential as well for chaos–look at Lenin's Russia and that brave new future now. Look as well at the American transportation system–can anyone really say it is better now than in the late 1950s or early 1960s, when you had recently-built interstate highways, a still (although marginally) viable national railroad system, a regulated network of airlines which served large and small communities, a decent bus system and safer subways? (For that matter, one can say the same thing about most American cities in general thirty years ago.)

Nevertheless, such negative examples to the contrary notwithstanding, I remain an optimist that the scientist will emerge the biggest beneficiary of changes over the next decade.

## *MARKET SIGNALS*

Stepping back from these broad generalizations, let me elaborate on some of the structural market changes at work, some of the experiences behind my beliefs. I have spent the last four years meeting with collection development librarians, library directors and university administrators. It has been perhaps the most rewarding period in my career, but not without its bumps and bruises.

I have watched librarians' progress in dealing with the "serials crisis" from: anger often rooted in significant misunderstanding or ignorance; to an understanding of the structural nature of the problems but hope for quick radical fixes; to the now more widespread realization that this is a complex issue with no easy solutions and no single villain, the elimination of whom will right all wrongs. As a former librarian and now publisher, I commend librarians for learning about publishing.

Publishers generally have been slower to learn about libraries. It has taken publishers at least the same four years to believe the world has changed. Perhaps I can best illustrate this with a recent example. In the fall of 1991 I had an opportunity to meet at a major research university with the associate provost's office responsible for library services. The provost described to me the university's concern over the growing journal literature–its volume and price– and said they had just completed an extensive study of the journal use habits of three different scientific disciplines. The goal was to identify ways of reallocating journal budgets to provide better service–"more bang for the buck," as the saying goes.

The provost said that as a result of their study they were considering some fairly radical options, including (1) much more formal resource-sharing agreements with four other area universities and (2) cancellation of many journal subscriptions, with a reallocation of some or all of the money to individual departments or professions for the purchase of individual articles from document supply companies. She anticipated that electronic networking would greatly facilitate such arrangements, whether resource-sharing or article purchase on demand. She then asked me how publishers would react to either of these actions (legally, economically, strategically) and what alternatives did *we* have to offer, what new services could *we* provide to meet her needs?

I gave her my best, most sincere answer, trying to put a positive spin on what is actually a pretty narrow, even paltry, range of alternatives offered by publishers. At that point she looked at me rather incredulously and said: "Wait a minute. You're not telling me that publishers think that they can go on doing business as usual, are you?" Unfortunately, an honest answer to that question would be: "Many publishers do, some don't." And those publishers who think they can go on through the decade with "business as usual" are likely to be wrong. Some publishers hope they--and their journals--can resist the changing technology and either continue on in paper in an admittedly declining market, the same way they have for the last twenty years, or alternatively decide unilaterally the speed and way in which electronic dissemination will occur. The technological changes are, I believe, too great for that level of publisher control.

## *TECHNOLOGY-PUSH*

The history of technological changes in communication media offers interesting examples of technology's impact on both the underlying content and on the distribution medium. For the first half of the century standard recordings were issued on 78 rpm records. One characteristic of this format was that popular music was typically issued on a 10" disk, which held about 3 minutes of music. As a result, all pop and traditional jazz tunes had arrangements under three minutes.

While 45s replaced 78s for pop tunes around 1950, the real technological revolution of that same period was the 33 1/3 LPs. Now the jazz musician, for example, was freed from the arbitrary length of a 78 record side. Creative expression took advantage of the new technology, so that some early jazz LPs have only one 25-minute composition per side. By contrast, nothing creative has really happened (other than expansion of dynamic and frequency ranges) with the switch from LPs to CDs. This is a distribution medium switch which has not seriously (or pleasantly) affected the content.

Staying with music for a moment longer, consider how the synthesizer has changed both the content and the economics of music. Synthesizers are perhaps the logical extreme of multi-track taping. Multi-tracking (use of 32 or 64 channels to record a single moment in sound) allows skilled tape editors to correct all errors. Have a squawk from the oboe? No problem, we'll edit the note out and substitute a new one. The result is what some complain are sterilized performances.

With the synthesizers you can not only program and correct the offending notes–you don't even need to have the original instruments to begin with. This is not just a question of technical virtuosity but plain economics. What theatre-goer would not like to have a pit orchestra of twenty-five? Five to eight are more likely, with one or two musicians (or more) at synthesizers. It is possible to produce a credible musical revival with an "orchestra" of two or three synthesizers. Technology has made possible the dramatic reduction of one cost component of such revivals.

Other examples of technology-push abound. Feature films are now largely standardized at under 120 minutes to fit on standard video tape cassettes, for the video aftermarket is essential to the financial performance of the film. Fax has driven Telex virtually out of business and has put a very serious dent in the overnight delivery/messenger services. Photocopying long ago eliminated most carbon paper in standard correspondence. And so forth.

There is one further communication-related technology change which deserves a little closer attention, as there may be parallels in what to expect with scientific journals. The second half of the Twentieth Century has witnessed a steady and irreversible decline in the number and vitality of newspapers in the U.S. Where thousands of newspapers flourished, hundreds or in some cases scores only now still publish. I am not a historian of newspapers and could only speculate on the many social and economic changes behind the decline of newspapers. But one significant factor certainly is television.

One need look no further than the Gulf War to see the difference between television and newspaper coverage. CNN reported the war literally as it was happening, winning its leader Ted Turner *Time's* Man of the Year award. Newspapers were left to get their late-breaking news first from CNN, then from AP and their own reporters. They could not report the "news"–they could record the history for archival purposes.

They broadened this role by trying to provide more in-depth analysis, more background data than CNN or the other television stations could provide. But in the long term, newspapers were recording events for later historical use, not for current awareness. The number of newspapers needed to provide this kind of archival record is limited–three, four perhaps. All others must survive on the local news, feature sections and advertising, a respectable business but not of more than regional significance. Newspapers which have survived the technology change–the globalization of instant satellite communication–have done so by specializing in niches, not by trying to do what they did for the past one hundred years.

## FUTURE ACTION

Where does this leave us, science librarians and publishers? Are we hapless chess pieces on the board, pawns manipulated by Adam Smith's economic "invisible hand," only this hand now being robotic and marked "made in Japan"? Only if we choose to be. On the assumption that librarians are best able to decide on the actions they need to take, let me conclude by suggesting four imperatives for scientific journal publishers who want to survive the next decade.

1. Get your material in a standardized, distributable (SGML) electronic form. Journals which want to be internationally recognized but which cannot be *easily* distributed electronically within the next 5-10 years will cease to have anything but local interest. The proceedings of a state medical society can stay in paper only. The *International Journal of Bear Research* cannot. Paper is not going to disappear in the next decade, which has its own costly consequences, as we will have to produce everything in two editions. The successful publisher will start with standardized electronic files, from which both paper and electronic versions can be created.

2. Speed up the publication process. As networks link the scientific community and its research, scientists will become increasingly impatient with delays in publication. The peer review process is and will remain essential and everything the publisher can do to assist in that stage is critical. But once that peer review is done, the information must become public–be "published"–rapidly as well.

3. Pay more attention to how scientists learn about your articles

and their ability to get copies. In other words, the successful publisher in the next decade will take on far more responsibility for being sure scientists receive current awareness information on what is published and have quick and reliable access to article copies. In many settings, this will be done via or in connection with the library. In other cases, the publisher may deal directly with the reader or via a non-library third party.

4. Learn to be flexible in product offerings and pricing. Traditional publishers have a great deal to learn from financial and legal publishers who have successfully developed electronic products. Publishers are used to producing a single product–a printed journal–and to selling it at a fixed price. Future success will require much greater marketing expertise and innovative pricing. Publishers have to learn to live in a world where they can actually give customers what they want, where they can listen to their customers and adapt their products. Publishers have not been intentionally stubborn or inflexible in their present journals. It simply has not been economically feasible to tailor a paper product to an individual customer. That *is* possible electronically and will be necessary in the next decade.

The future will be difficult and not all publishers–nor all libraries–will survive. Darwinism will have its say over the next decade and it will be the flexible, innovative and creative publishers who can look back on the 1990s as the period in which they made their greatest strides.

# Library Buildings: Their Current State and Future Development

Jay K. Lucker

## INTRODUCTION

I bring a strong bias to the subject of the future of the library as a physical entity. Despite predictions by others to the contrary, I firmly believe there is a future for libraries as places and while there will certainly be many changes in the ways that people acquire and use information, and many changes in the role and nature of libraries themselves, I find it impossible to conceive of a time when there will not be a physical, tangible, usable entity with real books and real people inside.

At MIT in 1988, we developed a long range, strategic plan for the Libraries as part of a campus-wide planning effort. A major component of that plan was a vision of the MIT Libraries in the 21st century. The four principal aspects of the vision were "The Library as Place," "The Workstation as a Window on the Library," "The Librarian as Information Guide," and the "The Libraries as Organization." The placement of these topics was no accident. I believe that the library building of the future is merely another stage, albeit a very critical one, in the continuing evolution of libraries. For MIT, the vision of "Library as Place" contained the following elements:

---

Jay K. Lucker has been Director of Libraries at MIT since 1975. He is active as a library building and library management consultant and also teaches courses in the literature of science and technology, academic libraries, and library architecture at Simmons College Graduate School of Library and Information Science. Mr. Lucker did his graduate library work at Columbia University.

© 1992 by The Haworth Press, Inc. All rights reserved.

"At the beginning of the 21st century, the MIT Libraries as buildings housing physical collections with convenient spaces for users to consult those collections will continue to be important elements of the Institute community. The Libraries will continue to be a place for self-education and discovery outside the classroom and laboratory; they will continue to be a haven from the pressure of academic life and communal living. They will be a place of particular importance to students, as a part of the social and intellectual experience of an MIT education.

"MIT scholars will continue to need to use the body of print materials collected by the Libraries. Indeed, as publishing on paper increases rather than declines, students and faculty will become increasingly dependent on the Libraries to acquire, preserve, and provide access to resources necessary to support research and teaching. The Libraries will also serve as a source of information about new technologies and as an access point to non-print materials outside the immediate holdings of the Libraries.

"The MIT Libraries, as subject libraries close to their user communities, will retain the advantages of that physical closeness while, through technology, providing access to collections elsewhere at MIT and in the outside world. New "libraries" on campus in academic departments and research centers will be created as "electronic library modules," with small collections of current journals complemented by electronic access to and delivery of materials housed elsewhere and by online communication with subject librarians.

"All materials will be represented in the online catalogue, including specialized materials such as archival and manuscript collections, maps, slides, machine readable data files and software. Through national and international cooperative programs for preservation and access, MIT users will be guaranteed access to any research materials required."[1]

## TWENTIETH CENTURY ACHIEVEMENTS

In tracing the recent history of academic library building in the United States, one needs to be reminded of a number of critical factors that affected the planning and design of these facilities. Later on, we will see that some of these issues, especially location and decentralization, have become less critical in the electronic age.

1. The academic library exists in the context of the total college or university campus. While often cited as the "heart of the university," the library building must nonetheless coexist with administration buildings, classrooms, laboratories, dormitories, athletic facilities, and, one would hope, open space. Whether architecturally harmonious or contrapuntal, the library building should belong on the campus.
2. The physical location of the building is important. Many academic libraries were located in or near the geographic center of the campus; this not only served to foster the concept of "symbolic" heart but also responded to the issue of physical convenience.
3. The idea of a main or central academic library runs counter to the intellectual organization of the university. Academic entities are arranged by department that has led historically to a system of departmental libraries. Professional schools, especially but not exclusively law and medicine, often have their own libraries. Even within large central libraries there are forces and arguments for some sort of disciplinary identification. This may manifest itself through the inclusion of subject reading rooms, seminar rooms and graduate studies, or a divisional system.
4. Libraries are primarily service buildings. They need to be accessible and open to users. At the same time, libraries are immense storage facilities and must be designed economically and efficiently. There is a constant tension between these two functionalities.
5. There is a wide range of activities that takes place in a library: browsing, reading and study, utilization of specialized equipment, teaching, group interaction, librarian-patron interaction, photocopying, multiple types of staff work, materials storage–to mention the most obvious. Interrelationships and conflicts are everywhere and there are no simple solutions.
6. The twentieth century library requires a wide range of equipment, much of which has specific physical, electrical, and environmental requirements. Machines are needed to access information–computers, microfilm readers, CD-ROM workstations; to store special kinds of information–microforms,

maps, slides, audiovisual materials; and to engage in specific tasks–binding, repair, copying.
7. The need for open access to staff and collections is countered by the need for a limited amount of secure space–for collections, staff, and storage. Some library materials require special storage facilities; for example, rare books and manuscripts.
8. Readers and librarians need to be able to interact openly and conveniently. This often creates a conflict with the requirement for quiet spaces conducive to study and reflection.
9. Space requirements expand as collections grow. While academic library collections no longer double in size quite as quickly as in the past, there is constant growth.
10. Libraries are usually open for extended periods of time and throughout the year requiring a range of lighting and environmental controls.

## *TRENDS IN RESEARCH LIBRARY BUILDING DESIGN*

A substantial number of academic and research library buildings were either constructed or added to in the past five decades (1950-1990). In general, buildings that were completed within the past ten years reflect both changes in the overall philosophy of libraries summarized below but also respond to the new challenges of computerized technology and information networks. Among the major characteristics that distinguishes post-1945 libraries from their predecessors are the following:

1. There has been a move from closed to open stacks and an increased intermingling of readers and books. There are relatively few closed stack academic libraries in North America and increasingly, libraries in other parts of the world have adopted this philosophy. Open stacks are seen as educationally advantageous as they lead to the serendipitous use of collections. Some of the labor costs associated with closed stacks, principally for paging, have been eliminated but there has been an increase in costs associated with shelf reading as well as

preservation and replacement. The existence of open stacks has also caused an increase in concern about collection security. Electronic book security systems have become commonplace in academic libraries and this technology has itself engendered a number of physical requirements in building design especially in the location and outfitting of circulation and reserve desks as well as building entrances and exits.
2. There has been a reduction in the size and number of large, cavernous, high-ceilinged reading rooms. This loss of monumentality, while mourned by some traditionalists, has resulted in more efficient use of space as well as lower heating and ventilation costs. There has, however, been a recent trend in the use of atria and light-courts which, if designed and integrated appropriately, can improve aesthetics and functionality.
3. Concomitant with the scaling down of reading room has been a shift from large, multi-user reading tables to individual reading stations. This change reflects an acknowledgment of the way that readers have tended to use libraries as well as another step toward more efficient use of space.
4. Library areas devoted to public services have been designed so as to promote interaction between patrons and staff. The location of information and reference desks and the relationship between these activities and collections of reference materials and catalogs is a key element in space planning.
5. Recent academic library design has emphasized the importance of browsing and serendipity in academic libraries. Not only open stacks, but well designed open stacks with good lighting and convenient reading spaces have become a critical building element.
6. There has been a dramatic increase in the range, number, and complexity of facilities that support the increasing role of the library in education and instruction, both formal bibliographic instruction and individualized teaching space.
7. Library buildings reflect a greater awareness of and a response to environmental concerns: lighting, air conditioning, humidity control, fire protection, and collection security. There has also been some response to the needs of handicapped users but clearly this is an aspect of library design that will become

increasingly critical in the next few years because of legislation and public awareness and activity.
8. Academic libraries built in the past 40 years have had a better capacity to accommodate a proliferation of new information formats: microforms, audio and video recordings, and machine readable information.
9. There were great improvements in building construction methods and materials including better fire protection, sound insulation, and underground construction.

## *STORAGE BUILDINGS*

Another major trend in the post-1945 period was the expansion and growth of library storage facilities. While the concept of cooperative storage never fully materialized in the way that many had predicted when the Midwest Interlibrary Center (later the Center for Research Libraries) and the New England Depository Library were envisioned, a large number of research libraries including most of the members of the Association of Research Libraries, planned and constructed storage buildings of some kind. Today, there are relatively few ARL libraries without some kind of on-campus or off-campus storage. Harvard, Princeton, Yale, Michigan, MIT, Ohio State, and Illinois all have major storage buildings and the University of California has constructed two regional facilities to accommodate the needs of its several campuses.

Many of these buildings utilize high density, fixed or movable compact shelving. The use of compact shelving in the libraries inevitably raises the question of using them in "standard" libraries. Several factors affect the use of movable compact shelving in active collections:

- Floor loading requirements are 300 pounds per square foot as compared to 150 pounds per square foot for standard shelving;
- The limited number of aisles restricts the number of simultaneous users;
- The per book cost of compact shelving is several times that of standard shelving;
- There are increased costs associated with lighting, air flow, and sprinkler systems;

- Fixed, high density shelving is not feasible in an open stack library under current building code requirements because of the use of narrow aisles and extra-high shelves, both of which preclude handicapped access.

There have been numerous studies of the relationship of open stacks to the quality of library use and to circulation. The relative cost effectiveness and cost benefit of browsing versus retrieval from storage is highly dependent upon a number of factors. One thing is quite evident: the higher the level of bibliographic control, the more use is made of the material regardless of whether or not it is in storage. Many research libraries have stored the oldest portion of their collections off-site. These materials were generally not included in their online catalogs. Since many readers tend to neglect the older card catalog once there is an online version, the use of stored items was much lower. As records for these materials were entered online, the circulation rose measurably.

The cumulated experience of libraries involved with storage facilities leads to the following generalizations:

- The larger the proportion of scientific and technical information in a collection, the higher the percentage that can be stored with minimal effect upon users.
- The larger the library, the higher the percentage that can be stored effectively. Libraries with holdings of under two million volumes are hard pressed to store much more than 15% without incurring negative user reaction; libraries with four to five million volumes have more flexibility and more options.
- Runs of periodicals are more efficiently stored than monographs. They are browsed less and requested more by volume and number.
- Creating browsability in storage buildings defeats their purpose. Open stack storage requires wide aisles, reading facilities, and stack maintenance that essentially mirrors services in a general research library.
- Use notwithstanding, off-site storage can serve as a means of protection for fragile material.
- Libraries should be able to reverse the storage process without

great expense or difficulty, that is, to move books back to active collections based on increased use, change in programs, or other causes.

## SHORTCOMINGS AND PROBLEMS

The major problems that one finds in existing academic library buildings may be grouped into four areas: the lack of space for collections, readers, and staff; an inability to expand on the existing site; physical and mechanical conditions; the lack of flexibility including especially the inability to provide for electronic information services.

Inadequate staff space is currently more a reflection of the quality of space rather than the quantity since there has been very little growth in the size of academic library staffs in recent years. Many libraries, unfortunately, were designed with less than adequate staff areas from their beginnings and they must deal with both quality and size issues. One of the most critical factors exacerbating the staff space problem is that there is generally insufficient accommodation for current technology. This is true in almost every area of the library but especially in technical services and reference and information services. The lack of space for books and other materials in many cases reflects an unwillingness on the part of the parent institution to plan for the future. Reader space is less likely to be in short supply except in those libraries where stacks and staff areas have encroached on spaces previously allocated to carrels and reading tables.

Site limitations may be a result of legal restrictions: building height, property lines, location of utilities; functional limitations: no space to expand; or intrinsic problems: the building was simply not designed for an addition. Remarkably, many university and college library buildings were planned with the idea of a future addition in mind and there have been numerous examples of successful projects that have greatly increased the size and lifetime of a library.[2]

Among the physical and mechanical problems plaguing older

libraries are those connected with heating, ventilation, and air conditioning including air filtration; the need to install or replace elevators; the presence of asbestos in ceilings, walls, and other areas that must be removed at great expense whenever there is a major renovation; the failure of the building to meet current building and handicapped code requirements.

The lack of building flexibility is often a severe limitation on the placement or relocation of library functions. A common example is in the replacement of card catalogs by online systems with public terminals. Almost universally, the catalog cases were located in areas that did not have electrical outlets or telephone conduit. The major limitations inherent in older buildings include inadequate or uneven floor loading; difficulty in providing easy means for running wires and conduit; lack of sufficient power; poorly designed and inefficient environmental systems. In many buildings it is expensive, often prohibitively, to relocate stacks because they are part of the structural system. In addition, national, state, and local building codes have changed significantly, especially with regard to handicapped access. Major renovations in the United States (involving more than 25% of gross square feet) usually require that the entire structure adapt to the current code. The introduction of computer technology into research libraries over the past two decades has highlighted the general deficiency of many buildings. Integrated library systems have brought with them a host of requirements in the quantity and quality of space required. These include:

- Hard wiring from computer to terminal.
- Conduit to carry both low power and high power lines.
- Computer rooms with adequate environmental controls.
- Connectivity for online catalog terminals.
- Power and space for CD-ROM workstations.
- Microcomputer laboratories and/or clusters of personal computers and/or terminals.
- Multi-purpose workstations that provide access to the library, the university, and beyond. (Online catalogs, online databases, national bibliographic utilities, campus networks, satellite communication, telefacsimile, full text databases, numeric databases, document delivery.)

## THE NEAR FUTURE

Beyond the developments that we have already seen, there are a number of major technological changes that can be anticipated over the next few years that will require even more adaptability in library buildings. Structures currently being planned ought to include the capacity for:

- Multi-media workstations
- Interactive computer systems
- Local area networks
- Inexpensive laptops
- Intelligent interfaces

I believe that within the next decade there will be an increasing impact on research library collections through changes in scholarly publishing. The following are most likely to happen:

1. Electronic journals will begin to replace paper journals slowly, with the primary impact on expensive, specialized scientific, technical and medical periodicals. There are today fewer than 30 scholarly journals published solely in electronic form.
2. Popular fiction may begin to be marketed like popular music but there will be very little publishing of scholarly monographs in electronic form. The average print run for a 1991 university press monograph is 750 units.
3. There will be an increasing number of reference tools published electronically but a good percentage of these will be "new" rather than "replacement" titles.
4. While faculty and research needs with be increasingly served by access rather than ownership of information, there will still be an ever growing volume of printed information. Library collections will be limited more by budget than by availability of information.
5. Undergraduate library collections, being principally monographic, and consisting of secondary rather than primary literature, will continue to be heavily print.
6. Electronic scanning and digitization of existing print collec-

tions will be of limited applicability by individual libraries because of:

- The cost of scanning including equipment and labor.
- The cost of indexing and tagging.
- The cost of data storage.
- The cost of distribution (machines to access, print, and download).
- Copyright restrictions.
- The lack of a good storage medium for a mixture of print, graphics, and color.

## THE ROLE OF THE RESEARCH LIBRARY IN THE 21ST CENTURY

Research libraries, in the 21st century, will continue to acquire, organize, and preserve information. They will also:

1. Provide extended cataloging through table of contents services, indexes to conferences and symposia, and in-depth description of all of the materials in their collections–all of this via the online information system.
2. Provide access to expertise required by users; that is, to librarians and other information professionals.
3. Provide access to equipment for specialized collections; not everyone will have personal access to a computer terminal or to equipment that accesses specialized formats like optically stored text.
4. Provide access to printed information–older material, rare books and manuscripts, plus most of what is yet to be published.
5. Be a place for study, reflection, and contemplation. Classrooms are large, expensive to heat and light, expensive to monitor. Students, at least undergraduates, do not have offices or laboratories and they live in an environment that is generally not conducive to quiet study. Therefore, libraries are essential.
6. Provide for group study, group access to technology, a gathering place for the exchange of ideas and for social intercourse.

7. Be the link to cooperative enterprises and resource sharing networks.
8. Provide a wide range of technology-based services: local and remote online catalogs; bibliographic databases; full text reference tools; online reference librarians; online document ordering; online interlibrary loan, suggested purchases, and university based information files.

## *ACADEMIC LIBRARY BUILDINGS IN THE 21ST CENTURY*

Most of the buildings that currently house the library collections of universities and colleges will continue to exist as libraries into the 21st century. Some of these structures will be added to in some physical forms. Others will have to cope with the demands of the future with little additional space. A relatively small number of universities and colleges will be able to afford new libraries. For those contemplating new buildings or additions, I would offer the following thoughts.

Changes in library building construction and in furnishings, equipment, and environmental capacity have occurred throughout history and will continue to occur in the future. Buildings should be designed as flexibly as possible but not so much as to eliminate a sense of organization.

Library collections will continue to grow but not as quickly as in the past because of economic constraints, electronic publishing, resource sharing, and the use of local and cooperative storage facilities.

There will continue to be a need for study space in libraries.

Energy conservation will be of great importance in the design of buildings. The physical environmental in a library is critical for readers and for the maintenance of the collections. Balancing these two competing forces will be difficult but essential.

For the majority of librarians, planning for the future including adapting our library buildings for the next generation, will require that we are cognizant of and responsive to decisions and trends over which we may have little or no influence. Some of these come from the larger world of higher education and technology; others from our parent university or college; and others from within our own organization. For a university like the Massachusetts Institute of Technology, several major trends were identified as part of a strategic planning process:

1. Identify user needs. Faced with an exponential increase in the amount of published information and in a variety of forms, research libraries will have to identify and respond to the particular needs of local clientele and to structure, market, and deliver services responsive to those needs.
2. Emphasize access to information. There will necessarily be a greater emphasis on access to information and less of an attempt to build comprehensive local collections. Rapid delivery of information, increasingly in electronic form, will become a critical measure of the effectiveness of the library.
3. Exploit new technology. Newer technologies will provide faster and more comprehensive access to information but will not quickly replace existing formats and technologies. This will increase the overall cost of operations and require innovative budgeting and new sources of funds.
4. Exploit local networks. The availability of personal computers and campus networks presents both an opportunity and a challenge as faculty, students, and research staff become more information-literate and their needs become more sophisticated.
5. Link library programs to academic programs. With limited resources and an ever growing universe of information, there must be a close mapping between library collections and services and the educational and research priorities of the university.
6. Monitor economic pressures. For the immediate future, a variety of economic pressures will cause a steady erosion in the buying power of academic libraries: general inflation in the cost of scholarly information, especially serials, and in operating costs; a spiraling number of new serial titles and their introduction in new formats; fluctuations in the value of the dollar abroad; the decline of government sponsored research.
7. Reallocate resources. There will be a continuing shift of bud-

gets away from staff and collections, toward the support of automation, telecommunications, and contractual arrangements for information access.

## THE NEW RESEARCH LIBRARY

By the year 2000, most internal library operations will be automated and staff members will use individual computer terminals to carry out their day to day responsibilities. There will be close collaboration among the library, academic computing, and administrative computing in the design and delivery of information. The campus network will provide a wide range of services, many of which will be developed in the library. There will be an international network of research libraries with each institution taking responsibility for acquiring and organizing local locally created information and for providing worldwide access to unique and specialized material in its collection.

The pace of change in the 21st century will require great flexibility in the way that libraries organize themselves and utilize their staffs and resources. Measures of quality of research libraries will transcend the traditional counting of volumes and titles and will instead look at their ability to match user needs with relevant information. Libraries will continue to exist as physical entities with collections, staffs, and services. They will, above all, be a vital factor in fulfilling the mission of the university in creating, preserving, and disseminating knowledge.[3]

## REFERENCES

1. *The MIT Libraries at the Beginning of the 21st Century: a Strategic Plan.* Cambridge, MIT Libraries, 1988.
2. Metcalfe, Keyes DeWitt. *Planning Academic and Research Library Buildings.* 2d ed. Chicago, American Library Association, 1986.
3. Lucker, Jay K. "The Research Library in the Information Age"; *MIT: Shaping the Future.* Cambridge, MIT Press, 1991.

# The Future of University Science and Technology Libraries: Implications of Increasing Interdisciplinarity

Julie M. Hurd

**SUMMARY.** Since the end of World War II scientific research has become increasing interdisciplinary as universities, government research facilities and corporations have sought solutions to societal problems and cures for life-threatening conditions. An integral part of the research process is information-seeking and that activity has been affected significantly by the emergence of interdisciplinarity fields. The materials both used and produced by interdisciplinary researchers have resulted in new demands on scientific and technical libraries. This paper will examine the problems of access to interdisciplinary information. It will explore some of the challenges facing scientific and technical libraries attempting to provide information services to scientists who are engaged in interdisciplinary research.

In 1977 Rustum Roy of Pennsylvania State University outlined some of the key aspects of interdisciplinary scientific research from his perspective as a university administrator.[2] He wrote of the growth of university-based, mission-oriented research in the decade of the 1960's and the impact this development had on university finance, organization and governance. Roy provided an example of a field that is highly interdisciplinary in nature: materials science, which draws upon the traditional disciplines of chemistry, physics,

---

Julie M. Hurd holds a PhD in chemistry and an MA in library science from the University of Chicago. She is currently Science Librarian at the University of Illinois at Chicago, Science Library (M/C 234), Box 8198, Chicago, IL 60680.

© 1992 by The Haworth Press, Inc. All rights reserved.

engineering, and mathematics. He also cited a number of other interdisciplinary fields and analyzed their relationship to traditional disciplines identified with university departments and degree programs. Since 1977 numerous other interdisciplinary fields have emerged and examples of these can readily be found: molecular biology, bioengineering, environmental chemistry, and more. Often these emerging areas of research are at very active, and highly visible, research fronts and are featured in popular press science writing and in other media. The focus on solutions to societal problems common to much interdisciplinary research makes such projects particularly newsworthy. A timely example is provided in a Chronicle of Higher Education report that describes the emerging field of "environmental mathematics" as "an attempt to get mathematicians to connect again with the natural world" in an effort to study pollution caused by idling auto engines, the decline in nesting sites for the spotted owl, or the settling of sulfur dioxide molecules in the human lung.[3]

## WHAT IS INTERDISCIPLINARITY?

Roy recognized the need to define the terminology used to discuss these ideas and observed that lack of agreement on terms has handicapped analyses of the sociology of interdisciplinary organizations. He defined a "discipline" as a field of knowledge for which some minimum number of universities (say, 12-20) have established departments labeled with the discipline name. The scope of the discipline is then defined by the activities of the departments, and his definition implies that there is reasonable agreement on the subject matter comprising the discipline. Roy's subsequent discussion acknowledged the existence of other approaches to defining a discipline and the inherent possibilities for confusion. The changes occurring in physics and chemistry in the period from 1920-1970 are used to illustrate his point that these fields could, in fact, be considered to consist of several disciplines because they now are made up of a number of discrete subject areas that are independent and noninteractive. Roy's definition of "interdisciplinary" activity specifies an "interactive mode of research (or study) where . . . each researcher's work demands the use of ideas, concepts, materials, or instruments from one or more other disciplines."[4] He adds that such work tends to be goal or mission-oriented.

Other authors have struggled with the definitions of basic terminology, and a recent book offers insights into this non-trivial problem. Julie Thompson Klein provides in-depth discussion on the nature of interdisciplinary discourse and devotes several chapters in her book to definitions of "interdisciplinarity."[5] Her book also includes an extensive classified bibliography that she considers to be a representative sample of a far larger body of literature. Klein discusses the terminology that has been employed by various authors and notes her preference for the terms "interdisciplinary" and "integrative" for work that seeks to "accomplish a range of objectives:

- to answer complex questions;
- to address broad issues;
- to explore disciplinary and professional relations;
- to solve problems that are beyond the scope of any one discipline;
- to achieve unity of knowledge . . . "[6]

Klein's and Roy's definitions of interdisciplinary research are similar and will reflect the usage in this paper.

Chemistry continues to provide examples of these shifting discipline boundaries. Rudy M. Baum describes a recent symposium on "Frontiers in Chemistry & Medicine" sponsored by the University of North Carolina, Chapel Hill and Glaxo, Inc., a pharmaceutical company.[7] He summarizes the presentations of organic chemists speaking at the meeting on their research in progress using synthetic and biosynthetic molecules to carry out chemical reactions and to investigate biological systems. Baum suggests that the view of chemistry presented at this symposium demonstrates the emergence of new paradigms and a sort of "sociological frontier" where chemists and biologists employ a shared methodology drawn from traditional theoretical and experimental organic chemistry but applied to complex biological systems. He argues a broadened focus for chemistry in which it overlaps not only biology but also materials science, high-temperature superconductivity and other pursuits; this seems to characterize chemistry as increasingly interdisciplinary in exactly the sense defined by Roy and Klein.

## *INTERDISCIPLINARY RESEARCH AND TECHNOLOGY TRANSFER*

The growth of interdisciplinary research has probably caused the most wide-reaching changes in universities, formerly sites for only the most basic research. Development of practical applications (except in such fields as engineering and medicine) were often formerly relegated to the profit-sector or to government laboratories. As the governmental funding base to support basic research has shrunk, universities have sought to establish new sources of revenue; this has led to increasing university alliances with profit-sector organizations either through collaborative activities or through grants from corporations in support of university-based research. In fact, the symposium described above grew out of a collaboration between the University of North Carolina's chemistry department and Glaxo that resulted in shared laboratory facilities on campus with funds for renovation supplied by the pharmaceutical company.

Evidence of the trend toward increasing interdisciplinarity is also seen in the establishment of new units on university campuses with titles including "center," "committee," or "institute." That universities now are establishing patent offices and sponsoring the development of research parks to aid in technology transfer also supports this observation. Patent offices are a relatively recent phenomenon on most university campuses and are being established to provide a structure through which the parent institution can license technological discoveries of university-affiliated scientists and profit directly from those innovations. *The Chronicle of Higher Education* recently reported that royalty revenues earned in 1990 by 21 of the country's largest research institutions were 28 per cent higher than in 1989; that trend was expected to continue and reflects the increasing involvement of universities in technology transfer.[8] The literature of higher education has reported these developments and many writers have expressed concerns about such issues as the potential for conflict of interest and erosion of universities' tax exempt status.

The impact of the technology transfer mission on university infrastructure will not be the focus of this article, however. Instead we shall examine its impact on university libraries and information services.

On many campuses the increase in the amount of interdisciplinary research carried out by faculty and their graduate students has resulted in new and different needs for library collections and services. These information needs may differ in significant ways from those of twenty years ago when research projects were more easily contained within the boundaries of single, recognized disciplines. There are certainly new journals and secondary services that have resulted from interdisciplinary research; university scientists publish in these journals and request that libraries acquire them and the publications that index them. In addition, scientists may be using increasing amounts of information from more than one field or in non-journal formats such as patents or standards. University libraries can expect in the future to serve growing numbers of users whose needs may not be confined by the boundaries of any single well-established discipline and who may experience difficulties in using information sources and services organized on a discipline-based model.

## *MEASURES OF INTERDISCIPLINARITY*

A. L. Porter and D. E. Chubin observe that "the absence of data on interdisciplinary research has been a bane to the study of this phenomenon."[9] In fact, a literature search that attempts to identify studies of interdisciplinarity is in itself an illustration of some of the problems of interdisciplinary research! Sociologists of science, information scientists, science librarians, and science policy specialists are some of the authors of research papers treating the topic. Their articles appear in a wide variety of journals and conference proceedings, including publications in the basic sciences. The scatter of this literature, and thus the need to consult more than one secondary service, is a feature common to other interdisciplinary investigations.

While there exists a large body of literature dealing with various aspects of interdisciplinarity, little of that material addresses the nature of problems faced by information seekers whose needs cross the boundaries of traditional disciplines. Even rarer are any studies that endeavor to measure interdisciplinarity in the sciences.

An exception is found in the writings of D. E. Chubin and associates who employed citation analysis techniques to develop a numerical measure of interdisciplinarity based on citations outside the discipline-affiliation claimed by the author(s) of the works examined.[10] He applied his measure, *Citations outside Category*, to the fields of demography, operations research and toxicology and asserts that use of this indicator is validated by his findings. Chubin suggests that his measure offers potential application in "micro-level" studies that examine the research programs of particular institutions, departments or laboratories.

Other citation-based efforts to characterize interdisciplinary research could be designated as "macro-level" in that they examine the literature of a particular discipline; these studies exist for several disciplines. K. E. Clark and W. R. Kinyon explored the influence of physics on other disciplines by analyzing the indexing of physics articles in eight major secondary services in other fields.[11] The extent of coverage of physics sources in such indexes as *Chemical Abstracts, Engineering Index* and *Mathematical Reviews* was considered by Clark and Kinyon as evidence of potential interdisciplinary information use. Jin Choi used citations in anthropology journals to assess the intellectual dependence of that discipline on others.[12] Her analysis supported a view of anthropology as a "receiver" discipline on the basis of figures revealing that 70% of the literature cited in a sample of anthropology journal articles was generated in other disciplines.

Katherine McCain has focused on various disciplines in her research and has included some that are considered to be interdisciplinary fields, the history of technology[13] and neural networks.[14] McCain and co-workers are employing co-citation analysis techniques to the neural networks journal literature to explore subject relationships to such other fields as philosophy, psychology, mathematics, computer science, biology, cognitive science, artificial intelligence, and engineering. Her approach should illuminate complex relationships among these disciplines from the perspective of a highly interdisciplinary and rapidly advancing area of research.

Studies such as those cited above focus on an entire field or population of scientists; they are not usually intended to provide details on a subset of scientists based at a particular institution. An understanding of the structure of the literature of various disciplines is essential for library managers, but it is also useful to have local information on a library's own patron population. This latter type of data can provide a context and allow comparisons to entire fields but also can identify the special interests of patrons of a particular library or information service that need to be taken into account in decision-making. An obvious example is that of journal usage by a university community; a detailed analysis of campus use may identify specific titles that are considered very important by a particular department even though these journals are relatively low circulation or not "high impact" as rated by *Science Citation Index*. These titles very likely reflect research specializations and academic programs at the individual institution.

User studies have long been carried out by libraries to gather data needed to inform managers' decisions; there are numerous descriptions of these in the professional literature and no doubt many others that are disseminated only locally. When published, user studies allow for inter-institutional comparisons and provide models for further investigation. In the aggregate they may even support some cautious generalizations. A small number of user studies have collected data that measure interdisciplinary information use.

One of the more extensive studies of cross-disciplinary information use is found in the work of Paul Metz who analyzed library circulation data at a large state university.[15] Data obtained from an online circulation system included information on library patrons' academic status and departmental affiliation as well as records on the library materials each had checked out during a two day period selected for study. This data provided a detailed "snapshot" of library use. Metz was able to analyze these statistics to measure faculty use of subject literatures, the extent to which such usage crossed discipline boundaries, and the implications for library organization and collection development. His study also provides a thoughtful discussion of the differences between information obtained from circulation statistics and that derived from citation analyses and concludes that the two approaches are complementary.

More recently several other investigators have initiated research into questions of interdisciplinary information use. Brett Sutton reported his preliminary findings at the 1991 annual meeting of the American Society for Information Science.[16] He is studying behavior of scholars at a research institute (the Beckman Institute at the University of Illinois at Urbana-Champaign) created specifically to foster interdisciplinary work. Sutton will be examining the Beckman Institute researchers as both producers and consumers of information and hopes to be able to identify how these scholars negotiate interdisciplinary boundaries.

Another study employs the measure of interdisciplinarity developed by Chubin and co-workers to the publication output of university departments.[17] A citation study of recent articles published by the faculty in science departments demonstrates a high degree of interdisciplinary information use. In the case of chemistry department faculty, almost 50% of the journals cited in their published articles classed in disciplines other than chemistry. A similar study of biological sciences faculty is in process. The sample of biologists' recent publications, upon preliminary analysis, suggests that these faculty will also be involved in highly interdisciplinary research. Thirty-three percent of the articles in the sample of biologists' publications offer evidence of interdisciplinary collaboration on the basis of the co-author affiliations. There are examples of university/research institute, university/industry, and multi-departmental collaborative efforts with co-investigators drawn from medicine, chemistry, chemical engineering, and biotechnology. A citation study is underway to investigate the detailed disciplinary origins of source materials used in this research.

Also under study at the present time is cross-disciplinary use of secondary services.[18] In order to provide a baseline for a subsequent study of faculty use of locally-mounted bibliographic databases, a recent survey of science, engineering and health sciences faculty solicited information on use of major indexing and abstracting services in both book and electronic format. The returns from this survey provide evidence of cross-disciplinary information use. College of Medicine faculty complement their searching of MEDLINE/ *Index Medicus* with *Biological Abstracts*; College of Nursing faculty make most use of *Current Index to Nursing and Allied Health Liter-*

*ature* (CINAHL) but also consult *Psychological Abstracts* and *ERIC*; College of Pharmacy faculty are heavy users of *Chemical Abstracts*.

The growing literature of interdisciplinarity will likely include more of these kinds of empirical studies directed toward particular populations. The information such studies provide to managers will be increasingly necessary to support decisions involving expenditures of limited resources. Institutions of higher education are expected to be accountable to all their primary constituencies, and data resulting from user studies offers insights into the interests and needs of constituents.

## *CONSEQUENCES OF INTERDISCIPLINARITY*

If current trends continue, it seems likely that growing numbers of universities will be engaged in mission-oriented, interdisciplinary research projects, often aimed at technology transfer and commercialization of university-generated discoveries. The irresistible appeal of direct monetary gain from either licensing agreements or spin-off companies has the potential to influence the inherent nature of research taking place on campus. The literature of higher education of the last decade recognizes both the opportunities and the pitfalls ahead if these developments continue.

Richard Anderson and Barry Sugarman writing in a publication of the Forum for College Financing identify some of the issues involved in commercializing university intellectual property.[19] They describe the process of licensing technology and discuss the entrepreneurial activities of universities in establishing start-up or spin-off companies to foster technology transfer.[20] They emphasize the organizational complexity of universities and assert that attempting to create a profit-center in a part of a university will profoundly affect the rest of the organization. Their paper summarizes some of the major concerns: negative effect on teaching programs, de-emphasis on pure science, decline in free and open communication and dissemination of research findings, increasing dependence on industrial support and accompanying loss of objectivity. These concerns should not be lightly dismissed and could be perceived by many as threats to the entire institutional culture of higher education.

In 1988 Virginia Polytechnic Institute and State University sponsored a national conference on the university spin-off corporation; selected papers presented at that meeting have been published in a book that provides numerous case studies as well as insights into the potential for stimulating institutional change.[21] Contributors represent many of the universities that have served as role models for technology transfer, and several of the papers discuss in depth the involvement of research universities in the process. Most of the authors see positive benefits that will enhance the academic environment, and their views are very likely shared by many other university administrators who hope to emulate the successes reported in this book.

## IMPLICATIONS FOR UNIVERSITY SCIENCE AND TECHNOLOGY LIBRARIES

University administrators and science press writers have documented the growth of interdisciplinary research on campus and identified many of the substantive issues that face the university at large. What is lacking in this literature is any analysis of the impact of interdisciplinary research on university libraries and information services. A recent issue of *Science & Technology Libraries* has addressed this topic by bringing together articles that address the role of librarians in technology transfer. Particularly germane to this paper is the contribution of Mary Pensyl who describes uses of commercial database services in support of technology transfer at Massachusetts Institute of Technology.[22] She observes that the university library is a resource frequently overlooked by administrators who are quick to cite the role of laboratories, computer centers, interdisciplinary programs and research consortia. Her paper offers some specific examples demonstrating the importance of information specialists in the technology transfer mission. Many of the activities she describes involve utilization of traditional skills possessed by science and technology librarians such as understanding of the disciplines and their literatures as well as technological expertise in manipulating information tools essential in the research process.

If future scientific research results in shifting discipline boundaries and fundamental changes in the entire university infrastructure, it seems likely that this will impact university library organization. Departmental and branch libraries are common in large research universities; frequently these have been science collections located in close proximity to laboratories and offices. Over the last century the merits and drawbacks of decentralized library collections have been discussed with regularity in the professional literature. This debate has been summarized by Leon Shkolnik who provides an historical context for the arguments used.[23] He notes the efforts to balance ease of access with ever-increasing concerns for cost containment. He also points out the need to serve scholars engaged in interdisciplinary studies and makes a case for some degree of centralization of resources.

In the case of those chemists described above whose citing behavior showed high usage of materials outside their own discipline, a "chemistry" library, narrowly defined and stocked, would only partially meet their needs. A broader, divisional science library seems better suited to support highly interdisciplinary research. When universities have operated with a departmental library structure there has often been considerable duplication of materials; a chemistry library would very likely feel pressure to duplicate some titles held in a physics or a biology library. If acquisitions budgets were open-ended and available titles less numerous, then duplication of subscriptions could be viewed as a reasonable approach to meeting need. Few institutions can now claim that extensive, or indeed any but minimal, duplication of any but a very small number of primary journals represents the wisest deployment of scarce resources. Duplication of expensive indexing and abstracting services is even less justifiable. This reality lends support to the divisional or central library over the more narrowly-focused departmental collection.

Another type of difficulty that may be encountered by scientists who are engaged in interdisciplinary research concerns the use of secondary services to identify materials relevant to their research. Many of the oldest and largest indexing and abstracting services are discipline-based; they frequently are published by professional associations and have developed to meet the needs of scientists in the parent discipline. Although a service such as *Chemical Abstracts* attempts to cover the field of chemistry comprehensively, economic factors eventually limit size and scope for any service. Journals in other disciplines may be indexed selectively; less important titles may be covered by fewer services or with longer time lags. In addition, many secondary services concentrate to a high degree on research journals covering to a lesser extent, if at all, the trade literature, engineering standards, or patents; all these types of publications are likely to be used by more applications-oriented research teams.

For scientists working in interdisciplinary fields a comprehensive literature search is likely to require the use of more than one index in order to locate all relevant literature. Increasingly, research libraries find themselves unable to support duplicate subscriptions to these very costly secondary services, and this fact, in an institution with decentralized science collections, results in inconvenience for interdisciplinary scientists. A university that might have once held subscriptions to *Chemical Abstracts* for the Chemistry Library, Engineering Library, and Health Sciences Library can no longer justify such an expense. Pharmacists and medicinal chemists in the medical school as well as chemical engineers will very likely find themselves compelled to visit the Chemistry Library to use this abstracting service.

The emergence in recent years of cross-disciplinary indexes serves those well for whom a "match" occurs, e.g., *Pollution Abstracts* or *Engineered Materials Abstracts*, but there are many more interdisciplinary fields than there are currently covered by indexing services. Here overlap studies could provide insights into the thoroughness of coverage of these new discipline-spanning indexes and, if directed toward examination of interdisciplinary topics, also provide guidance on which discipline-based services provide most effective access to interdisciplinary sources. Given these difficulties of access, what can science libraries do to assist the growing numbers of interdisciplinary researchers? Several services seem capable of "bridging" discipline boundaries and merit consideration.

Online databases offer capability for searching the electronic equivalents of several indexes and abstracts simultaneously and comparing coverage. Although variations in both indexing vocabulary and authors' terminology occur across the files, a carefully designed search strategy will likely offer appreciable time-saving over manual searches of the same indexes. Online access to files not represented in book form in a library's reference collection is also available. Furthermore, the use of master indexes to a vendors' files allows a strategy to be tested for retrieval effectiveness prior to entering the databases. For example, use of Dialog's DIALINDEX[SM] can be an important early step in identifying databases likely to contain relevant citations. Recent enhancements to retrieval software now offer the ability to reduce duplication in multi-file searches and this feature, while not always able to eliminate all duplication, does result in lower print costs. Smaller libraries may benefit particularly from online services in that these provide access to large costly files that might not be justifiable as subscriptions; special libraries have recognized this benefit of online services for some time. Any library may discover an online database for which it holds no paper equivalent (or even for which none exists) that seems particularly suited to support an interdisciplinary query.

End user searching can be an attractive alternative to mediated searching for those scientists working at active research fronts, a frequent characteristic of interdisciplinary investigations. When a field of study is growing rapidly, terminology tends to be in flux and indexing vocabularies may be unresponsive to effective strategy development. In such situations suitably trained scientists can find it most efficient to be directly involved in information retrieval; they may then make relevance judgments while online and modify strategies to reflect their assessment of citations found. Science librarians can serve as resource persons and consultants to these end user searchers and may also direct them to suitable databases, thesauri and search guides.

Science libraries that operate in a decentralized environment with several departmentalized collections serving the sciences will very likely hear complaints from their users engaged in interdisciplinary research; these are the patrons whose journals and indexes are scattered over two or more campus locations. These may also be the patrons most inconvenienced by cancellations of duplicate journal subscriptions; what was once in the library in their building can now be consulted only by a trip across campus! Services to consider that address these problems include:

- intra-campus exchange programs for new journal issues or photocopied title pages for browsing use
- photocopy services employing campus mail, couriers, or use of telefacsimile transmission to provide timely document delivery of needed materials between sites
- use of campus local area networks for e-mail to remote libraries for transmission of reference questions, online search requests, delivery of books or journals, circulation services, interlibrary loan initiation, etc.

Of course, these enhancements bear a price tag and few library budgets are sufficiently expansive to launch such new services without careful projections of staffing and equipment needs. Even if user fees must be assessed, however, for many patrons the convenience factor can encourage use of departmental or grant funds.

Finally, the importance of being aware of new research initiatives on campus cannot be underestimated. In this regard, library committees and faculty liaisons are sources of valuable early information on new research centers developing on campus. Library directors and librarians serving on faculty senates are also in good positions to learn about new initiatives on campus that will impact the library. While some universities require a sort of "environmental impact statement" for the university as each proposed new program is reviewed, unhappily this is not universally true. It can be much too late if a library learns from a university press release that an interdisciplinary research center to foster technology transfer has been established! Such programs have been known to be planned without librarian input on available library resources to support them or without opportunity for library staff to begin long-range planning for acquisition of materials or development of support services.

## REFERENCE NOTES

1. Rustum Roy, "Interdisciplinary Science on Campus-the Elusive Dream" *Chemical & Engineering News.* 55: 28-40 (August 1977).

2. David L. Wheeler, "Mathematicians Develop New Tools to Tackle Environmental Problems" *Chronicle of Higher Education*, 38: A7, A10-11 (January 22, 1992).

3. Roy, p. 32.
4. Julie Thompson Klein, *Interdisciplinarity: History, Theory and Practice* (Detroit: Wayne State University Press, 1990).
5. Ibid., p. 11.
6. Rudy M. Baum, "Traditional Boundaries of Chemistry Pulled Wider by Changes in Science" *Chemical & Engineering News.* 69(47):18-22 (November 25, 1991).
7. Karen Grassmuck, "Major Research Universities Report Big Increases in Royalty Revenues from Patented Discoveries" *Chronicle of Higher Education.* 37: A23, 25 (March 6, 1991).
8. A. L. Porter and D. E. Chubin, "An Indicator of Cross-Disciplinary Research," *Scientometrics* 8(3-4): 161-176 (1985).
9. Daryl E. Chubin, Alan L. Porter, and Frederick A. Rossini, "'Citation Classics' Analysis: An Approach to Characterizing Interdisciplinary Research," *Journal of the American Society for Information Science.* 35: 360-368 (July 1984)
10. K. E. Clark and W. R. Kinyon, "The Interdisciplinary Use of Physics Journals," *College & Research Libraries News* 50: 145-150 ( Fall 1989).
11. Jin M. Choi, "Citation Analysis of Intra- and Interdisciplinary Communication Patterns of Anthropology in the U.S.A.," *Behavioral & Social Sciences Librarian* 6(3/4): 65-84 (1988).
12. Katherine W. McCain, "Cross-disciplinary Citation Patterns in the History of Technology," In ASIS '86, edited by Julie M. Hurd. (Medford, NJ: Learned Information, Inc., 1986) p. 194-196.
13. Katherine McCain and P. Joy Whitney, "Understanding Interdisciplinarity." Conference presentation, ASIS Special Interest Group on Biological and Chemical Information and Special Interest Group on Foundations of Information Science. American Society for Information Science, 54th Annual Meeting, Washington, DC, October 27-31, 1991.
14. Paul Metz, *The Landscape of Literatures: Use of Subject Collections in a University Library*. ACRL Publications in Librarianship, no. 43 (Chicago: American Library Association, 1983).
15. Brett Sutton, "Understanding Interdisciplinarity." See reference 13.
16. Julie M. Hurd, "Interdisciplinary Research in the Sciences: Implications for Library Organization," Submitted for publication.
17. Karen L. Curtis, Julie M. Hurd, and Ann C. Weller, "Access to Current Research Literature: Information Seeking Behavior of Faculty," Accepted for presentation. Medical Library Association Annual Meeting, Washington, DC, May 1992.
18. Richard E. Anderson and Barry Sugarman, "Options for Technology Transfer," *Capital Ideas.* 4 (1 & 2): 1-16 (July 1989). Also available from ERIC as ED311839. For a more extensive discussion, see also: Gary W. Matkin, *Technology Transfer and the University* (New York: Macmillan, 1990).
19. An example familiar to most in our profession is Northwestern University's successful spin-off of NOTIS, Inc. to market its library automation system of that name. NOTIS, Inc. was recently acquired by Ameritech.

20. Alistair M. Brett, David V. Gibson and Raymond W. Smilor, editors, *University Spin-off Companies: Economic Development. Faculty Entrepreneurs, and Technology Transfer,"* (Savage, MD: Rowman & Littlefield, 1991.)

21. Mary Pensyl, "Emerging Roles for Academic Librarians in the Technology Transfer Process," *Science & Technology Libraries.* 11(2):29-38 (Winter 1990).

22. Leon Shkolnik, "The Continuing Debate over Academic Branch Libraries," *College & Research Libraries* 52:343-351 (July 1991).

# Knowledge Diffusion and U.S. Government Technology Policy: Issues and Opportunities for Sci/Tech Librarians

Thomas E. Pinelli
Rebecca O. Barclay
Stan Hannah
Barbara Lawrence
John M. Kennedy

---

Thomas E. Pinelli serves as Assistant to the Chief, Research Information and Applications Division, Mail Stop 180A, NASA Langley Research Center, Hampton, VA 23665-5225. He received his PhD in Library and Information Science from Indiana University, Bloomington, IN.

Rebecca O. Barclay is Research Associate with the NASA/DoD Aerospace Knowledge Diffusion Research Project. She is pursuing a PhD in Communication and Rhetoric from Rensselaer Polytechnic Institute in the Department of Language, Literature, and Communication, RPI, Troy, NY 12180.

Stan Hannah is Assistant Professor in the College of Library and Information Science at the University of Kentucky, Lexington, KY 40506-0039. He is pursuing a PhD in Library and Information Science from Indiana University, Bloomington, IN.

Barbara Lawrence is Director of the Technical Information Division of the American Institute of Aeronautics and Astronautics (AIAA), New York, NY 10019.

John M. Kennedy is Principal Investigator of the NASA/DoD Aerospace Knowledge Diffusion Research Project and Director of the Indiana University Center for Survey Research, 1022 East Third Street, Bloomington, IN 47405. He received his PhD in Sociology from the Pennsylvania State University.

This paper is an intellectual product of the NASA/DoD Aerospace Knowledge Diffusion Research Project and was funded under NASA Grant NAGW-1682. The views expressed are the authors and may not represent those of their respective institutions or the funding agencies.

© 1992 by The Haworth Press, Inc. All rights reserved.

**SUMMARY.** Federal involvement in stimulating economic growth through the development and application of technology policy is currently the subject of serious debate. A recession and the recognition that an internationally competitive economy is a prerequisite for the attainment of national goals have fostered a number of technology policy initiatives aimed at improving the economic competitiveness of American industry. This paper suggests that the successful implementation of U.S. technology policy will require the adoption of a knowledge diffusion model, the development of user oriented information products and services, and a more "activist" approach on the part of sci/tech librarians in the provision of scientific and technical information (STI). These changes will have a dramatic impact on the sci/tech library of the future and the preparation of sci/tech librarians.

## INTRODUCTION

Traditionally, the Federal government has limited itself to activities either directly or explicitly tied to an existing responsibility of a specific government agency. Since the early 1960s, however, government has taken an increasingly active role in stimulating technological change and innovation in the civilian economy. Federal attempts at stimulating and nurturing technological innovation represent a dramatic departure from earlier policy positions which were based on a strict interpretation of the "general welfare" clause of the U.S. Constitution.[1] Economic vulnerability, lagging productivity, unfavorable trade balances, loss of traditional markets, and unemployment are the primary reasons for government intervention.

### Federal Involvement in Applied Research and Development (R&D)

The Federal government has successfully stimulated aerospace, agriculture, and biomedical R&D, as well as broader generic applied R&D in the National Institute of Standards and Technology (NIST). Scholars cite Federal intervention in aerospace and agriculture as models for government involvement in civilian R&D and precommercial research cooperation between industry and government. In fact, Vannevar Bush's[2] proposed model for the creation of his National Research Foundation was based on the land-grant colleges and the National Advisory Committee for Aeronautics (NACA). "Both offered science, applied science, technology, and a system for coupling knowledge with people who would use it in the field."[3]

By and large, Federal programs designed to stimulate civilian R&D have been unsuccessful. (This is not to say, however, that these programs did not contribute substantially to stimulating technological innovation.) Averch[4] suggests that these programs represent political rather than technical failures. Mowery[5] believes that the failure is both political and technical and attributes it to the application of an inappropriate theoretical economic framework, one that ignores or does not account for the effective transmission and utilization of complex research results and technological information. In particular, these programs overlook the abilities and limitations of organizations engaged in innovation to exploit extramural research, thus ignoring the relationship between knowledge production, transfer, and utilization as equally important components of the innovation process.

Unlike Japan, which has a managed and centralized approach to R&D, the U.S. funds R&D using various methods through numerous agencies of the executive branch. Federal R&D activities are undertaken by thousands of engineers and scientists in academia, government, and industry, and receive oversight, but not coordination, from many committees and subcommittees in both the executive and legislative branches of government.[6] Although considerable research into technological innovation and policy analysis has been conducted by various disciplines and from numerous perspectives, policy implications from the results of this research and investigation are inconsistent and contradictory, and are simply not used for policy development. In fact, Tornatzky and Fleischer[7] suggest that the "United States has no coherent innovation or technology policy. The United States does, however, have many programs and numerous policies which cut across political jurisdictions and the idiosyncratic missions and mandates of single agencies which are more or less responsive to a series of shifting political alliances and imperatives."

There is general consensus that current conceptual and empirical knowledge regarding both the process of technological innovation and U.S. government intervention is lacking. According to Curlee and Goel,[8] recognition is growing that technology transfer and diffusion is the "key" to the success of technological innovation. Consequently, understanding the influences that motivate innovation and channel its direction is necessary if government intervention is to successfully increase the production of useful innovation. Nelson[9] and Pavitt and Walker,[10] in their review and analysis of government policies and programs toward technological innovation, state that Federal innovation policy and prescription encourage innovation, not its adoption; knowledge transfer and utilization [diffusion] are "very inadequately served by market forces and the incentives of the market place." They conclude government would better serve public policy by assuming a more active role in the knowledge diffusion process and formulating policies and programs that encourage and improve communications between users and producers of knowledge.

## *Implications for Successful Federal R&D Intervention*

An examination of aerospace and agriculture as successful Federal intervention programs suggests several points that should be considered by those involved in formulating Federal technology policy. Although primarily technical, these points have an obvious political component. *First*, any attempt at intervention and stimulation of civilian R&D must take into account the unique characteristics of the various industries, their previous experiences with the Federal government, and their abilities and limitations to exploit the results of extramural research. The market system specific to aerospace and agriculture exerts substantial pressure to innovate in order to maintain economic competitiveness. Consequently both industries devote considerable effort to experimenting, screening, and adapting new technology to their own specific needs. Few, if any, aerospace companies can afford to invest in long term, high risk R&D, thus making them ideal clients for a federally funded R&D program which produces new technology, works on specific-discipline related problems, and makes the results available to the companies.

*Second*, the character of the industry which is the presumed beneficiary of the R&D program is central to its potential for success. The structure of the industry must lend itself to taking advantage of the programs' results, the leaders of the industry must be interested in and not opposed to the programs, and the government/industry relationship needs to be based on long standing trust and the perception of mutual benefit. Both aerospace and agriculture have established relationships with the Federal government dating back to 1917 with the creation of the NACA and its first research laboratory and the Hatch Act of 1887 which created the agricultural experiment stations. Industry leaders support government involvement and perceive Federal research programs to be mutually beneficial.

*Third*, careful attention needs to be given to the balance between user (industry) needs and the institutional/technical capabilities of the R&D institutions in designing the programs. The conduct of research in and of itself is not sufficient to assure that it will be used productively and put to use in commercial applications. Both aerospace and agriculture use mechanisms such as committees and peer review to ensure that the federally funded research undertaken is relevant, desirable, and needed.

*Fourth*, there must be a system for coupling knowledge with people who would use it in the field. Both aerospace and agriculture have established programs for collecting, controlling, and disseminating the results of federally funded R&D. Within both programs the U.S. government technical report is used as a primary means of transferring the results of this research to the user community. Additionally, both systems have components that include collecting, translating, evaluating, and disseminating the results of foreign R&D to U.S. academic, government, and industry users. This point has particular relevance for the implementation of a knowledge diffusion model and a more activist role for the sci/tech librarian in knowledge diffusion.

*Fifth*, successful technology policy includes both "supply-push" and "demand-pull" elements. In the case of aerospace, the use of Federal policy to supply and push aerospace knowledge began with the creation of the NACA by Congress to "supervise and direct the scientific study of the problems of flight with a view to their practical solutions and to give advice to the military air services and other aviation services of government." In its wind tunnels and laboratories, the NACA worked on problems of aerodynamics and aeronautics common to both military and commercial aviation, guided by committees composed of representatives from the aviation industry, the military services, and academia.

The demand-pull was accomplished through the passage of various legislation including the Kelly Air Mail Act of 1925, the McNary-Watres Act of 1930, and the creation of the Civil Aeronautics Board in 1938. This legislation had the combined effect of furthering the demand for state-of-the-art aircraft and fostering the rapid diffusion and adoption of innovations that drew upon federally funded research results.

## DIFFUSING THE RESULTS OF FEDERALLY FUNDED R&D

There is general agreement among policymakers that STI derived from federally funded R&D can be used to enhance technological innovation and economic competitiveness. Studies show a positive relationship between federally funded STI and successful innovation, technical performance, and increased productivity. What is unknown, however, is how STI is linked to the various components of the R&D process. Obtaining this knowledge is critical for formulating U.S. government technology policy. Such policy would, of course, recognize the inherent relationship between technological innovation and STI resulting from federally funded R&D.

Three models or approaches have dominated the "transfer" of federally funded R&D.[11,12] While variations of the models or approaches have been tried, Federal R&D transfer and diffusion activities continue to be driven by a "supply-side" model.

### The Appropriability Model

The *appropriability model* emphasizes the production of knowledge by the Federal government that would not otherwise be produced by the private sector and competitive market pressures to promote the use of that knowledge. This model emphasizes the production of basic research as the driving force behind technological development and economic growth and assumes that the Federal provision of R&D will be rapidly assimilated by the private sector. Deliberate transfer mechanisms and intervention by information intermediaries are viewed as unnecessary. Appropriability emphasizes the supply (production) of knowledge in sufficient quantity to attract potential users. Good technologies, according to this model, sell themselves and offer clear policy recommendations regarding Federal priorities for improving technological development and economic growth. This model incorrectly assumes that the results of federally funded R&D will be acquired and used by the private sector, ignores the fact that most basic research is irrelevant to technological innovation, and dismisses the process of technological innovation within the firm.

## The Dissemination Model

The *dissemination model* emphasizes the need to transfer information to potential users and embraces the belief that the production of quality knowledge is not sufficient to ensure its fullest use. Linkage mechanisms, such as information intermediaries, are needed to identify useful knowledge and to transfer it to potential users. This model assumes that if these mechanisms are available to link potential users with knowledge producers, then better opportunities exist for users to determine what knowledge is available, acquire it, and apply it to their needs. This model, which is used in aerospace, grew from recommendations of several "blue ribbon" committees such as those documented in the Weinberg Report (1963) and led to the creation of the Federal "clearinghouses" including the National Technical Information Service (NTIS). The strength of this model rests with the recognition that STI transfer and use are critical elements of the process of technological innovation. Its weakness lies with the fact that it is passive, for it does not take users into consideration except when they enter the system and request assistance; however, user requirements are seldom known or considered in the design of information products and services. This model employs one-way, source-to-user transfer procedures that are seldom responsive in the user context.

### The Knowledge Diffusion Model

The *knowledge diffusion model* is grounded in theory and practice associated with the diffusion of innovation and planned change research and the clinical models of social research and mental health. In terms of Federal support for applied R&D, the Agricultural Extension Service, with its network of extension agents who work directly with farmers, closely approximates this model. Knowledge diffusion emphasizes "active" intervention as opposed to dissemination and access; stresses intervention and reliance on interpersonal communications as a means of identifying and removing interpersonal barriers between users and producers; and assumes that knowledge production, transfer, and use are equally important components of the R&D process. This approach also emphasizes the link between producers, transfer agents, and users and seeks to develop user-oriented mechanisms (e.g., products and services) specifically tailored to the needs and circumstances of the user. It makes the assumption that the results of federally funded R&D will be under utilized unless they are relevant to users and ongoing relationships are developed among users and producers. The problem with the knowledge diffusion model is that (1) it requires a large Federal role and presence and (2) it runs contrary to the dominant assumptions of the established Federal R&D policy system.

## U.S. GOVERNMENT TECHNOLOGY POLICY AND KNOWLEDGE DIFFUSION

It is accepted *a priori* that STI resulting from federally funded research in science and technology can nurture and stimulate technological innovation. Therefore, it must be included as a component of U.S. government technology policy. Federal policymakers have expressed concern that STI may be underutilized and have suggested that the linkages between technology and STI be closely examined as part of the policy formulation process. In fact, a body of knowledge exists to support the claim that the existing model and mechanism used to transfer STI may contribute to its under utilization.[13] Finally, there are those who believe that the existing structure and organization of STI as manifested in present day libraries and technical information centers may actually impede its transfer.[14]

## STI and Technology Policy

By and large, the relationship between STI and the process of technological innovation is not well understood by policy and lawmakers. The U.S. has no overall strategy regarding the use of STI to stimulate technological innovation and currently lacks a focal point for developing one.[13] At the Federal level, the transfer and utilization of STI goes uncoordinated; there is no centrality concerning issue identification and resolution. Although the Office of Science and Technology Policy (OSTP) has a mandate to "promote the transfer and utilization of STI for civilian needs, to consider the potential role of information technology in the information transfer process, and to coordinate Federal STI policies and practices," in general, OSTP has not fulfilled this legislative directive.[6]

At present, the U.S. lacks a coherent or systematically designed approach to transferring the results of federally funded R&D to the user.[13] The very low level of support for knowledge transfer in comparison to knowledge production suggests that transfer efforts are not regarded as an important component of the R&D process.[14] Roberts and Frohman[15] claim that most Federal approaches to "transfer" are simply ineffective in stimulating technological innovation because they "start to encourage the utilization of STI only after the R&D results have been generated" rather than during the idea development phase of the innovation process.

Scholars such as Branscomb[16] argue that the current "supply-side" approach to knowledge production and the "trickle down" benefits associated with the funding of basic research and mission-oriented R&D are inadequate for developing a U.S. technology policy. They will simply not restore the U.S. to a more competitive footing with other industrialized countries such as Germany and Japan. These industrialized nations are adopting "diffusion-oriented" or "capability-enhancing" policies which increase the power to absorb and employ new technologies productively. U.S. technology policy efforts, on the other hand, continue to encourage innovation, not its adaption; remain product, not process oriented; and rely on a "dissemination-oriented" approach to the transfer of STI.

A strong technology policy would commit the U.S. to building a technology infrastructure that includes an STI transfer component based on a knowledge diffusion model. This model should have an "activist" component that emphasizes both domestic and imported STI, and it should be responsive in a "user" context. In short, this policy would be committed to "Total Quality Information Management." In addition to performing data and information evaluation, it would be coordinated across Federal agencies by the OSTP using a mechanism similar to the now defunct Committee on Scientific and Technical Information (COSATI).[16]

## Limitations of the Existing Federal STI Transfer Mechanism

The existing Federal STI transfer mechanism is composed of two parts–the *informal* that relies on collegial contacts and the *formal* that relies on surrogates, information products, and information intermediaries to complete the "producer to user" transfer process. The producers are the Federal R&D "mission" agencies and their contractors and grantees. Producers depend upon surrogates and information intermediaries to operate the formal transfer component.

Surrogates serve as technical report repositories or clearinghouses for the producers and include the Defense Technical Information Center (DTIC), the NASA Center for Aero Space Information (CASI), and the National Technical Information Service (NTIS). Information intermediaries are, in large part, librarians and technical information specialists in academia, government, and industry. Those representing the producers serve as what McGowan and Loveless[17] call "knowledge brokers" or "linking agents." Information intermediaries connected with users act, according to Allen,[18] as "technological entrepreneurs" or "gatekeepers." The more "active" the intermediary, the more effective the transfer process.[19] Active intermediaries take information from one place and move it to another, often face-to-face. Passive information intermediaries, on the other hand, "simply array information for the taking, relying on the initiative of the user to request or search out the information that may be needed."[20]

The major problem with the total Federal STI system is "that the present system for transferring the results of federally funded STI is passive, fragmented, and unfocused." Effective knowledge transfer is hindered by the fact the Federal government "has no coherent or systemmatically designed approach to transferring the results of federally funded R&D to the user."[13] Approaches to STI transfer vary considerably from agency to agency and, with any given agency, have changed significantly over time. These variations reflect differences between agencies (i.e., legislative mandates), the interpretation of their missions, and budgetary opportunities and constraints. In their study of issues and options in Federal STI, Bikson and her colleagues[14] found that many interviewees considered dissemination activities "afterthoughts, undertaken without serious commitment by Federal agencies whose primary concerns were with [knowledge] production and not with knowledge transfer"; therefore, "much of what has been learned about knowledge transfer has not been incorporated into federally supported STI transfer activities."

The specific problem with the *informal* part of the system is that knowledge users can learn from collegial contacts only what those contacts happen to know. Ample evidence supports the claim that no one researcher can know about or keep up with all the research in his/her area(s) of interest. Two problems exist with the *formal* part of the system. First, it employs one-way, source-to-user transmission. The problem with this kind of transmission is that one-way, "supply-side" transfer procedures do not seem to be responsive to the user context.[14] Rather, these efforts appear to start with an information system into which the users' requirements are retrofit.[21] The consensus of the findings from the empirical research is that interactive, two-way communications are required for effective information transfer.[14]

Second, the *formal* part relies heavily on information intermediaries to complete the knowledge transfer process, but a strong methodological base for measuring or assessing the effectiveness of the information intermediary is lacking.[22] The impact of information intermediaries is likely to be strongly conditional and limited to a specific institutional context. To date, empirical findings on the effectiveness of information intermediaries and the role(s) they play in knowledge transfer are sparse and inconclusive.[23]

The *formal* part of the transfer mechanism is particularly ineffective because STI is not organized and structured according to problem relevance. More to the point, putting STI to use frequently requires transferring it in a use context that is quite different from the context in which it was produced or originally packaged. This problem is complicated by the fact that STI is organized along traditional disciplinary lines as are subject matter indexes, abstracts, and key words. This organizational scheme makes multidisciplinary retrieval extremely difficult for users and (typically non-technical) information intermediaries alike. The *formal* part of the transfer mechanism becomes even less effective when the user's environment is not well aligned with the standard disciplinary taxonomies.[14]

## The Existing Structure, Organization, and Management of STI

The existing structure, organization, and management of STI may restrict or inhibit the process of technological innovation. Consequently, changes must be made as part of any effort, national or otherwise, to nurture technological innovation and to stimulate economic growth through the development of technology policy.

*Passivity of libraries.* Traditionally, libraries and technical information centers that house STI are passive structures that require the user to initiate a request for information. They employ one-way, source-to-user transfer procedures that are seldom responsive to the user context. The consensus of findings from empirical research is that interactive, two-way communications are required for effective STI transfer.[14] Complaints from STI users indicate that these findings have not been incorporated into the design of STI products and services and the operations of most libraries and technical information centers that house STI.

Passivity may be attributable to two historical causes. *First*, for the most part, libraries and technical information centers that house STI are funded as cost centers: their cost is charged to the overhead of the organization. Constant attempts by organizations to reduce overhead result in passively structured and staffed operations. Such a low level of support for knowledge transfer prohibits interactive, two-way communications. In the new structure, organization, and management, STI must become more of a strategic resource and less of an overhead burden. *Second*, the paradigm governing library and information science education is based on a dissemination model which stipulates that libraries provide documents instead of supplying information; thus, library and information science graduates remain tied to information artifacts and do not learn to take active roles in the STI transfer process. Simply stated, libraries and technical information centers that house STI manage information resources (those things which carry information) rather than manage information.[24]

In the new structure, organization, and management of STI, passivity must become activism. The need for more frequent and more effective use of STI characterizes the strategic version of today's competitive marketplace. There are several reasons for this. Information technology is making the same STI available at the same time to all competitors. The marketplace is increasingly characterized by a growing number of stakeholders that are constantly changing. This implies that a broader array of STI will be needed for decision making and that simply providing retrieval and access without providing interpretation and analysis is meaningless. The need to provide STI interpretation and analysis is critical because there is less time available for making decisions and the half-life of information is getting shorter.[25] Finally, increasing U.S. collaboration with foreign producers will result in a more international manufacturing environment. These alliances will result in a more rapid diffusion of technology, increasing pressure on U.S. companies to push forward with new technological developments and to take steps designed to maximize the inclusion of recent technological developments into the (R&D) process.

*Lack of user responsiveness.* STI is just not organized, structured, and delivered in ways that take into account the characteristics of individuals involved in the process of technological innovation, the majority of whom are engineers. Technological innovation implies a knowledge-producing activity embedded within a larger problem-solving activity.[26] Throughout the innovation process, ideas and knowledge are pursued and transferred. The fact that these ideas and knowledge may be "physically or hardware encoded" does not alter the fact that the process of innovation is fundamentally an information processing activity.[18] To facilitate information processing, STI transfer mechanisms should be user-responsive, giving users greater control over and involvement in the knowledge diffusion process.[14]

STI is currently structured and organized around a (basic) science rather than an (applied) technology model that consequently better serves scientists, not engineers. Fundamental differences between science (scientists) and technology (engineers) have significant implications for planning information services for these two groups. Typically, the goal of the scientist is to build theory and advance knowledge by making original contributions to the literature. The goal of the engineer is to produce or (re)design a product, process, or system. Engineers, unlike scientists, work within time constraints; they are seldom interested in theory, source data, and guides to the literature so much as they are in reliable answers to specific questions.[27]

Engineers tend to read less than scientists, consult literature and libraries less frequently, and seldom use the information products and services which are directly oriented to them. What engineers usually want is a specific answer, in terms and format that are intelligible to them, not a collection of documents that they must sift, evaluate, and translate before they can apply them. Their search for information seems to be based more on the need for a specific problem solution than around a search for general opportunity.[27]

*Limitations of STI retrieval systems.* Contemporary STI retrieval systems may exacerbate the problems of the existing structure, organization, and management of knowledge and its lack of user responsiveness. In fact, STI retrieval systems may now be contributing to the very problems they were designed to solve. Few would argue with Lancaster[28] that "while technological advances have undoubtedly increased physical access to sources of information, it is very doubtful that intellectual access has increased significantly, if at all." Although advances in computer hardware may provide greater access to available STI, they do not provide an effective means of filtering the STI in terms of quality or problem relevance.

The rapid growth in the volume of STI that must be stored and retrieved is not the only problem confronting users of STI retrieval systems, however. There is a growing awareness that contemporary STI retrieval systems " . . . are primitive and prevent the full utilization of the information . . . "[29] The traditional STI retrieval system " . . . does not inform (i.e., change the knowledge of) users on the subject of their inquiry. It merely informs them on the existence (or nonexistence) and whereabouts of information packages relating to their request."[30] In other words, current STI retrieval systems are misnamed. They do not retrieve STI; rather they retrieve citations. The bibliographic citations, of course, do not reflect the rich network of inter-relationships that exist in any scientific discipline. In fact, the resulting citations are so devoid of structure that they are usually arranged chronologically by year or by authors' last names.

Researchers involved in technological innovation see their work in terms of STI that is problem-oriented and organized according to products, procedures, and processes. To meet their STI needs, they want a source that exhibits an understanding of the major topics and paradigms in their field. What they do not need is a bibliography produced by a librarian who typically has little, if any, education or experience in the subject being searched.

Librarians and information scientists usually discount the preceding criticisms by noting that most users cannot accurately or adequately define their information needs. Moreover, they assert that these individuals are information "illiterate." The fact is, however, that users of STI do not approach information searching in the same way that librarians do. Whereas a librarian might begin a search by consulting the appropriate index or guide to the literature, card catalog, or electronic database, STI users consult colleagues and personal collections of information.

## The Promise of Intelligent Databases

The pressing need is to develop a new paradigm for structuring, organizing, and managing STI that will allow researchers to retrieve ideas–not bibliographic citations. Conceptually, the next step is to develop databases that will store not only facts about individual documents but also the linkages that exist among the documents. These "intelligent" databases would provide an abstract model of the subject specialty that would closely resemble the researcher's working model. In a very real sense such a database could be correctly termed an intelligent database. Such databases would equip sci/tech libraries with a retrieval tool that would equal the power of Vannevar Bush's famed Memex, the individualized, private file organizer and personal library that would act as "an enlarged intimate supplement" to the researcher's memory.[31] Most importantly, Memex would, like the human mind, be able to retrieve information by associating ideas and not by matching index terms.[31]

Intelligent databases are quite real. They are the outgrowth of the confluence of two key technologies. The first is the traditional online retrieval system with its processing and mass storage capabilities. The second is a subset of artificial intelligence: expert systems. Expert systems are now sufficiently developed to allow the construction of online retrieval systems that can represent documents in terms of concepts rather than keywords; in short, the technological tools needed to build databases that can truly represent the intellectual framework of a discipline are now available.[29]

The design of the complex knowledge representation schemes needed to construct intelligent databases will be a difficult and costly task. However, the availability of "shells," a software package that facilitates the building of knowledge-based systems (also called expert systems), by providing a built-in knowledge representation schema and inference engine, means that the builders of intelligent databases no longer need the advanced programming skills required for developing artificial intelligence applications.[32] In effect, the shells put the expertise needed to construct a knowledge-based system into a software package, thus reducing " . . . the levels of skill required by developers."[33] Advances in shells have so dramatically reduced the cost and risks of developing an intelligent database that Klein and Methlie state that the technology is now both practical and available.[34] The advent of intelligent databases will dramatically change " . . . how we do research, how we look for ideas, how we make decisions, and how knowledge is transmitted."[29] For Feigenbaum, McCorduck, and Nii, the benefits of intelligent knowledge databases are so compelling that there is no question that such systems will be built in next decade; " . . . the only open question is when."[35]

## The Need for a New Paradigm

For practicing sci/tech librarians there is another "open question" that is important to answer: who will build and manage the new intelligent information retrieval systems? Hopefully, the information science component of the sci/tech library profession will play a central role in their design, construction, and management. However, there are several important and fundamental impediments that the profession must overcome before they can be important players in the development of intelligent databases. Information scientists must rethink many of their current practices and change many of their procedures. But, what is most urgently needed in the profession, as Dougherty notes, is "a dramatic break with the past" coupled with " . . . new initiatives that will enable [sci/tech] librarians to make fuller use of information technologies and the talents of library professionals."[36]

The need for breaking with the past is not mere rhetoric. This break with the past requires a new paradigm for structuring, organizing, and managing STI that allows for the retrieval of ideas; emphasizes sci/tech librarians interpreting and analyzing information rather than accessing and retrieving documents; and enables information scientists to play an active and central role in the design, construction, and management of intelligent STI knowledge-based databases using expert systems. Breaking with the past is never easy, however. The new paradigm may necessitate a complete restructuring of library and information science education, "support of basic information science, including research leadership in the field, and constant self-renewal through some drastic form of continuing education, e.g., joint commitment by school and student to lifelong cyclic return to the school, following the first degree."[37] To do less, according to Heilprin, will "probably lead to [the] absorption of functions and personnel of the [sci/tech] library by other, more competitively adaptive information communities."[37]

Sci/tech librarians have been educated and socialized to maintain, care for, and love the library and its enormous collection of documents. Since so much of the daily operation and activity of today's sci/tech libraries revolve around inventorying, housing, and maintaining the collection of documents, these libraries have inevitably been more concerned about preserving the collection than in accessing the collection. As Heaps has stated, the needs of the traditional library " . . . led to the development of standard procedures for manual cataloguing, use of card indexes, bibliographies, and the circulation and ordering of books, journals, and reports."[38] As a natural result, " . . . the traditional library was oriented more to managing the things which carry information than managing information as if it were a resource."[38]

While it is easy to point out obstacles that will prevent information scientists from participating in the development of intelligent STI retrieval systems, it is important to note that they also possess the type of skills that would qualify them to work as knowledge engineers. The term "knowledge engineer" was first coined by Edward Feigenbaum in 1977 to describe the person who would be responsible for identifying pertinent information, developing a knowledge framework through a combination of representation and inference, and implementing this framework using software tools.[35] The skills needed by the knowledge engineer include a solid working knowledge of systems design and "a fairly high degree of computer literacy;" in addition, the future knowledge engineer must possess " . . . a fairly wide range of skills, many of which are behavioral in nature."[39]

Clearly, many information scientists already have most of the skills that would be needed by a knowledge engineer. One fact is certain: intelligent databases will be developed in the near future, and they will offer the kind of context sensitive access that will transform Bush's visionary Memex into a practical research tool. What is less clear, however, is the role that information scientists will play in the development of intelligent databases. Hopefully, they will seize the opportunity and adapt their professional and educational institutions so that they can take full advantage of the enormous opportunities offered by intelligent database technology.

Unfortunately, library and information science education reflects the same uneasy mixture of traditional values overlaid with a soupçon of information technology that characterizes so much of the professional life of information scientists. A large part of the curriculum is designed to turn out students qualified to operate document warehouses, while a set of specialized courses that are usually introductory in nature, attempt to turn out information professionals equipped with the skills needed to take advantage of the new information technologies. In a very real sense, library and information science education is struggling, perhaps unsuccessfully, with an attempt to amalgamate two incompatible and competing paradigms.[40]

## CONCLUDING REMARKS

In a *Wall Street Journal* editorial,[41] Peter Drucker stated that to be competitive and successful in the global marketplace requires a strategy that includes a commitment to change, leadership in the management of technology, and the wise use of knowledge. He further states that the Japanese are "willing to pay large sums to gain access to the knowledge their foreign partners will produce and control over it-or at least priority in using it."[41] In doing so, the Japanese have adopted a "diffusion-oriented" approach to technology policy. Every major Japanese industrial group has its own research institute, whose main function is to bring to the group awareness of any important new knowledge in technology developed world-wide.

U.S. technology policy must be based on the belief that the production, transfer, and use of STI is inextricably linked to successful technological innovation; that the process of technological innovation is best served by a "knowledge diffusion" based model; and that an STI transfer infrastructure, funded and coordinated as a partnership between American industry and the Federal government, is required for the nation to become competitive in the global marketplace in the 1990s and beyond.

For years land, labor, and capital were perceived to be the forces propelling the economic growth of industrialized nations. With the advent of a global economy, information has been added to the traditional sources of wealth.[42] In international industries, the successful firms will be those that produce, transfer, and utilize STI for marketplace and strategic advantages. "Comparative advantages of organizations are to be found more in knowing the *how* and *when* to use information rather than in simply having it."[25] Given that the *how* of information use is "inadequately developed and poorly applied in nearly all private and public organizations,"[42] American industry must reexamine its approach to the management and utilization of STI as part of a strategic version directed toward successful participation in the global economy.

A commitment by the sci/tech library community to change and to a new paradigm is required. While the exact shape of the new sci/tech library paradigm cannot be seen in minute detail, its major features are clear. The paradigm will embrace many of the same principles of success that have been identified in successful firms in the private sector. *First*, the paradigm must recognize that the sci/tech library's clients are striving to meet the demands of a rapidly changing competitive scene. *Second*, to meet their clients' needs, sci/tech library services will take on many of the characteristics common to the most successful private sector firms, such as, a proactive stance that emphasizes value-added services that are tailored to meet the individual needs of each user or groups of users, innovative services that are the result of intensive listening to the customer, exceptional services and responsiveness to customers, and a love and appreciation for change . . . "at least as much love for change as we hated it in the past."[43]

## REFERENCE NOTES

1. Tiech, Albert H. "Federal Support of Applied research: A Review of the United States Experience." Paper commissioned for a workshop on *The Federal Role in Research and Development,* November 21-22, 1985, held in Washington, DC and sponsored by the National Academy of Sciences, National Academy of Engineering, and Institute of Medicine.

2. Bush, Vannevar. *Science: The Endless Frontier.* (Washington, DC: Government Printing Office, 1945.)

3. Shapley, Deborah and Rustom Roy. *Lost at the Frontier: U.S. Science and Technology Policy Adrift.* (Philadelphia: ISI Press, 1985.)

4. Averch, Harvey A. *A Strategic Analysis of Science & Technology Policy.* (Baltimore, MD: The Johns Hopkins University Press, 1985.)

5. Mowery, David C. "Economic Theory and Government Technology Policy." *Policy Sciences* 16 (1983): 27-43.

6. Pinelli, Thomas E. "Enhancing U.S. Competitiveness through Federal Scientific and Technical Information: Issues and Opportunities." *Government Information Quarterly* 7:2 1990: 219-228.

7. Tornatzky, Louis G. and Mitchell Fleischer. *The Process of Technological Innovation.* (Lexington, MA: D.C. Heath Company, 1990.)

8. Curlee, T.R. and R.K. Goel. *The Transfer and Diffusion of New Technologies: A Review of the Economic Literature.* ORNL/TM-11155. Oak Ridge, TN: U.S. Department of Energy, June 1989. (Available from NTIS, Springfield, VA; N90-11655.)

9. Nelson, Richard R. "Government Stimulus of Technological Progress: Lessons From American History." In *Government and Technical Progress: A Cross-Industry Analysis,* Richard R. Nelson, ed. (NY: Pergamon Press, 1982), 435-463.

10. Pavitt, K. and W. Walker. "Government Policies Toward Industrial Innovation: A Review." *Research Policy* 5:1 (January 1976): 11-97.

11. Ballard, Steven et al. *Innovation Through Technical and Scientific Information: Government and Industry Cooperation.* (NY: Quorum Books, 1989), 39-45.

12. Williams, Frederick and David V. Gibson, eds. *Technology Transfer: A Communication Perspective.* (Newbury Park, CA: Sage Publications, 1990), 14-15.

13. Ballard, Steve et al. *Improving the Transfer and Use of Scientific and Technical Information. The Federal Role: Volume 2–Problems and Issues in the Transfer and Use of STI.* Washington, DC: National Science Foundation, 1986. (Available from NTIS, Springfield, VA; PB-87-142923.)

14. Bikson, Tora K.; Barbara E. Quint; and Leland L. Johnson. *Scientific and Technical Information Transfer: Issues and Options.* Washington, DC: National Science Foundation, March 1984. (Available from NTIS, Springfield, VA; PB-85-150357; also available as Rand Note 2131.)

15. Roberts, Edward B. and Alan L. Frohman. "Strategies for Improving Research Utilization." *Technology Review* 80 (March/April 1978): 32-39.

16. Branscomb, Lewis G. "Toward a U.S. Technology Policy." *Issues in Science and Technology* 7:4 (Summer 1991): 50-55.

17. McGowan, Robert P. and Stephen Loveless. "Strategies for Information Management: The Administrator's Perspective." *Public Administration Review* 41:3 (May/June 1981): 331-339.

18. Allen, Thomas J. *Managing the Flow of Technology: Technology Transfer and the Dissemination of Technological Information Within the R&D Organization.* (Cambridge, MA: MIT Press, 1977.)

19. Goldhor, Richard S. and Robert T. Lund. "University-to-Industry Advanced Technology Transfer: A Case Study." *Research Policy* 12 (1983): 121-152.

20. Eveland, J. D. *Scientific and Technical Information Exchange: Issues and*

*Findings.* Washington, DC: National Science Foundation, March 1987. (Not available from NTIS.)

21. Adam, Ralph. "Pulling the Minds of Social Scientists Together: Towards a World Social Science Information System." *International Social Science Journal* 27:3 (1975): 519-531.

22. Kitchen, Paul and Associates. *A Review of the Feasibility of Developing a Methodology to Demonstrate the Value of Canadian Federal Libraries in Economic Terms.* Canada: Paul Kitchen and Associates, March 1989.

23. Beyer, Janice M. and Harrison M. Trice. "The Utilization Process: A Conceptual Framework and Synthesis of Empirical Findings." *Administrative Science Quarterly* 27 (December 1982): 591-622.

24. Diener, AV Richard. "A Tale of Two Paradigms, or Whatever Happened to IRM?" *Bulletin of the American Society for Information Science* 18:2 (December/January 1992): 26-27.

25. Barabba, Vincent P. and Gerald Zaltman. *Hearing the Voice of the Market: Competitive Advantage through Creative Use of Market Information.* (Boston, MA: Harvard Business School Press, 1991), 23-25.

26. Vincenti, Walter G. *What Engineers Know and How They Know It: Analytical Studies From Aeronautical History.* (Baltimore, MD: Johns Hopkins University Press, 1990.)

27. Pinelli, Thomas E. "The Information-Seeking Habits and Practices of Engineers." *Science & Technology Libraries* 11:3 (Spring 1991): 5-25.

28. Lancaster, Frederick W. "Has Technology Failed Us?" *Information Technology and Library Management: Festschrift in Honour of Margaret Beckman.* 13th International Essen Symposium, 22-25 October 1989, ed. by Ahmed H. Helal and Joachim W. Weiss. (Essen: Essen University Library, 1991.)

29. Parsaye, Kamran et al. *Intelligent Databases: Object-Oriented, Deductive, Hypermedia Technologies.* (New York: John Wiley, 1989,) 256.

30. Lancaster, Frederick W. *Information Retrieval.* (New York: John Wiley, 1968), 1.

31. Bush, Vannevar. "As We May Think." *Atlantic Monthly* 176:1 (July 1945): 107.

32. Edwards, John S. *Building Knowledge-Based Systems: Towards a Methodology.* (NY: Halsted Press, 1991), 242.

33. Beynon-Davies, P. *Expert Database System: A Gentle Introduction.* (London: McGraw-Hill, 1991), 39.

34. Klein, Michael and Leif B. Methlie. *Expert Systems: A Decision Support Approach.* (Wokingham, England: Addison-Wesley, 1990), 2.

35. Feigenbaum, Edward; Pamela McCorduck; and H. Penny Nii. *The Rise of the Expert Company.* (NY: Vintage Books, 1988), 266.

36. Dougherty, Richard M. "Needed: User-Responsive Research Libraries." *Library Journal.* 116:1 (January 1990): 59-62.

37. Heilprin, Laurence B. "The Library Community at a Technological and Philosophical Crossroads: Necessary and Sufficient Conditions for Survival."

*Journal of the American Society for Information Science* 42:8 (September 1991): 566-573.

38. Heaps, H.S. *Information Retrieval: Computational and Theoretical Aspects.* (NY: Academic Press, 1978), 1.

39. Beerel, Annabel. *Expert Systems: Strategic Implications and Applications.* (Chichester: Ellis Horwood, 1987), 129.

40. Blaise Cronin observed that library and information science programs are, like the human brain, split into two hemispheres that have different functions; *Vibrations.* "Cronin Urges Technological Upgrade." 30:1 (Fall 1991): 1.

41. Drucker, Peter F. "Japan: New Strategies for a New Reality" *The Wall Street Journal.* October 2, 1991.

42. Badaracco, J.L., Jr. *The Knowledge Link: How Firms Compete Through Strategic Alliances.* (Boston, MA: Harvard Business Press, 1991), 1-2.

43. Peters, Tom. *Thriving on Chaos: Handbook for a Management Revolution.* (NY: Knopf, 1987), 45.

# Collection Development vs. Access in Academic Science Libraries

Gary Wiggins

**SUMMARY.** The academic science librarian of today faces many challenges as we move toward a new century. Not the least of these is the transition from a collection which is primarily print-based to information sources which will exist substantially in electronic formats. This paper examines some of the concepts and dilemmas which an academic science library must consider in order to align its collection development activities with the changing environment of scientific and technical librarianship. In particular, the problem of serials access versus ownership is considered.

Of prime importance to collection development in large academic science libraries are the faculty, for it is their research programs and endeavors which determine the collection's scope and depth and the services offered by the library. Science faculty at academic institutions are generally engaged in 3 activities: research, teaching, and service. The larger the academic institution, the more the faculty are likely to concentrate their efforts on research. It is that activity which garners the research grants to fund the personnel and equipment needed to explore matters of interest in the laboratory. Ulti-

---

Gary Wiggins is Head of the Indiana University Chemistry Library, Bloomington, IN 47405. He holds a BA degree in chemistry, masters degrees in Slavic Languages and Library Science, and a PhD in Library and Information Science. Dr. Wiggins is a member of the American Chemical Society and the Special Libraries Association.

© 1992 by The Haworth Press, Inc. All rights reserved.

mately, the results of the experiments will be published and contribute to the archival record of science which is vital for its survival.

Tuck et al. have identified four categories of research activity:

- collecting and analyzing published information
- collecting and analyzing primary data (including experiments and field work)
- writing (reports, theses, etc.)
- communicating results of research through seminars, conference papers, journal articles, and books.[1]

Experimental results are typically presented at symposia or conferences before appearing in published primary sources of information. In a sense, the oral presentations are part of the second activity: teaching. Teaching requires organizational skills and the ability to present concepts in a way that will be easily understood by the audience. Good teachers also have the capacity to test the target audience in a meaningful way to see if (and to what degree) they have grasped the material which has been selected for presentation.

Finally, academic faculty are engaged in service. The service may take the form of a post within the department (for example, chairing the laboratory safety committee) or within the larger academic community at the home institution (such as service on the faculty senate), or, more likely nowadays, service to the profession through a role in one of the professional societies. The last activity may involve arranging a symposium at a national meeting or serving on any of the many committees which most professional organizations generate. An academic science library will typically be heavily involved in the faculty's research and teaching enterprises, but much less so in the activities which center around service.

There are some services which academic libraries traditionally have provided free, and which will undoubtedly continue to be free. Among them are ready reference, circulation, and open access to materials. However, both librarians and users must recognize that information is not a free commodity. Fees for certain services which have traditionally been free should be considered. In-depth reference service, mediated online searching, and on-campus delivery of materials are examples of services where the labor costs have often been absorbed by the academic institution. Yet it is the labor costs which form a significant barrier to the provision of wider access services. Therefore, it is essential to define the core services and collections which ought to be offered at no charge to the user. In particular, much attention needs to be devoted to collection development and access services, for it is the access to published material which is still of utmost concern to the faculty at the beginning of this last decade of the twentieth century.

What used to be called the "acquisition" function in libraries has now been designated "collection management and development." This reflects the realities imposed by economics over the last two decades. Science librarians today do not simply acquire materials suggested by the faculty and other users. They actively evaluate the body of available sources, comparing them to the research and teaching interests of their primary clientele and selecting the material which will satisfy as much as possible of the current demand from the on-site collection. Even the mass of material from previous, more affluent decades of "acquisition" work does not escape their scrutiny, for collection management also encompasses weeding. The desirability of keeping a collection of little-used older material on-site must be measured against a rapidly dwindling amount of empty shelf space for newer material. Off-site storage facilities may be utilized, but increasingly, withdrawal (weeding) is the choice made by the collection manager.

Another buzzword which emerged in the 1980s is "access," a term generally applied to information sources which are not held at the geographic site of the academic institution. Calls for more use of access services are increasingly heard from library administrators, especially that new breed of assistant or associate deans of large academic libraries, the "chief collection development officers." Part of their job is to control expenditures and find space for all of the materials collected. One need only read the titles of a few "Specflyers" (publications of the Association of Research Libraries Office of Management Studies Systems and Procedures Exchange Center) to gauge the direction of modern acquisitions work: "Cooperative Collection Development" (no 111, February 1985) and "Serials Control and Deselection Projects" (no 147, September 1988). The recent report of the ARL Task Force on a National Program for

Scientific and Technical Information lists five priorities, among them, "accelerating research libraries' efforts to coordinate programs in acquiring, maintaining, and preserving serials literature."[2]

The management of science serials collections has often been approached in the last two decades by assigning each serial subscription to a subject fund (chemistry, physics, biology, medical sciences, etc.). The responsible librarians were then given the charge to "manage" the fund, that is, to make the necessary cancellations when the allocated budget was exceeded, which frequently happened in the last 20 years. The difficulty with this approach is that it tends to ignore the interdisciplinary nature of science, an aspect which is becoming increasingly important in many areas of research. Too often the fund managers (librarians) were forced to cancel serial titles which were of less immediate need by their own faculty, but were critical to an emerging new area of study in another field. An often-used criterion is the "cost/benefit" of a particular serial title.[3] Elaborate usage studies have been devised to prove that such venerable reference titles as the *Beilstein Handbook of Organic Chemistry* or translation journals simply were not contributing to the immediate mission of a given fund. Unfortunately, little weight is given to the effort and expense required to produce such works and the cost of obtaining the desired information via alternate paths when such sources are not available.

Collection development in academic science libraries has bordered on the chaotic in recent decades. This has resulted in part from a failure to adequately define "cooperative collection development" and "access" and in part from the lack of a coherent plan for integrating machine-readable sources into our collecting profiles. There are some ground rules which must be accepted before order can be achieved in collection development.

Rule number 1: Buy no material for *any* program/department until its priority in the institution's plan for the 1990s is clearly defined. This must be clearly and openly stated by the highest levels of the academic administration.

Rule number 2: Invest the resources available for collection development (including access) in a manner which reflects the long-term priorities of the academic institution. This rule must be enforced by the library administration.

It seems sensible to define the access/ownership expenditure ratio on the basis of actual university priorities. There should be at least a two-tiered division of expenditures for *acquisition,* that is, for actual material held (or leased) on-site, regardless of format. This could be defined in terms of the percentage of times that a researcher should expect to find a needed item at the home institution, perhaps 90% of the time for the top level of support, and 75% of the time for those supported at a lesser level.

Many academic institutions subsidize the costs of access to materials or electronic forms of information which are not locally owned (or leased). That may take the form of a flat fee for a photocopy (or telefacsimile) of journal articles, a subsidy for costs associated with searching an online database, etc. It could be argued that academic institutions should provide a uniform level of subsidy for access according to membership in user groups, regardless of the priority which the university places on the programs or departments from which the users come. There are significant annoyances in using many of the access services, despite the great strides in the technology which serves these areas. Not the least of those is the delay in obtaining the material. It is likely that for a good while to come, the time necessary to acquire information via information products accessible through a library will exceed the time it takes to find the same information in a library which actually owns the information source. Thus, an academic institution must reserve a significant portion of what was once called the acquisitions budget for access to alternate sources of information, both print and electronic. Costs which might be subsidized from this source of funds include interlibrary loan fees, search costs for remote online databases, and purchase, license, or royalty fees for electronic forms of information provided on-site in lieu of paper counterparts.

The basic problem with cooperative collection development programs in the sciences, if not in all disciplines, is that there is a core of material and information sources which all significant research libraries want to own or have access to. This is nowhere better illustrated than in the Research Libraries Group "4+ Project" for Chemistry. Starting with a list of journals which contribute the most references each year to *Chemical Abstracts,* the participants in the project supplemented the titles with rankings from *Science Citation*

*Index* and other sources. The list was then pared down to 541 titles, and an agreement was reached that for each title on the list, n subscriptions would be maintained, where n varies from 1 to the maximum number of participants.[4] The participating universities were seeking a long-term commitment for the maintenance of the titles, at least 5 years. Needless to say, there was a large group of titles for which all libraries chose to continue to maintain subscriptions.

Ralli has stated that "There is no substitute for direct access by scholars to the materials they require."[5] But direct access is no longer limited to a user who physically retrieves books and journals sitting on library shelves. Information is becoming fully transportable to a user's workstation. In the future, it should be easier to transport information in computer-readable form from a library or other source than it is to make a photocopy today. Electronic formats of information will have the greatest and most far-reaching impact on academic research over the next decade. Libraries should, therefore, embrace a broader definition of access to include all document delivery techniques which use appropriate technology to easily deliver information from the location in which it is held to the user. As telefacsimile services become more widely available, the options for enhanced document delivery services increase dramatically.

Some recent research projects and new commercial services provide useful insights into the ingredients necessary for the successful transition to an electronic library. These are Cornell's CORE project, the British Library's Project Quartet, and the Colorado Alliance of Research Libraries UnCover services.

The Chemistry Online Retrieval Experiment (CORE) at Cornell University is an extensive investigation of the impact of an electronic chemistry library.[6] Equipped with a database of ten years of online journals from the American Chemical Society and the indexing of those articles from Chemical Abstracts Service, the project has several ambitious goals. One of them is to determine the users' perception of the effectiveness of the electronic form of the primary journal as compared to paper. Another is to identify the most desirable traits of the user interface to an electronic system of journals. The CORE project also attempts to address the most severe limitation to online use of chemical journals–the lack of pictorial information in online files of full-text science journals. Drawings of apparatus, spectograms, chemical structures, reaction diagrams–all standard features of printed chemical journals–would be lost if the only access in the CORE project were to the ASCII text. In order to include such graphical matter, the pages with images were scanned from the microfilm versions of the printed ACS journals.

Among the potential benefits cited for an electronic chemistry library are superior distribution methods, cheaper, less-cumbersome methods of storing and archiving the material, and more effective access to library resources by end users.[7] A key technology for the CORE project is the computer network, since the delivery of graphic images to a workstation requires considerably more network capacity than does textual data.

Project Quartet, so named for the four British academic participants (University of Loughborough, University of Birmingham, Hatfield Polytechnic, and University College, London), also included as participants the British Library Document Supply Centre and the ADONIS consortium of publishers.[8] The project ran for three years, 1986-89, and had objectives similar to those of the CORE project, among them, to determine just how far the newer electronic media could replace traditional print sources and where the management of print-on-paper systems might be enhanced by such media.

Project Quartet focused on 4 distinct areas: online information systems, computer-based message systems, computer conferencing systems, and document delivery systems. Two hundred and twenty high-use biomedical journals on CD-ROM (the ADONIS collection) formed the major database used in the experiment. User studies conducted on the ADONIS portion of the project showed that there was no overwhelming demand for the service. A possible explanation offered by the researchers is " . . . that the service provided was not really sufficiently better than that obtainable using conventional methods for the user to be willing to make the switch."[9] To be successful, a new service must provide sufficient incentive to the user to make its use routine. The Project Quartet researchers suggest that the document delivery function needs to be integrated with related services–end-user searching, current awareness bulletins via e-mail, one-stop ordering and delivery.[10] Only then do they feel that the users will be persuaded to change their information search and request habits.

The Colorado Alliance of Research Libraries (CARL) has developed such an integrated system with its UnCover services. With CARL, the users can perform searches over the Internet in a bibliographic database of journal articles. Either word or author searches are possible. They can also scan contents pages of recent journals, select articles, and have them sent to a telefacsimile machine. The FAX document delivery service is generally provided within 24 hours, but the remarkable aspect of the service is that CARL retains the FAX image, thereby providing the next user who selects that article with a virtually instantaneous copy. It remains to be seen whether masses of end-users with credit cards in hand will avail themselves of CARL's UnCover services. Competition from Faxon Finder and Faxon Xpress, similar services from Faxon Research Services, Inc., will soon be available.[11] Such integrated services point the way to the future of science librarianship. It is the implementation of services based on increased access which will define the science library of tomorrow.

In the mid-1970s, Eugene Garfield noted that a collection of 100,000-200,000 books and articles can form the active core of a library able to provide copies of 90 percent of all future citations.[12] This contention was even more dramatically illustrated by Garfield in discussing the 1988 *Science Citation Index*. In that year, only 900 journals received 83 percent of the 8,000,000 citations processed for *SCI*'s *Journal Citation Reports*.[13] In the earlier article, subtitled "Pulling Weeds with ISI's *Journal Citation Reports*," Garfield proposed that only reprints of highly cited articles be retained by libraries. Although Garfield's company, the Institute for Scientific Information (ISI), had plans at that time to identify, collect, publish, and market a core collection of heavily-cited articles, such a product never materialized.

One can conjecture that the idea of a library of repackaged paper articles was ultimately deemed by ISI to be too radical a departure from the normal acquisitions patterns of the time to be marketable. However, times have changed. There exists today the technology to create a library of electronic articles tailored to the needs of a particular clientele. What is missing from the current scene is the motivation to do so. As long as libraries continue to measure quality in terms of complete physical volumes held, the idea will not take hold. However, a few bold success stories could change the value systems of both academic librarians and users. A library equipped to store and retrieve images received from a document supply source such as CARL or Faxon could begin to build a database of document images with a modest investment in equipment.[14] A LAN-based FAX product could serve as the waystation for incoming images. An archival copy could be created before forwarding to the end-user, and eventually a collection of documents of particular relevance to the primary clientele would be amassed. Of course, a fee would have to be paid to the publisher for the retention of the image, but appropriate accounting software could keep track of the costs and also determine which records had failed to be productive in a given time span (perhaps 10 years).

The obvious benefit of such a scenario from the librarian's viewpoint is that the acquisitions budget could be used to acquire *and retain* both complete volumes of the core journals and additional individual units (articles) which are truly needed by the clientele. There would be an incentive for the publishers to weigh more carefully the items accepted for publication. Articles which no one cites or wants to read could not be easily concealed in a journal volume sold only as a complete product. In terms appropriate to the automobile industry, a library would have the option of purchasing the "foreign" (off-site) economy model or the "domestic" (locally-owned) fully-equipped model.

The science library community is poised to make a fundamental change in collecting policies in the 1990s–to move from the exclusive collection of journal *volumes* to a more flexible collecting profile that allows the permanent addition to their collections of individual *articles* from journals not locally held. What is needed to facilitate the collection of individual articles is a unique item identifier for each journal article, a code which is universally understood by librarians and users. With the development of the Serials Item and Contribution Identifier (SICI), we now have such a tool.[15] SICI is the ANSI/NISO standard Z39.56 (1991) which defines a string of numbers and/or letters to uniquely identify a particular item (issue) and/or contribution (article) of a serial. The SICI code provides the capability to construct a database of locally held journal articles instead of (or in addition to) journal issues and volumes. The SICI standard will enable the precise indexing and searching of a file of article images. Some of the major scientific publishers, including Elsevier, Pergamon, and Wiley have pledged to print the barcoded version of the SICI item/issue identifier on the cover of journal issues starting in 1992. In effect, the SICI has the potential to revolutionize serials transactions in much the same way that Chemical Abstracts Service Registry Numbers for chemical compounds have revolutionized the searching of chemical databases–by providing a uniform access point to all references to a unique item. The SICI will surely become a standard data item in the records of the serials abstracting and indexing services. Then it should be straightforward to link the references retrieved from such searches to the file of original documents, whether in a remote or local database.

What is being proposed differs substantially from the system of document delivery and document use which is now in place. How can we enlist the support of the major players (publishers, document suppliers, librarians, and users) in order to transform the current system?

The two most difficult groups to convince will be the publishers and the users. Publishers will probably raise the threat of copyright infringement in order to preserve the journal volume instead of the journal article as their smallest marketable unit. The legal aspects of the reuse and repackaging of electronic data are murky at best. Libraries and publishing companies must confront and solve the copyright questions before significant progress toward the electronic library can occur. The owner of a nightclub who permits musicians to perform copyrighted music without paying royalties to the composer of the work is liable for damages. So too might librarians be held liable if we create databases which allow our patrons to illegally use the data without proper compensation to the copyright holder. Nevertheless, librarians must move the concept of cooperative collection development to its logical conclusion: that individual libraries will no longer be the customers of journal publishers. Instead, the publishers must deal with library consortia (alliances) whose members will collectively decide what titles to buy and in what numbers within the consortium. In that regard, the Research Libraries Group 4+ Project provides a good model for defining the core collections in various disciplines.

Another approach, involving Elsevier Science Publishers, is TU-

LIP, The University LIcensing Program.[16] The 3-year program, scheduled for 1992-94, is described as the first step by Elsevier and 12-16 participating U.S. university libraries to develop a "viable" means for the electronic distribution of scientific information, defined as "economically and functionally acceptable to all parties in the distribution value chain."[17] Limited to 35 materials science and engineering journals, the TULIP collection of Elsevier titles is said to encompass approximately half of the core journals in this area. Tapes will be shipped to one or more of the participating institutions who will make the data available to the others over the Internet. Interestingly, usage statistics in future reports about the use of the journals distributed electronically through the TULIP program must not identify specific journals and articles within journals. An open enrollment option will be available from January-June 1992 only to members of the Coalition for Networked Information who subscribe to at least half of the titles in the program. These two facets of the program perhaps reveal the publisher's concern about maintaining journal subscriptions. Participants in TULIP will make a single annual payment to cover single campus uses of the titles, with no further per-use payments required. However, there is an option to sell individual articles on demand to non-campus customers.

The TULIP program is significant in that a consortium of academic libraries with common interests has engaged in a research project with a major publisher. Publishers must find ways to work with library consortia to define the "most marketable unit" of a journal title, the collection of articles which will have the greatest chance of being purchased by all members of a consortium of large academic libraries. Just as scientific authors seem to have embraced the concept of "least publishable unit" for maximum exposure of their research results, so too must the publishers develop the concept of the "most marketable unit" for the continued survival of the scientific journal as we know it today. The "least marketable unit," the journal article, will be defined by the libraries who import the images of individual journal articles into their own local databases. Publishers must decide how and to whom the least marketable unit will be sold. Will it be available from document suppliers or libraries or simply be deposited in an archive at the publisher's location to be ordered at will by whoever needs it?

The users of journal articles must next be convinced that it is to their advantage to accept the concept of access. In order to succeed, librarians must define access in a much broader sense than is currently employed in the library world (access to materials not held locally). We must extend the concept of access to our own local collections and provide better (electronic) delivery even of the material we own. It is a fact that the single most valued service in an academic science library today is the provision of well-functioning photocopy machines. Science faculty expend enormous amounts of effort, directly or indirectly, to copy articles and to enter the bibliographic records for them into their personal information systems. The paper copies themselves generally are added to the considerable store of filing cabinets maintained in most faculty offices to house their "personal libraries."

It is this cycle of information gathering that science librarians must tap into in order to win faculty support. We must turn our attention to building local electronic repositories of document images and the attendant bibliographic records which will serve our primary clienteles better than is possible with the current system. More importantly, we must enlist the support of our users in the design of local multi-purpose document archives and indexing systems. The design must incorporate incentives to channel the energy and money currently being expended on photocopying into the production of the local database.

The source of the document images received by the user could be the library's local collection, as well as the collections of consortium partners, document suppliers, or publishers. The database would be searchable over a local- or wide-area network, with images delivered simultaneously to the user's workstation and to the locally maintained library database. Eventually, initiation of document delivery orders for items not locally held could be a shared responsibility with the users. A copy of the image would go into the local database as well as being shipped to the user. With an appropriate scanning device to substitute for the photocopy machine and a network link to their own private files, the end-user might even be persuaded to forego making paper copies of older articles in favor of the document images. Once the images enter the database, other legitimate users should have access to them with no more authorization than the barcodes commonly affixed to user IDs for circulation purposes nowadays. To increase the attractiveness to the users, the database must have value added by providing pipelines to the word-processing packages employed by them. The users must be able to easily query the database, to call forth the retrieved images, and to capture bibliographic information that meshes with their own method of manuscript production. Thus, a program for fitting the bibliographic references into manuscripts at appropriate points and in appropriate formats is essential.

One might ask why all of this activity should be taking place in each local science library. Why not assign some central agency, such as CARL, Faxon, or the Center for Research Libraries to perform the work once for all of us? In addition to the obvious need to have multiple collections of significant scientific work for archival purposes, there is the economic aspect to consider. At this point in time, the scientific publishing enterprise cannot survive if we tell the publishers to sell one copy to a document delivery counterpart of OCLC and let us affix our "access symbol" to the record as needed. It is unlikely that there will be a sudden shift from commercial publishers to university presses or to free or low-cost electronic formats for scholarly journals in this decade. For the foreseeable future, there must continue to be a diverse group of subscribers to share the publication costs of scholarly journals. Sanford G. Thatcher, Director of the Penn State Press and long-time Chair of the Copyright Committee of the Association of University Presses, has spoken to this issue.[18] He argues that scientific journal publishing requires substantial resources in staff expertise and capital. While anyone with the ability to start a forum on a listserver can conceivably become an electronic journal "publisher," this is not devoid of costs, both human and real. The value added by publishers cannot be denied. The scientific community needs the scholarly review process which is coordinated by the publishers. Likewise, publicity and the maintenance of a subscription service are not without cost.

Be that as it may, it must be admitted that a portion of the cost of the current scientific publishing enterprise is due to financial incentives given by the publishers to the organizers of professional society symposia and conferences. Sometimes the expense of presenting a symposium is more than offset by the royalties paid by the publisher in exchange for the right to publish the papers.

There is a pressing need for a reassessment of the values and costs in scholarly publishing. The process has begun, and it will not be a painless one. The document access system proposed in this paper is transitional. It seeks to shore up and redefine the library customer base of the scientific publishers by promoting the concept of the article as a marketable unit. Librarians, publishers, and users need to work together to define acceptable subscription prices for journals, fees for the retention and reuse of document images or abstracting/indexing data, *and* fees for the value-added services provided by librarians. Then we will move toward a truly electronic library.

## REFERENCE NOTES

1. Tuck, Bill [and others]. *Project Quartet.* (British Library. Library and Information Research Report; 76); Cambridge: Cambridge University Press; 1990. (p.249)

2. *Report of the ARL Task Force on a National Program for Scientific and Technical Information.* Washington, DC: Association of Research Libraries; 1991 May. (p.6)

3. See for example: Blick, Dawn; Sinha, Reeta. Maintaining a high-quality, cost-effective journal collection. *College & Research Libraries News* 51(8): 485-490; 1991 September. Chrzastowski, Tina E. Journal collection cost-effectiveness in an academic chemistry library: results of a cost/use survey at the University of Illinois at Urbana-Champaign. *Collection Management* 14(1/2): 85-98; 1991.

4. The RLG lists in chemistry, business, and mathematics are available from: Distribution Services Coordinator, The Research Libraries Group, Inc., 1200 Villa Street, Mountain View, CA 94041-1100.

5. Ralli, Tony. Performance measures for academic libraries. *Australian Academic & Research Libraries* 18(1):1-9; 1987 March. (p.4)

6. Egan, Dennis E. [and others]. Creating and using an electronic library: Progress report on the CORE project. In *Proceedings of EDD '91; Belcore/BCC Conference on Electronic Document Delivery*; 1991 March 25-28; East Brunswick, NJ. (pp.238-251)

7. *Ibid.* (p.239)

8. Tuck. *Op. cit.* (p.3)

9. *Ibid.* (p.244)

10. *Ibid.* (p.248)

11. For more information on CARL's UnCover service, contact: CARL Systems, Inc., 3801 E. Florida Avenue, Bldg. D, Suite 300, Denver, CO 80222 Phone: 303-758-3030 FAX: 303-758-0606.

The Minutes of the September 24-25, 1991 OCLC Research Libraries Advisory Committee indicate that OCLC is jointly developing a serials table of contents and document delivery project with Faxon. The database will contain bibliographic records from about 10,000 journal titles and will be linked to library holdings information. Members of the committee noted that "Faculty will not want to pay individually for such documents and will want the institution to cover charges." (p.6) They also note that "Un-mediated document supply requests directly from the user are inevitable." (p.6) For further information, contact: Faxon Research Services, Inc., 14 Southwest Park, Westwood, MA 02090 Phone: 617-329-3350 ext. 407; FAX: 617-329-6291.

12. Garfield, Eugene. No-growth libraries and citation analysis; or, pulling weeds with ISI's *Journal Citation Reports*. In *Essays of an Information Scientist*; v. 2: 1974-1976; Philadelphia, PA: ISI Press; 1977: pp. 300-303. (p.301)

13. Garfield, Eugene. How ISI selects journals for coverage: quantitative and qualitative considerations. *Current Contents* 33(22): 5-13; 1990 May 28. (p.6)

14. The equipment and software necessary to establish a document archive database are available commercially. For example, Compulink's LaserFiche LAN can store document images and be integrated into a Novell network. The system handles computer files, paper documents, and FAX transmissions. The so-called "hydra" machines, multi-function devices for printing, faxing, scanning, and copying, could also be adapted for such an application. See *Byte* 16(4): 217; 1991 April for a list of companies that provide document imaging solutions.

15. Feick, Tina. SISAC news: ANSI/NISO Z39.56 1991 has passed! and SISAC update. *Newsletter on Serials Pricing Issues* NS 13; 1991 November 13.

16. Elsevier Science Publishers B. V. TULIP, The University LIcensing Program. Working Plan 1; 1991 October 10.

17. *Ibid.* (p.2)

18. Thatcher, Sanford G. Letter, 1991 December 3, to Ann Okerson, Office of Scientific and Academic Publishing, Association of Research Libraries.

# Which Life Science Journals Will Constitute the Locally Sustainable Core Collection of the 1990s and Which Will Become "Fax-Access" Only? Predictions Based on Citation and Price Patterns 1979-1989

Tony Stankus
Carolyn V. Mills

**SUMMARY.** The arrival of royalty-paying, inexpensive fax delivery networks will greatly ease concerns of copyright law and faculty goodwill on the part of librarians when cancelling journals. Librarians realize that it will be cheaper to give free fax delivery of individual articles to their faculty than to take subscriptions to many of the typically voluminous and expensive journals that faculty have come to expect on library shelves. Some journals of high demand will always be locally held, but subscriptions to others will likely continue only as long as taking them is cheaper than repeatedly requesting faxes. Since publishers will still greatly prefer to get advance subscriptions (with all the revenue up front), rather than after-the-fact piecemeal payments, they may actually have a financial incentive to publish fewer but higher demand articles in their existing journals so as to tip purchasing calculations in favor of maintaining

---

Mr. Stankus is Science Librarian, and Ms. Mills is his assistant at the Science Library, College of the Holy Cross, 1 College Street, Worcester, MA 01610-2395. Mr. Stankus graduated *Summa Cum Laude* from Holy Cross and from the University of Rhode Island Graduate School of Library and Information Studies. Ms. Mills took her bachelor's degree at Allegheny College and is currently a master's degree candidate at URI.

subscriptions to them. Ironically, through article-specific fax royalty reports, smart publishers will have a tool that enables them to concentrate only on authors who are likely to sustain subscription loyalty through genuinely interesting papers. The warning signs of "at risk" journals have actually long been available to both publishers and librarians through studies of pricing and citation data, but often have been ignored. We report a long term analysis of citation data with some reference to pricing from 1979-1989, and predict which journals have the best chances to remain locally held in the 1990s, and which are likely to go to "fax-access-only." We invite working librarians who make frequent use of fax as a substitute for cancelled journals to report to us any correlation of their experiences with our forecasts.

## *THE PROMISE OF FAX*

Librarians facing rapidly escalating journal costs have been cancelling more and more journal subscriptions. They have sometimes been restrained from further cancellations by irate faculty, who complain about interlibrary loans which are late in coming. Senior financial administrators who have urged librarians in their cancellation campaigns, have nonetheless felt justifiably nervous about legal liability for photocopies requested through interlibary loans that may be beyond "fair use." With the advent of document delivery via licensed fax delivery services, librarians will have a much greater sense of freedom in deciding which journals will be locally held, with subscriptions paid in advance, and which will be accessed only occasionally from remote collections or databases, on a "pay-as-you-go-for-only-what-you-use" basis. This sense of liberation stems from four reasons.

First, fax is fast, substantially answering faculty complaints about speed. Even the slowest fax delivery service is easily four or five times faster than most interstate ILLs going through conventional mails, and generally beats overnight express mail as well. Faculty who are tempted to complain about 24hr. turnaround for a document to be delivered–many faxes arrive even more quickly–will probably not gain a favorable hearing from senior university financial officers. They will be seen as being unreasonable.

Second, fax can be made free of legal worry rather easily. Publishers have agreed to cooperate with many fax-delivery services and accept the royalty fees that have been negotiated. The royalty charges for the publisher are included alongside the service charge for the fax-delivery service in the bill. They are collected for the publishers by the fax-delivery service. When the fax service assumes the role of an honest broker, it is procedurally impossible to obtain these legal faxes and not pay the royalties, a built-in enforcement method that involves no nasty complications or public relations dilemmas for the much-derided-of-late publishers.

Third, fax is cheap when compared to the cost of taking a very voluminous and expensive journal. Such a journal could easily cost a thousand dollars. A fax of a paper will typically cost between $10-$25, depending on the fax-service chosen. It could take between 40 and 100 faxes to equal the cost of taking the journal for a single year.

Fourth, fax access is a natural in this electronic age. More and more often, fax-access is not viewed as a procedure apart from the literature searching process, but as a ridiculously easy and logical extension of it. Scientists and their librarians in the course of running a subject search on-line, on-disc, or on diskette, often obtain fax ordering information at the same time that they find their needed references. In many on-line cases, only a few keystrokes more will let them order the article electronically, with a minimum of paperwork.

## *LETTING LOCAL LIBRARY COLLECTIONS FOCUS ON WHAT IS ACTUALLY READ*

Over the years we have noted two interrelated facts. First, that the time that faculty have for actually reading anything has not appreciably expanded, despite all sorts of advances in the automation of their laboratories, in the use of computers, etc. Second, we note that within each specialty, there are some journals that seem to actually get read as opposed to being lightly scanned or held for occasional article retrieval. We think that these "actually read" journals are the materials that science collections must continue to collect locally, perhaps even in duplicate or triplicate subscriptions if the simultaneous demand is there. Figure 1 portrays our general theory. We estimate, for example, that within the basic life sciences, most scientists actually closely follow a handful of major multi-science journals (*Cell, FASEB Journal, Nature,* and the *Proceedings of the National Academy of Sciences*) plus a handful of journals actually in their specialty. There may be at most, one or two more subspecialty journals that scientists value as much as their specialty journals. If anything, subspecialty journals further limit the time a faculty member has for actually reading the main specialty titles. Although working faculty members have a sense of guilt about it, they are so time-pressed, that they really do just scan the rest, either through the journals' own tables of contents or through services such as Current Contents™ in print or on diskette. We suggest that this scanning-only situation makes fax-only provision a desirable alternative to local holding for some titles. We suspect that specialty journals ranking below the top two or three titles may even now be vulnerable to a fax-only status. This is particularly the case if they are expensive and do not effectively add the only geographical coverage that Americans really value: a heavy preponderance of papers from Canada, Western Europe, and the scientifically advanced Pacific Rim.

## *FACTORS USED IN DEFINING THE LOCALLY SUSTAINABLE CORE COLLECTION*

We chose to examine life sciences literature because it is very complex and generally expensive. Problems in its management are relevant to many academic, medical, and corporate biotech special library collections. We will discuss only sets of journals for original research that are matching in major specialty. Neither review journals nor conference abstracts journals are included owing to their structural "over-citedness" and "undercitedness" in comparison with most journals of original research papers. Three factors that appear to be related to the desirability of original research journals as materials for local holdings are compared. Two factors relate primarily to faculty perspectives; one to the budgetary concerns of

## FIGURE 1: OUR THESIS:
A LIFE SCIENTIST HAS TIME FOR ABOUT 10 "MUST READ" JOURNALS THAT IS OFTEN ALL THAT TODAY'S LIBRARY CAN AFFORD PER SCIENTIST

| DOMINANT MULTISCIENCE JOURNALS (MUST READING FOR ALL LIFE SCIENTISTS) | MAJOR SPECIALTY JOURNALS (MUST READING FOR THIS SPECIALTY) [FOCUS OF THIS STUDY] |
|---|---|
| Cell | 1st Choice Specialty Journal |
| FASEB Journal | 2nd Choice Specialty Journal |
| Nature | 3rd Choice Specialty Journal |
| Proc. Natl. Acad. Sci. | 4th Choice Specialty Journal |
| Science | 5th Choice Specialty Jornual |

+

librarians. Our sequence in dealing with these factors is portrayed in Figure 2. We seek to identify:

*The journal with impact factor leadership within a major specialty, 1979-1989.* We suggest that being the world's most cited journal on a per-item basis is a good indicator of the one journal that faculty in the U.S. are most likely to insist on having within their library. The impact factor leader within a major specialty in any year gets a score of 100; the followers get a score at some percentage of the leader's score. This data is derived from the section entitled "Journals by Category-Ranked by Impact Factor" within the annual volumes of *Journal Citation Reports*.[1] In our figures, this factor is labeled "Impact."

*The other journals that the leading specialty journal has regularly cited, 1979-1989.* We take this behavior to approximate how much scientists who succeed in getting into the leading journal also need the competing journals to document their work on a frequent basis. We suggest that these other journals are good candidates for "also-must-read-titles." Typically, the leader cites itself the most, getting a score of 100, the remaining journals get a percentage score. This data is derived from the "Citing Journal Packages" of annual volumes of *Journal Citation Reports*. In our figures we use the abbreviation "CBLJ" for "Cited By the Leading Journal."

*Relative prices for current subscriptions to the specialty journals under discussion, a figure drawn from FAXON catalogs.*[2] We feel that even among the leading journals chosen for comparison studies here, the most expensive journals are likely to be those more vulnerable to cancellation and fax-access *vs.* the less expensive titles, unless the more expensive ones are shown in some other way to be particularly outstanding. Cost is a surprisingly relative notion. In a field where the leading journal costs $100, a competitor of lower citation rank that costs $500 might well be viewed as unreasonable, and likely to be consigned to "fax-access-only." In another specialty, $500 would be seen as a bargain. Further, since in some fields all the competitors are closely matching in price, price loses some of its utility as a negative sorting device. Nonethelesss, in our figures, the most expensive title is set at 100, the less-expensive at some percentage. The label is simply "Cost."

## FIGURE 2: OUR PROCEDURE FOR RANKING JOURNALS FOR A LOCALLY HELD CORE COLLECTION

| STEP ONE | → | STEP TWO | ⇄ | STEP THREE |
|---|---|---|---|---|
| Identify the most persistent Impact Factor Leaders over the last 10 years. | | Identify several other titles cited significantly by the Impact Factor Leader. | | Consider Costs. Are they out of line for "IMPACT" or "CBLJ"? Use excessive $ as negative selection factor. |

"IMPACT" → "CBLJ" ⇄ "COST"

## LAYING OUT THE DISCUSSION OF RESULTS

In each of the sections that follow, we describe the subject specialty involved with a slant to indicating which specialty journals qualify for inclusion in our comparisons. This clarification is important because in some cases, we have a differing slant than the *JCR* on what constitutes an appropriate cluster of comparable journals. Moreover, the *JCR* consistently reports on many more journals in any specialty than the 3-5 titles that we will deal with in our comparisons

In the figures that accompany the discussion, we graphically depict the situation at the start of our study, 1979, and at the end, 1989. The year 1989 was chosen as the most recent for which citation data was available. The discussion, however, is not limited to these years. We attempt to explain how the rankings of 1979 changed during the ten intervening years to give us the situation in 1989, and how stable these 1989 standings are likely to be during the 1990s, given no new journals in that specialty. With comparative subscription rate information, we are looking for situations in which there is a substantial discrepancy between the standing of a journal and its price. We predict a turn to fax-only status for journals where this discrepancy is too great.

In our discussions, we sometimes indicate what journals might be moving from outside the comparison list into the core zone, challenging those that started within the core but are shifting to fax-only status. We show that there is a dynamic situation in some fields and stability in others. While most journals hold on to their leadership, few of the also-rans stay in exactly the same place. Citation data ought to be reviewed annually even if selection decisions based on citation data ought to be based on more than a single year's citation experience. Our exercise is in no way a substitute for ongoing citation-based analyses. Indeed, we also wish to strongly emphasize that libraries that use local circulation records and fax requests without reference to fresh citation data may find themselves with an eccentric collection that is out of touch with global shifts within a field. When fresh new faculty arrive at an institution they may find the collection out of synch with modern needs even if it seemed to serve retired local faculty quite well in the past.

We also feel that any decision to exclude a genuine Eurojournal may be unwise. There are at least two reasons for this. First, along with the ongoing political and economic merging of Europe is a good deal of pan-European scientific cooperation. The European scientific community has every potential for rivaling the formerly preeminent standing of the U.S. in life sciences research.[3] North American competitiveness will not be helped by excluding close familiarity with its most capable geoscientific rival. Second, life sciences work from Japan[4] and the rest of the scientifically competitive Pacific Rim[5] appears in the best western European journals on those occasions when it does not appear within North American outlets. Once again, Americans cannot afford to remain ignorant of this work, although thankfully, in most life science cases they can gain access to it without subscribing to many Asian titles.

A final note relates to British journals. The British have long had many excellent journals: some from their Royal Societies and some from prominent publishers like the erstwhile independent Pergamon. Both Royal Society and old Pergamon-type journals tend to be composed primarily of UK content, secondarily of content from the former Commonwealth countries, and then finally, content from Continental Europe and the U.S. The problem in selecting British journals is not in any way the quality of the British papers. It lies in the underrepresentation of the Continental papers in those journals in favor of many papers from the old Commonwealth. The problem is not with any formal British rules against Continental authors. There are none of these of which the authors are aware. Indeed, fairness in refereeing is typically British. (Their insistence on archaically formal sentences and spelling is admittedly annoying.) The problem is of perceived attitudes. The British are widely seen by Continental Europeans as having the strongest cultural resistance to blending in with Continental Europe. This resistance has been wearing down and one is finding more and more British papers in Eurojournals. But the reverse–more Continental papers in UK journals–is still not common. Continental authors may "know where they are not wanted," and just avoid British journals. The result is, that while there may be some exceptions like *Nature,* when buying journals for European coverage, one does not often get a genuine "Eurojournal" when one gets a good British journal. This means that, for now, given a hard choice between a distinctly British title and a genuine Eurojournal, we are inclined to give the nod to the Eurojournal. This preference is subject to change along with changes in British publishing. Consider that Pergamon, arguably the most prestigious of all historically British for-profit publishers, is now owned by Elsevier, arguably the most cosmopolitan publisher among all for-profit publishers.

## SPECIALTY-BY-SPECIALTY RESULTS

### Biochemistry

Either biochemistry or molecular biology is considered the foundation discipline for all other modern life sciences. Both closely related disciplines are now characterized by dozens of titles, and the use of biochemical or molecular approaches dominates many other life science specialties. Most collections currently have a large number of titles in either discipline. These titles are quite expensive, and in times of budget pressure, many librarians are likely to consider dropping some complete subscriptions and going to fax delivery for some titles.

The line between biochemistry and molecular biology both as disciplines and as journal categories is a fine one, and is being blurred with each passing year. This is clearly indicated by the name change of the society supporting the *Journal of Biological Chemistry*. It has become the American Society for Biological Chemistry AND Molecular Biology. Nonetheless, there are some persistent differences. A good many biochemists gain their training through programs of chemistry, and maintain professional identity with the chemistry community. Even many medical school and agricultural school biochemists still tend to work on the separation of biological fluids, a specialty largely developed out of chemistry. Biochemists tend to deal with many more kinds of fluid components than do most molecular biologists. These components include not only the sexy proteins and nucleic acids that molecular biologists dote on, but also mineral ions, lipids, and carbohydrates. Moreover, biochemists work with a wider variety of experimental conditions involving many differing buffers, temperatures, pressures, and rates of reaction.

In 1979, the *Journal of Biological Chemistry* was the undisputed impact factor leader among journals of biochemistry. It has never been seriously challenged (see Figure 3). Until 1986, it seemed that its rival from the American Chemical Society, *Biochemistry*, had just as secure a lock on second place, and until 1984, it seemed as if Springer's *European Journal of Biochemistry* was just as certain of third place. But the span beginning with 1985 saw tremendous competition for the remaining two spaces. No less than five titles competed for them. Some based their claim on impact factor, others on being cited by the leader, and others on more reasonable prices.

In the impact factor competition, relatively trivial percentages separated the (British) *Biochemical Journal* from two sets of journals from rival for-profit publishers. Each for-profit set contained a journal primarily for full-length papers and a journal for brief letters. Academic Press featured the *Archives of Biochemistry and Biophysics* (full papers) and *Biochemical and Biophysical Research Communications* (letters). Elsevier fielded its titanic *Biochimica et Biophysica Acta* (full papers) and *FEBS Letters* (brief communications). (The "FEBS" stands for Federation of European Biochemical Societies, a group which, to complicate matters, also sponsors the *European Journal of Biochemistry* which it allows Springer to handle.)

The late 1980s eventually saw something of an impact factor shakeout. The winners for the slots after the stalwart *Journal of Biological Chemistry* included a mix that favored two titles that had seemed fairly secure earlier: the *European Journal of Biochemistry* and *Biochemistry* and the short papers version of the Academic and Elsevier lines. Judging on impact factors alone Academic's *Biochemical and Biophysical Research Communications* and Elsevier's *FEBS Letters* looked a little stronger, and the *Archives* and *Biochimica et Biophysica Acta* looked a little weaker. But what about the other important factors?

The citing behavior of the leader, the *Journal of Biological Chemistry*, was not as helpful in making decisions as one would hope. *JBC* tended to clearly confirm only itself and *Biochemistry* as must-hold titles. A "cited-by-the-leader-pack" appeared instead, with members

## FIGURE 3: BIOCHEMISTRY

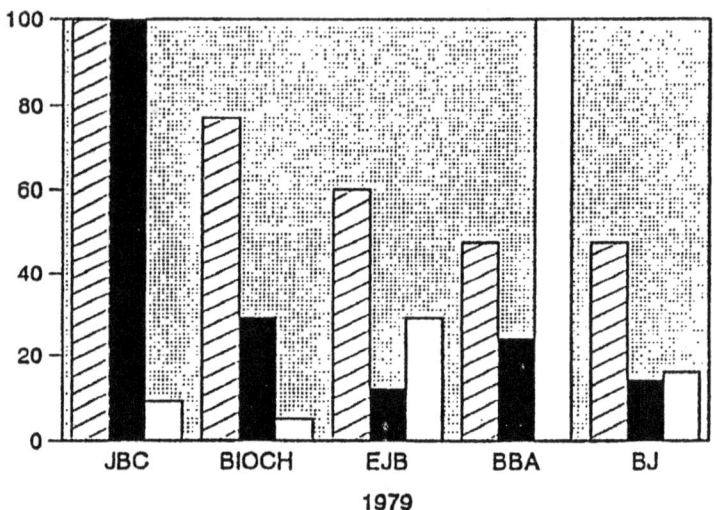

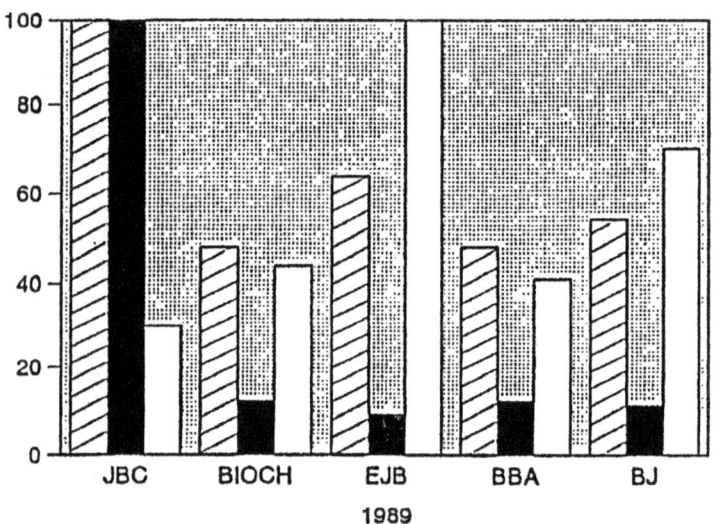

once again separated by only a few percentage points. Membership in the pack included the very journals we had hoped to sort out earlier using impact factors! *Biochimica et Biophysica Acta* which had far and away the most papers to cite understandably did a little better within the pack, while the *Archives* and *FEBS Letters* did somewhat more poorly than expected. One could argue that *Archives* had now failed twice to make the top five, and could be dropped, but *BBA* had earned a reprieve, even as *FEBS Letters* had been put on a kind of probation. The middle range of the CBLJ pack was occupied by *BJ, BBRC,* and *EJB*. Recall that they had decent impact as well, and seemed secure at this stage of evalution. With both *BBA* and *FEBS Letters* still contending, there was nonetheless still too many journals for many collections. It seemed as if a competition of price comparisons would have to be decisive for those who could support only a limited number of journals.

Price became clearly decisive in ruling out *BBA*, and somewhat decisive in ruling out *FEBS Letters* as well. *BBA* costs about ten times as much as the *Journal of Biological Chemistry* and three times as much as the most important Eurojournal competitor, the *European Journal of Biochemistry*. While *Biochemical Journal* is certainly cheaper than the *European,* the latter, Continental title has a wider mix of papers from scientifically advanced Western countries and for most years of this study, had a higher impact factor as well, so that it should rank higher than *Biochemical Journal. Biochemical Journal,* nonetheless, still makes it as the fifth journal, because its costs are marginally better than *FEBS Letters,* and the need for the Eurocoverage that *FEBS Letters* features as a strength is somewhat reduced by having the *European Journal of Biochemistry* already secure in the collection.

### Journals of Molecular Biology

Molecular biology has historically had a much greater emphasis on nucleic acids and proteins than on other substances. If the separation of fluids has been a chemistry domain, the sequencing of long strands of nucleic acids and proteins has been a hallmark of molecular biology. Molecular biology in 1979 was dominated in impact factor leadership by a relative newcomer to the field, *Cell,* from

MIT Press. (The title has since been further "privatized" by its publisher, Ben Lewin, under the banner of Cell Press.) (See Figure 4.) Three journals formed its most significant impact-factor competitition at that time: the *Journal of Molecular Biology,* pretty much an Anglo-American enterprise from Academic Press, *Gene* from Elsevier, and *Nucleic Acid Research* from another Anglo-American combine, IRL Press. For the early 1980s, *Cell* cited the *Journal of Molecular Biology* and *Nucleic Acids Research* much more significantly than it did *Gene,* putting *Gene* in trouble early on. In the meanwhile, three new titles have entered the competition. These are the *EMBO Journal* handled by IRL Press on behalf of the European Molecular Biology Organization, *Molecular and Cellular Biology* from the American Society for Microbiology, and *DNA* from Mary Ann Liebert. Each has cut into the relative impact factor standings of the old competition without knocking off *Cell.* By 1984, the *EMBO Journal,* a genuine Eurojournal, had locked up second place for the rest of the decade. By 1986, *Molecular and Cellular Biology* was ensconced in third for the rest of the decade. The *Journal of Molecular Biology* has dropped from a tie for second place to what amounts to a tie for fourth with *DNA.* We feel that this impact factor competition will continue at approximately an even pace, at these relative standings, for the foreseeable future. *Gene* has dropped to seventh place. We feel that this means a real decline for *Gene* and it may even continue further downward. The situation for *Nucleic Acids Research* might also seem bleak--it has gone from fourth to sixth, but not all the factors have been considered. In particular, we looked to the CBLJ contest for clarification.

In the category of being cited by *Cell,* the leader, the results are highly parallel, with one exception: *Nucleic Acids Research* is doing surprisingly well relative to its impact factor standings. Since 1983, it has actually been consistently beating out the *Journal of Molecular Biology* by a modest amount, and by a decisive amount, *Gene.* *DNA,* the youngest journal, and the one with the smallest number of papers in this group, does about as well as *Gene,* a situation that does not bode well for *Gene,* which publishes many more papers, leading one to believe that it should be more cited.

Price comparisons are also particularly striking: *Gene* is far and away the most expensive journal, about ten times as expensive as

## FIGURE 4: MOLECULAR BIOLOGY
◨IMPACT ■CBLJ ☐COST

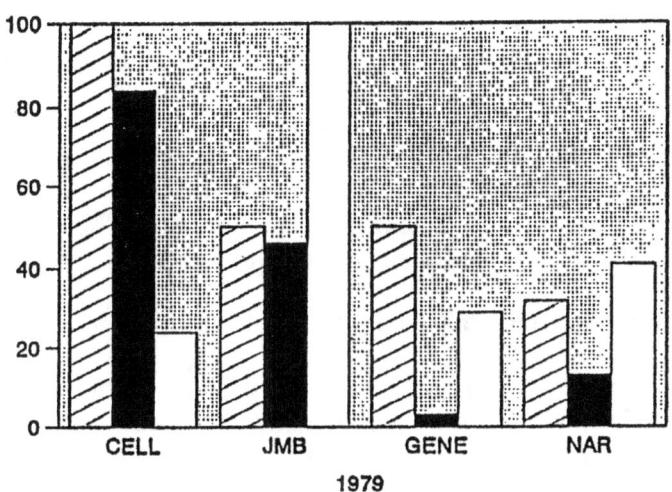

1979

◨IMPACT ■CBLJ ☐COST

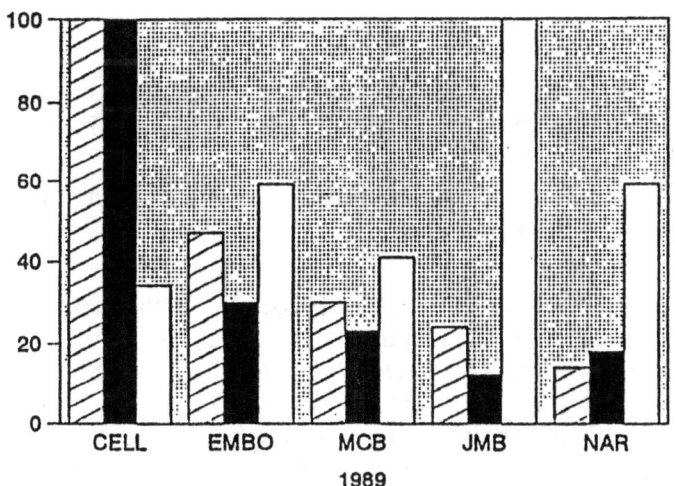

1989

the overall specialty leader, *Cell*. Three other titles are also substantially above average. The *Journal of Molecular Biology* is about six times as expensive as *Cell,* and both the *EMBO Journal* and *Nucleic Acid Research* are about three times as expensive.

Taken together, this data suggest that *Gene* is highly vulnerable to becoming an essentially fax-only journal in many collections. The *Journal of Molecular Biology* is next in line for this distinction, but probably at a much later time. *Nucleic Acids Research* is not particularly vulnerable because while it does not share the impact of the *EMBO Journal,* its price-matching competitor, it has a healthy CBLJ. Nonetheless, *DNA* is definitely the title to watch.

## Journals of General Cell Biology

Cell biology has undergone three generations of interest that are important for understanding membership in this category. In order of their historical development, these interests have been cell microanatomy, cell physiology, and cellular events involving the encoding of proteins by nucleic acids, essentially "molecular" cell biology. This journal assortment deals with journals that feature papers in all three areas, and avoids journals explicitly concentrating on any one of them. Consequently, journals explicitly devoted to cell physiology ( the *Journal of Cellular Physiology,* the *Journal of Cellular Biochemistry,* and the *American Journal of Physiology: Cell Physiology*) are not included, nor are those which are frankly molecular (*Cell* and *Molecular and Cellular Biology,* titles already discussed above). Moreover, while there are many minor cell titles, this list is focused only on those that command a serious major-scientific-power following.

In 1979, the *Journal of Cell Biology,* a Rockefeller University Press title published on behalf of the American Society for Cell Biology, was the clear leader in impact factors, and held this distinction throughout the 1980s (see Figure 5). It has been followed by two competitors of roughly equal impact factor standing throughout the 1980s. These were the *Journal of Cell Science* from the (British) Company of Biologists and *Experimental Cell Research,* a joint Swedish-American venture from Academic Press. By the early 1980s, a title that formerly had a somewhat limited appeal

## FIGURE 5: GENERAL CELL BIOLOGY

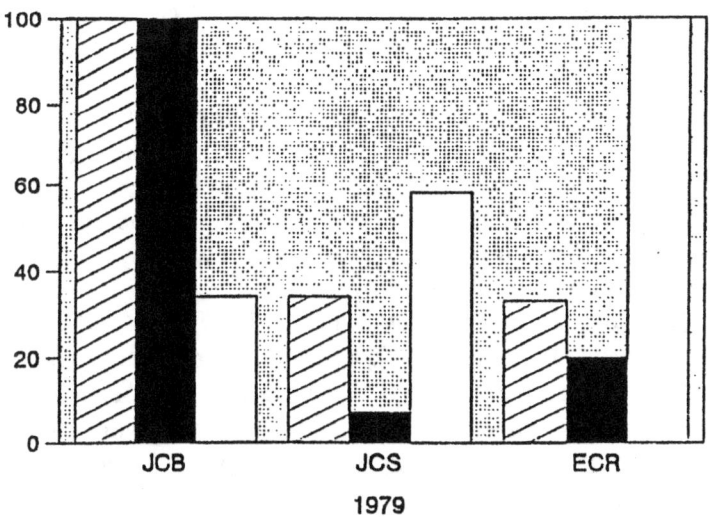

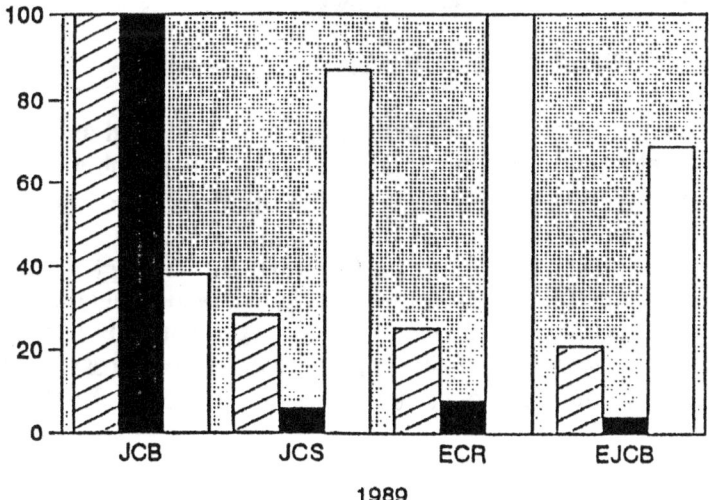

among German readers, *Cytobiologie* from Wissenschaftliche Verlag, gained the sponsorship of the European Cell Biology Organization, and began to challenge the British and Swedish/American entries, as the revamped *European Journal of Cell Biology.* It did not, however, so much consistently beat them, as merit a place alongside them.

In terms of being cited by the leader, the *Journal of Cell Biology,* roughly the same ranking sequence has occurred. *Experimental Cell Research,* the journal with the most papers published, has generally maintained a small but persistent lead, while the *European Journal,* which has generally published the fewest papers, is always at a small but persistent deficit in this group.

Price data show that the *Journal of Cell Biology* has been the best bargain in the group, and that *Experimental Cell Research* has always been the most expensive. The *Journal of Cell Science,* while always somewhat cheaper than *ECR,* has been relatively close to it in price so that no strong competitive disadvantage for *ECR* appears to have resulted. Only prices for the *European Journal* appear to have been markedly lower, and this advantage may ultimately work against *ECR,* although with fewer papers, it is once again, not a clearcut advantage for *EJCB.*

Taken together, the data suggest that this assortment of four titles is likely to persevere in the short run with all titles selected for local subscriptions in most collections. Only severe financial distress in many libraries over a long period will hurt *Experimental Cell Research* and consign it to fax-only access.

## Journals of Developmental Biology

For our purposes, developmental biology is defined as the study of the genetic and environmental events that give sophistication of shape and function to a primitive cell up to the point of its full differentiation as an adult or as a functioning component of an adult organism. For the bulk of the 1980s, work on the surgical manipulation of multicellular embryos was in decline and molecular procedures on unicellular or few-cell embryos, permanently ascendant.

In 1979, *Developmental Biology,* from Academic Press on behalf of the largely American member International Society for Developmental Biology, was the clear impact factor leader (see Figure 6). For most of the 1980s, it had three competitors of persistently lower impact factor status: *Differentiation* and *Roux's Archives of Developmental Biology,* both from Springer, and the *Journal of Embryology and Experimental Morphology,* from the (British) Company of Biologists. Two of these, *Differentiation* and *JEEM* tended to trade second and third place, but *Rouxs Archive* displaced *Differentiation* in one of the eleven years. *JEEM* took steps to challenge *Developmental Biology* through a series of changes of format and publishing schedule, eventually reinventing itself as the highly dynamic *Development.* While it clearly improved, the British leader did not overtake the American leader, *Developmental Biology.*

By 1989, however, a tremendous development overtook all the journals in this field: the rise of *Genes and Development. Genes and Development* came from a partnership of the Cold Spring Harbor Laboratory Press in the U.S. and the Genetical Society of Great Britain. Within a year or two of its birth it earned impact factors twice as high as those earned by the former leader, *Developmental Biology.* Such a stunning turnaround was reminiscent of the arrival of *Cell* in the 1970s, and while it may appear foolhardy to venture a prediction so soon, *Genes and Development* is just as likely to dominate its field as has *Cell* its domain.

In terms of being cited by the traditional leader, *Developmental Biology, JEEM* (and its successor, *Development*) have been the perennial second place journals among those in this assortment. *Roux's Archives* maintained third place with just as much constancy, as did *Differentiation* its lower fourth place standing. The arrival of *Genes and Development* pushed all of these journals down a single notch relative to the total assortment of journals of developmental biology. The descent relative to all journals of biology cited by *Genes and Development* has been much more dramatic than this one-place demotion might at first appear, since *Genes and Development* cites journals of molecular biology at a much higher rate than it does other journals of development. This means that librarians might be inclined to spend more on preserving more titles of molecular biology than on preserving a full array of traditional journals of development. There is some danger of having the lower end traditional journals, *Rouxs Archive* and *Differentiation,* appear to

## FIGURE 6: DEVELOPMENTAL BIOLOGY

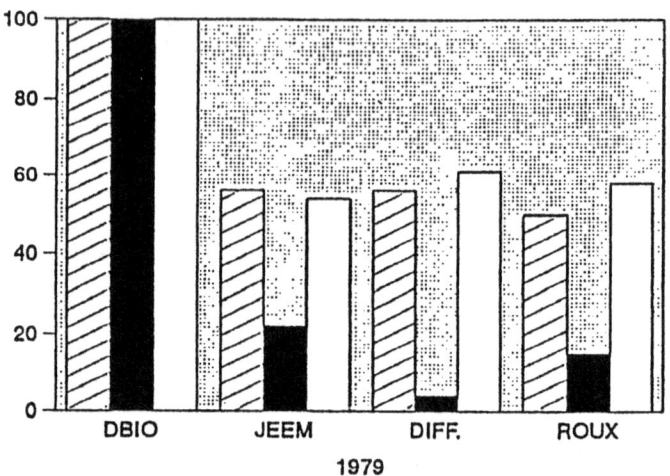

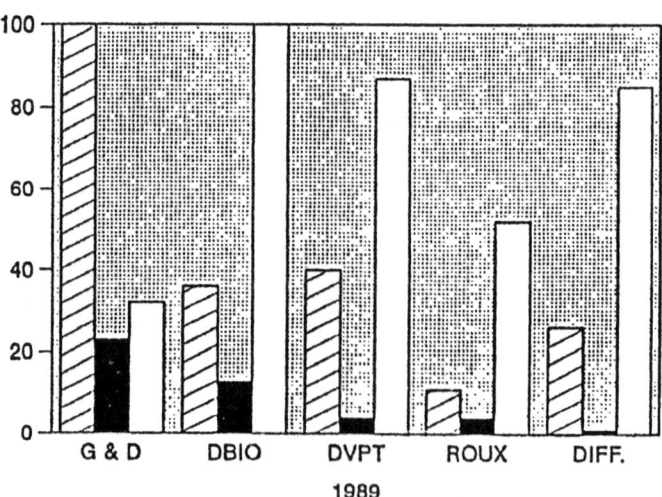

be dispensable. Price data may help sort out which of these two titles is most vulnerable.

*Genes and Development* is the best bargain in this group. Unfortunately, the two titles which are otherwise strongest in impact factors and in being cited by the leader, *Developmental Biology* and *Development,* are rather highly priced but of such price comparability that they are not otherwise vulnerable. Cost factors may also save *Rouxs Archive* from going to fax-only status immediately. This title is markedly cheaper than any other of the traditional developmental journals cited by the new leader, *Genes and Development.* By contrast, *Differentiation* has been priced at about the same level as *Developmental Biology* and *Development* but has not done as well as either of them lately in other factors suggesting demand. We suspect that it may be the most vulnerable to fax-only status.

## Journals of General Genetics

By 1979, genetics was a field undergoing intense "molecularization" and an explosion of well-funded adherents. The discoveries of Franklin, Watson, Crick, Wilkins, and their competitors were by then 20 years old and had generated enough papers to sustain a substantial number of journals in the related, but financially independent field of molecular biology. Nonetheless, genetics journals that also included traditional Mendelian genetics, microscopic analyses of chromosomes, clinical and sometimes agricultural genetics, environmental mutations, as well as population genetics, within their covers did not fade away. In 1979, three journals which had a somewhat more molecular mix of papers were battling for leadership in impact factors (see Figure 7). By a slight but reasonably persistent margin, Springer's *Molecular and General Genetics* actually held the lead for much of the 1980s over *Genetics* from the Genetics Society of America. *Chromosoma,* another Springer title, seemed to stress its microscopy angle more strongly in the early 1980s. In 1982, it actually held the impact factor leadership, but *Chromosoma* has clearly fallen since then. While part of this settling down is undoubtedly due to its heavily microscopic article mix, part may also be due to positive changes in the contender from the Genetics Society of America, *Genetics. Genetics,* which formerly had a fairly

## FIGURE 7: GENERAL GENETICS

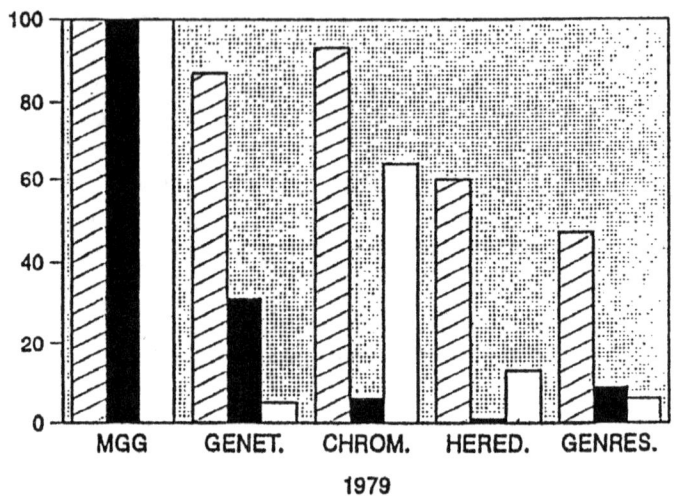

1979

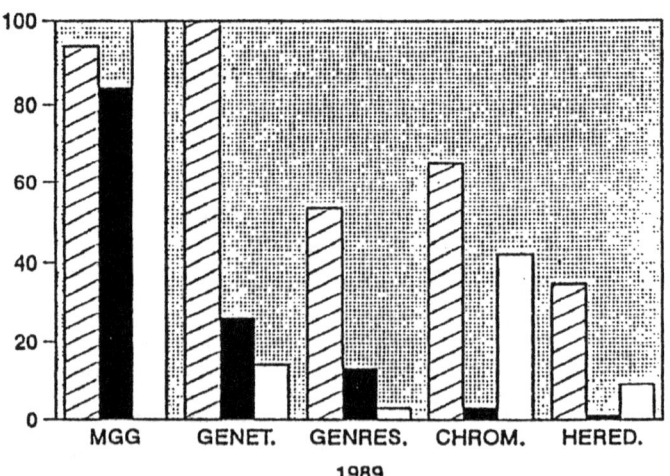

1989

conservative mix of topics and had an ancient, less-attractive format began to revamp itself in the mid 1980s. By 1985, it was once again a serious contender, and swapped impact factor leadership back and forth with *MGG*. The three journal race turned into a two journal race. *Chromosoma* began to join a number of impact-factor also-rans, most notably *Hereditas* from Almqvist and Wiksell and *Genetical Research* from the Genetical Society of Great Britain. These latter journals roughly swapped third through and fifth place back and forth throughout the 1980s, but have not, and will not contend for the top two places. *Genetical Research* has been, in fact, undercut by the migration of some of its trendier papers to *Genes and Development,* another journal in the related area of developmental biology, discussed above, which the Genetical Society copublishes with the Cold Spring Harbor Laboratory. *Hereditas,* by contrast, appeared to have matched its microscopical focus to that of *Chromosoma* and suffered the same generally diminished returns as *Chromosoma*. Indeed, a new contender from further back in the pack, has appeared. *Genome,* the slickly revamped *Canadian Journal of Genetics and Cytology,* may well surpass *Hereditas*. The CBLJ provides some clarification.

In terms of being cited by the leader, whether it was *Genetics* or *MGG, MGG* was the consistent winner. Even in years when it was itself the impact factor leader, *Genetics* tended to cite *MGG* much more than it self-cited. Perhaps an even greater surprise has been the poor showing of *Chromosoma*. It has been essentially tied for fourth place with *Genetical Research* for most of the 1980s, and beats *Hereditas* only marginally. All three of these journals–*Chromosoma, Genetical Research,* and *Hereditas*–have been somewhat marginalized by the propensity of both *MGG* and *Genetics* to cite journals in molecular biology much more than they do other journals of genetics. Will cost factors save any of these three journals?

Cost factors have greatly favored *Genetics* and *Hereditas*. They look clearly unfavorable for *MGG* and somewhat unfavorable for *Chromosoma*. *MGG*'s outstanding performance will probably save it from becoming a fax-only journal. We predict however, that *Chromosoma,* will become just such a title in the near future. The future of *Hereditas* is endangered not so much because of the price, which is reasonable, but because of marginal relevance. It confers no special advantage over the next three or four general genetics titles in line. Costs make *Genome* at least as attractive as any of the other little three, and make it the title to watch.

## *Journals of Microbiology*

In 1979, microbiology was a crowded field which had already booted out most papers on specific diseases caused by microbes into journals of clinical microbiology or pathology. Even then a list entitled "general microbiology" would not be completely homogenous because internationally each journal had slightly different lists of remaining allowable topics. Some publishers took papers on applied microbiology, some took papers on virology, environmental mutations, and so on. Other publishers developed separate publications for each of these topics. For the purposes of this paper, the journals included are the flagships of their geographic constituencies and all primarily emphasize bacteria, whatever else they may include.

A tremendous consistency marked impact factors in microbiology for the eleven years of this study. In 1979, the U.S. entry, the *Journal of Bacteriology* was firmly first (see Figure 8). Except for 1985, the Springer entry, the *Archives of Microbiology* remained solidly in second place. Third place was just as secure for the British entry, the *Journal of General Microbiology*, which was responsible for the single, 1985 upset. Fourth belonged to *FEMS Letters*, a title from the Federation of European Microbiological Societies, handled by Elsevier. Fifth went to the *Canadian Journal of Microbiology* from the National Research Council of Canada.

There was some jockeying in the category of being cited by the leader, the *Journal of Bacteriology*. The *Journal of General Microbiology* came in second place, consistently over the *Archives of Microbiology*, which held third. More aggressively, *FEMS Letters* moved up on the *Canadian Journal* and surpassed it by 1983. Nonetheless, the Canadian entry is secure in its spot. Few journals outside the group look like serious contenders.

Price data suggest that while two journals, the *Archives* and *Letters* are substantially more expensive than their peers, their status,

## FIGURE 8: MICROBIOLOGY

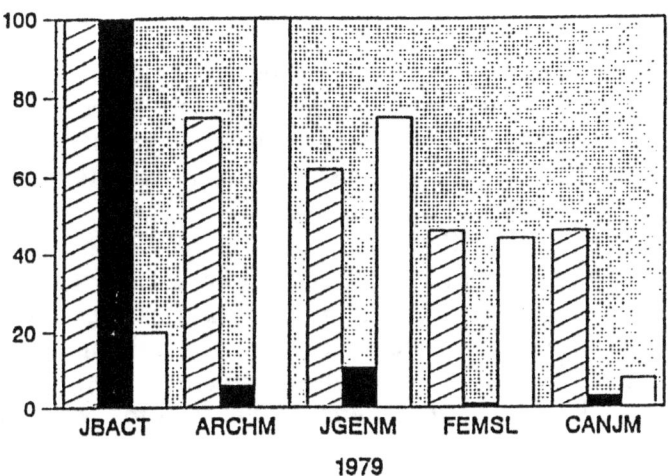

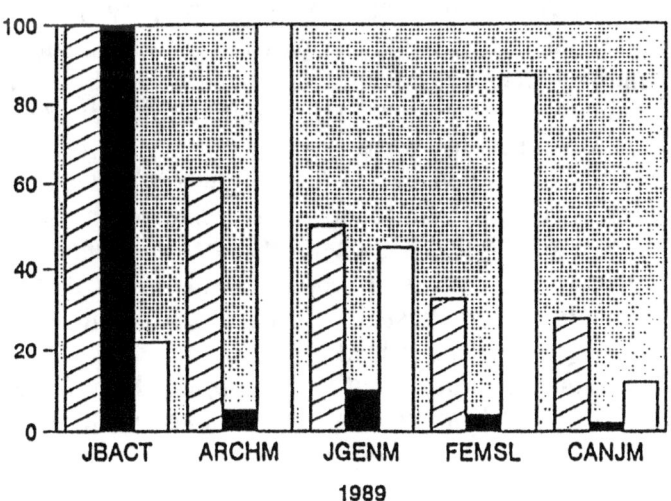

## Journals of Basic Immunology

Immunology has a strongly clinical side represented by titles such as the *Journal of Experimental Medicine* and the *Journal of Clinical Investigation,* and a mixed basic-science/clinical-science side represented by titles in the following list. Curiously, infection is not the strongest point even in a title like *Infection and Immunity* from the American Society for Microbiology. AIDS may prompt some realignment of topics, but the basic science underlying that infective disease is in many ways similar to the basic science underlying noninfective diseases now realized to have autoimmune aspects: lupus, multiple sclerosis, arthritis and rheumatism. "Mixed" immunology journals will continue to be dominant in many life science collections.

In 1979, impact factor leadership was held by the American Association of Immunologists through its *Journal of Immunology* and has yet to be relinquished (see Figure 9). In a similar manner, the *European Journal of Immunology* from the German chemical publishers, VCH, has held on to second. Third place has seen some contention. Until about 1983, the *Scandinavian Journal of Immunology* from Blackwell was the third-place tenant, but by 1985, it was clear that a title from the American Society for Microbiology, *Infection and Immunity* had taken over. But this was not the end of the descent of the Scandinavian entry. *Immunology*, another Blackwell title, has taken over the fourth spot. For the time being, however, the *Scandinavian* is secure in its last spot.

In terms of being cited by the leader, the *European Journal of Immunology* is securely in second place. *Immunology* was secure in third place until about 1983, when *Infection and Immunity* sprang into hot contention. The two currently have about equal status. The *Scandinavian Journal of Immunology* has declined substantially in its rate of being cited by the leader.

Price data show the *Journal of Immunology* to be a bargain. The *European Journal of Immunology* appears quite expensive by comparison. The three other titles in the group are roughly intermediate

## FIGURE 9: GENERAL IMMUNOLOGY
◨ IMPACT ■ CBLJ ☐ COST

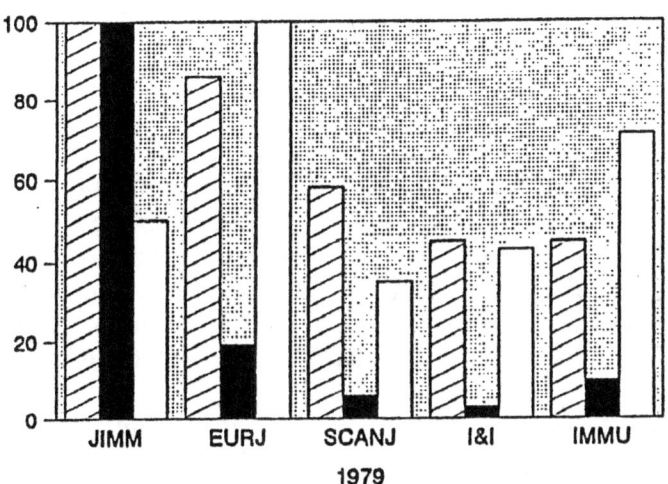

1979

◨ IMPACT ■ CBLJ ☐ COST

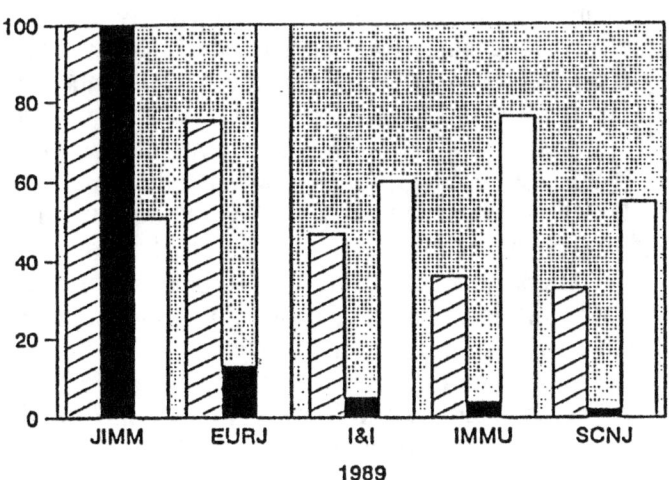

1989

in price, with *Immunology* being the most expensive of the three but still 25% cheaper than the *European*. Taken together three factors suggest that *Scandinavian Journal* is in some trouble because of marginal interest and that *Immunology* might be vulnerable because of cost. Neither, however, is likely to go to fax-only status soon.

*Journals of Physiology*

Physiology is nominally concerned with the function of the body on all levels of size and with all organ systems. In fact, in recent years, molecular and cellular levels of explanation have been paramount, particularly as addressing neuroscience systems. While the assortment discussed avoids frankly specialized organ-system journals, some titles, like the *Journal of Physiology* (London), clearly have a strong neuroscience orientation.

In 1979, the leader in impact factor was the *Journal of General Physiology* from the U.S.-based Society for General Physiology, as handled by Rockefeller University Press. It has never budged from this position (see Figure 10). Likewise, the *Journal of Physiology* (London) has a lock on second place. Third place had been fairly secure for the *American Journal of Physiology* from the American Physiological Society until 1983 (when there was a tie) and then again in 1988 (when there was again a tie). By 1989, *Pfluger's* was rising to challenge the *American Journal* for third place. This was not too surprising since this venerable and formerly German-language journal had long since evolved into the highly modern and largely English-Language Eurojournal of choice. A number of other journals might qualify for the next spot. We chose the *Canadian Journal of Physiology and Pharmacology* over the *doyenne,* the *Journal de Physiologie* (Paris), largely because the much younger Canadian title had already acquired a greater foothold in American libraries and was cheaper. While containing a small amount of Quebecois French content, it is largely an English language vehicle with a fair number of American papers. Despite this progress, its impact factor was rather modest, and it consistently anchored this fifth slot with few signs that it would advance further during the decade.

In terms of being cited by the leader, the *Journal of General Physiology,* the *Journal of Physiology* (London) would seem to be

## FIGURE 10: PHYSIOLOGY

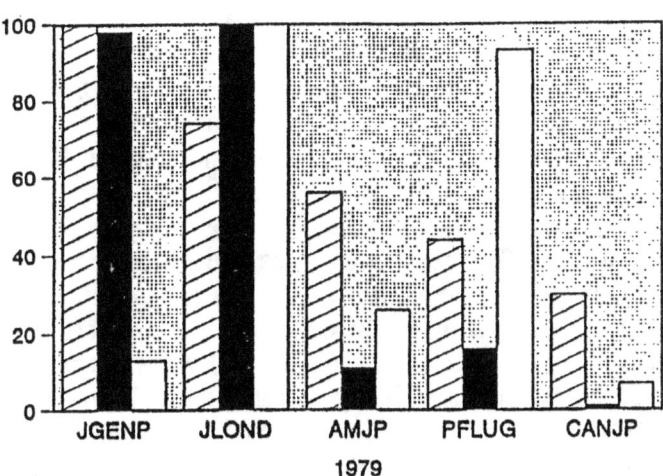

1979

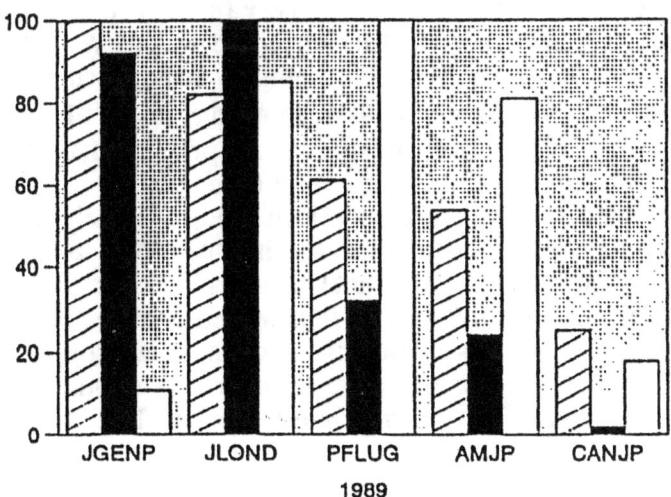

1989

the natural leader. It generally had the most papers to cite and might be expected to win based on raw probability. But by the mid-1980s, the *Journal of General Physiology* was self-citing often enough to overtake the voluminous British entry, leaving it in second by decade's end. Third is well on its way to being secured by the rising *Pfluger's,* once again bypassing the *American Journal of Physiology.* The *Canadian* entry is being challenged somewhat by a modernized *Journal de Physiologie* (Paris), but does not appear likely to be dislodged on a regular basis.

In financial terms, the *Journal of General Physiology* is a tremendous bargain. The next three titles are much less so, but no comparative disadvantage for any of the trio appears likely to result because amongst themselves they are quite close in price. The *Canadian Journal,* like the *Journal of General Physiology* is quite a bargain. This assortment is likely to remain stable in the fax age. The vulnerability of the fifth place journal, the *Canadian,* is more apparent than real since it is rather inexpensive. The next most vulnerable title, the *American,* is unlikely for reasons of professional society affiliation, to be cancelled despite its higher costs.

## *Pharmacology*

Pharmacology is the science of the interaction of drugs on the body or upon its component organ systems, usually pursued in conjunction with the alleviation of some disease. It is a discipline formed from the intersection of chemistry (usually natural products or synthetic organic chemistry) and physiology. In more recent years it has formed closer bonds with biochemistry and molecular biology, as the explanation of illnesses has descended to levels of the disruption of the synthesis or metabolism of given proteins, fats, or carbohydrates, with much of this disruption based on some DNA transcription defect. While this comparison group is largely composed of journals nominally devoted to all levels of pharmacological explanation, biochemical approaches are becoming increasingly common. Certain subspecialty journals (e.g., *Biochemical Pharmacology*) have a strong potential for disrupting this assortment in terms of current utility if not yet in terms of fair historical comparison.

By 1979, *Molecular Pharmacology* handled by Williams and

Wilkins for the (American) Society for Pharmacology and Experimental Therapeutics, had risen to the top of the impact factor pile (see Figure 11). *Molecular Pharmacology* is in many many ways a bridge journal deliberately created by that society for the more biochemical papers that had begun to fill its venerable main organ, the *Journal of Pharmacology and Experimental Therapeutics*. Was splitting off this molecular section a good idea? Four journals give evidence that this was not the case. First, the parent journal, *JPET*, has actually drifted downward in the rankings, shifting around third to fifth place. Three European journals have jockeyed with it successfully in impact factors. The *British Journal of Pharmacology* from the British Society for Pharmacology has done the best, actually rising to the top in four of the ten years. Two Continental journals, the *European Journal of Pharmacology* from Elsevier, and *Naunyn-Schmiedeberg's Archives of Pharmacology* from Springer have been contending for the nominal crown of genuine Eurojournal, the title that concentrates the best of European research. As a practical matter, *Naunyn-Schmiedeberg's* has the loyalty of the Swiss and Germans and has done slightly better in impact factors in eight out of eleven years, and probably is the Eurojournal of choice. The *European* publishes a tremendous number of papers, ironically including many American ones which, for some reason, did not make it into the two U.S. titles in this group. To summarize a somewhat fluid situation, we rank the impact factor leadership group as follows: tied for 1-2, *Molecular Pharmacology* and *British Journal of Pharmacology*; tied for 3-5, *Naunyn-Schmiedeberg's Archive,* the *European* and *JPET*.

Results in the category of being cited by the leader depended very much on whether *Molecular Pharmacology* or the *British Journal of Pharmacology* was the leader. *Molecular Pharmacology* self-cites and cites *JPET* much more heavily than does the *British*. The *British* self-cites and cites the *European Journal* and *Naunyn-Schmiedeberg's* rather more heavily. While there is some scientific crossover of citations streams, there really appears to be two fairly distinct citation whirlpools based on geoscientific differences. Most libraries would wish to cover both eddies. Can they afford to do so?

Dipping into the American current is safely manageable. Both *Molecular Pharmacology* and *JPET* cost but a small fraction of any

## FIGURE 11: PHARMACOLOGY

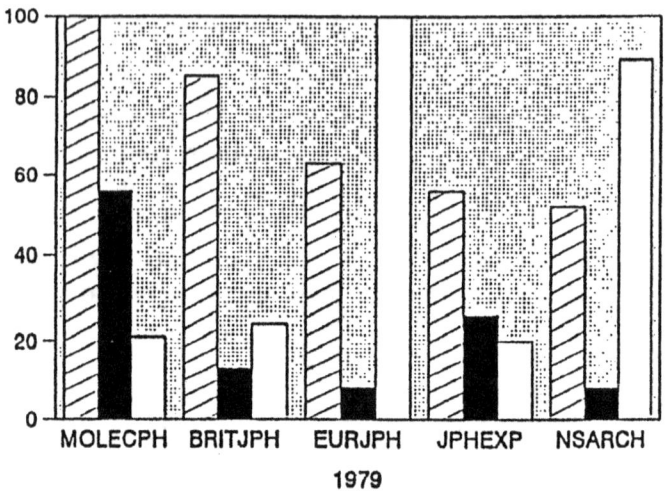

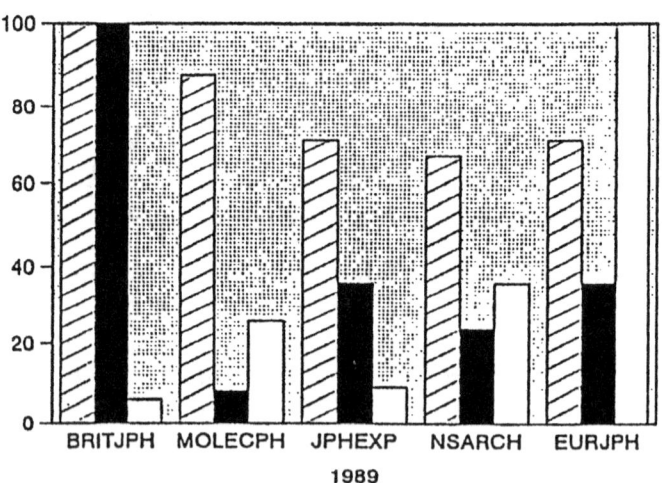

of their competitors. The water is up to one's ankles. The foreign vortex is somewhat more unsettling. The *British Journal* and *Naunyn-Schmiedeberg's* are from two to three times more expensive as the American titles, putting the water level at one's waist. The *European Journal,* however, is clearly over one's head: ten times as expensive as the American entries and three times as expensive as its European competition. While the *European Journal* is doubtlessly voluminous, it is, at best, a third place journal. It cannot decisively claim even to be the Eurojournal of choice, despite its title. With such extraordinary success for the British title and such heavy participation by the pharmaceutically-intense Swiss and Germans in other journals in this group, one is left wondering just who does send in those hundreds and hundreds of papers that the journal should be worth all that extra cost. We suggest that despite its prominence, the *European Journal of Pharmacology* may well be headed for fax-only access.

## *Fundamental Neuroscience*

Neuroscience features a variety of disciplinary and clinical *leitmotifs.* There is the experimental psychologist's concern with perception and memory. Clinical neurologists need to evaluate brain damage caused by accident, stroke, or tumor. Physiologists see the nervous system as an integrator of other organ systems and as the principal coordinator of the body's response to the environment. Preclinical professors in the departments of both anatomy and neurology at medical schools have long given their microscopes over primarily to neuroanatomy. Not all of these historic themes have achieved equal prominence in today's neuroscience journals. They are largely dominated by the last, "microanatomic," constituency in conjunction with cellular physiologists and molecular biologists. It should be noted that many journals entitled "neurology" are not discussed here because they are almost exclusively clinical and out of scope for most basic science collections.

In 1979, neuroscience was dominated by five journals (see Figure 12). The Americans had the microanatomic leader: the *Journal of Comparative Neurology.* It had a history of being taken over from the Wistar Institute by Alan Liss, an entrepreneur who had left

## FIGURE 12: NEUROSCIENCE

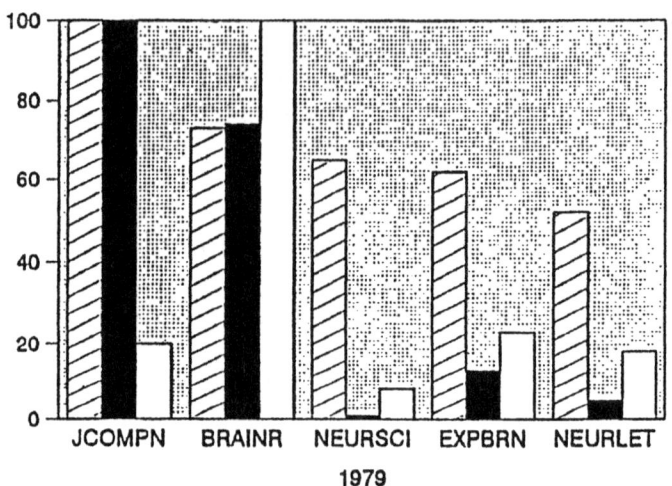

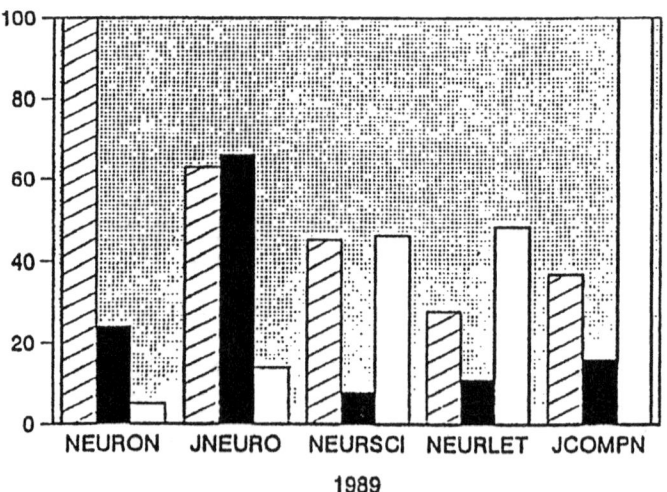

Academic Press, and who eventually sold the *Journal* to Wiley by decade's end. The British had *Neuroscience,* a Pergamon title, which as we now know, would eventually become the minion of Elsevier. Elsevier had one of the most massive, omnibus journals of our times: *Brain Research* which was largely devoted to full-length papers and reviews, and another journal for shorter papers: *Neuroscience Letters.* Springer had fielded *Experimental Brain Research.*

During most of the 1980s, *Neuroscience* and the *Journal of Comparative Neurology* traded off impact factor leadership between themselves. Likewise, *Brain Research* and *Experimental Brain Research* stayed very close to one another in third or fourth place respectively. *Neuroscience Letters* slowly showed improvement in impact factors, largely because it was the most molecular of the three European titles. It actually began to catch up with *Brain Research* and *Experimental Brain Research* but this seemed a fairly calm and gradual development.

But a serious change in the citation weather was coming in the mid-1980s. One of the then few alternative American entries in the field, the *Journal of Neuroscience,* a title founded by the Society for Neuroscience, back in 1981, had corrected a publication defect that devalued its ratings. They had noticed that their impact factors had been tremendously diluted by the inclusion of many rarely-cited abstracts in the impact-factor calculations. They reorganized the journal so that basically only full-length articles got counted, making its baseline comparable to its competitors. A new editor also made a number of other aggressive improvements. A reevaluation disclosed that by 1987, the relative newcomer was in fact, the new impact factor king. Every other journal in the assortment got bumped down a peg. But no sooner had this citation storm settled when a veritable impact factor hurricane hit town in 1988. Its name was *Neuron* and it came from Cell Press, the source of *Cell,* itself the most influential new life sciences journal of the last twenty years. After only one year, it bumped all its competition down one more peg. The impact factors of the 1980s ended up quite differently than they began!

The initially sleepy story of neuroscience journals was repeated in the cited-by-the-leader category. Either of the two most voluminous journals, the *Journal of Comparative Neurology* or *Brain Research* was the most cited, even when the impact factor leader was

*Neuroscience.* But only a year after the *Journal of Neuroscience* made its 1987 impact-factor breakthrough, it rose to number two. It did not yet dethrone *Brain Research* but it did beat out the *Journal of Comparative Neurology.* The *Journal of Neuroscience* continued to fare well even after *Neuron* had taken control, finally displacing not only *Brain Research* but *Neuroscience* as well. It may still take time to see whether or not *Neuron,* which is still quite new and does not have anywhere near the gross numbers of potentially citable papers of its principal competitors, cites itself enough to rise to the top in this category. It seems that it would be highly likely to at least make second place after the *Journal of Neuroscience. Experimental Brain Research* was particularly hard hit by *Neuron's* highly molecularized citing pattern, doing its worst in eleven years. *Neuroscience Letters* actually benefitted from *Neuron's* rise and clearly passed *Experimental Brain Research* as a more necessary title, and at least in this CBLJ category, *Neuroscience Letters* is also challenging *Neuroscience.*

What will it take to financially cover this field? If one wishes both *Brain Research* or the *Journal of Comparative Neurology,* erstwhile contenders for early choices for the local collection, the answer is a stunning $11,000! By contrast, first place *Neuron* is currently less than $300, second place *Journal of Neuroscience* is about $600, and even the $2100 for third place *Neuroscience* or fourth place *Neuroscience Letters* looks fairly reasonable. Fifth-place finishers that cost in excess of $4000 (*JCN*) and now seventh-place finishers (*BR*) that cost in excess of $6000 are extremely likely to be turned into fax-access-only journals in many, many collections. While *Experimental Brain Research,* at about $2400, is more reasonable than either of these blockbusters, it has been pretty much marginalized in the other citation-based categories, and so seems also headed for fax-only access. A brand new journal, the *European Journal of Neuroscience,* is coming into the fray, at less than $500. It has intellectual ties to both *Neuron* and to the *Journal of Neuroscience.* It is definitely the journal to watch. It may well threaten both *Neuroscience* and *Neuroscience Letters* as a locally-held title. Indeed, of all the major specialties in this study, neuroscience is the very most chaotic. Here, more than anywhere else, are long-established titles that are very likely to go to fax-access only.

## WILL FAX MEAN THE DEATH OF LOW-CITATION-RATING AND/OR OVERLY EXPENSIVE PRINT JOURNALS?

There are several practical reasons why a rating in this article consigning a journal to fax-access will not lead to its extinction:

First, the authors are not so vain as to assume that everyone will agree with our analysis of the last eleven years nor with our view of the future, and then act on it.

Second, there will still be a few hundred universities and/or medical centers who will still try to collect all these titles comprehensively, even after well over a hundred middle-sized universities and competitive liberal arts colleges have finished their cancellectomies.

Third, even within some small schools, personal eccentricities and preferences will have some say. It is extremely difficult for a working science librarian to argue with the only faculty specialist on campus about a given journal in that scientist's own specialty. Unless a significant amount of price differential that favors the librarian is involved, the top administration is likely to take the view of the professor over that of the librarian.

Fourth, even in some schools that do not attempt to collect comprehensively, four or five journals per major specialty would be considered too small, particularly if there are several faculty in nominally the same specialty. Our response is that having a large number of specialists still tends to lead to a reasonable consensus on the major specialty journals, with subspecialty journals serving to indicate distinctions among individual scientists. Indeed, we think there is less chance of eccentricity in schools with several matching specialists, than in those with only one, because the less eccentric faculty will outvote the eccentric.

Fifth, our perspective is American. We fully realize that the British may well think that the *Biochemical Journal* is the world's first or second best biochemistry journal and are extremely likely to go on supporting it whether or not small American institutions prefer it or not. The same is true for other local loyalties.

Sixth, we suspect that some of the wealthier European publishers, most notably Elsevier, may feel that they can indefinitely postpone fundamentally reforming their print journals until print journals become irrelevant for reasons of more general disadvantages against electronic competition. For them, fax money may constitute a mild boost to their plans to go more fully electronic. By that time they may hope to bypass librarians altogether and sell electronically conveyed articles directly to end-users. Such a strategy is less true of some of the American for-profit publishers whose tales of corporate woe have become legend. American for-profit publishers must reform to sustain subscriptions because fax revenues are not likely to make up the income difference before any cash reserves they have are depleted. They'll take any fax money but really need the subscription money now. Otherwise they may not be around for whatever electronic future there is to be.

## COULD FAX DATA JOIN CITATION DATA IN REFORMING JOURNALS?

### *How a Threat to Profits Might Lead to a Restructured Journal*

For at least 15 years, and despite some ongoing controversy, a good number of librarians have been using citation data as an aid in journal evaluation, particularly with regard to cancellations. Publishers who do well in impact factor have been using this data routinely in their ad campaigns for many years. Publishers who do poorly have tried to ignore these indicators, or, at best, mildly quiz their editors as to their validity. Editors with journals that performed badly in citation comparisons, could argue with some validity in the short run, but somewhat disingenuously in the long run, that all sorts of nonscientific or prejudicial elements could account for these unfavorable reports. Moreover, editors could tell publishers that judgements of citation data, just like judgements of scientific data, are best left to experts like the editors themselves. As long as sales are good, the publisher has no reason to doubt the editors: it makes no difference to journal revenues. Indeed many editors looked at the occurrence of citation star papers or citation star authors as a kind of critical mass phenomenon: if you publish more and more papers each year, you increase the chances of eventually getting some citation stars of your own. Alternatively, editors argued that journal subscriptions were supported largely by the demand for authors for outlets. If one published many papers by many authors, one would have many subscriptions from people who wanted to see their papers in print. But that argument has been clearly undercut by cancellations made by librarians who are no longer taking their marching orders from faculty, whom they fear somewhat, when they have contrary orders from financial administrators, whom they fear even more. It may now occur to publishers that it is worthwhile to listen to librarians about what to do with their print journals.

Next to complaints about journal price, complaints about journal bulk have been the most frequent on the part of librarians. Cost cutting on journal bulk may be one of the few ways for publishers to preserve subscription loyalty on the part of librarians while preserving profit margins for a product whose price they can no longer raise without fear of cancellations that offset income that was supposed to be generated by these price increases. And while it may seem strange to consumers in other walks of life, few librarians would object to receiving print journals with steady state or even reduced bulk for about the same money each year.

The central question might seem to be, how to decide which papers to cut back on so as to achieve this reduced or steady state? Indeed some publishers complain that they would be at the mercy of their editor's opinion. What independent tool is there, ask the publishers, that would enable them to evaluate the judgement of their editors in any campaign to cut out the fat in their journals? The answer involves a wonderful irony: article-specific or author-specific fax royalty reports. A part of the tool that threatens current subscriptions can be made to guide cuts in bulky journals in a way that should reinforce subscription loyalty. Fax reports will clearly bear out what citation data has been saying for so long, and will do so in readily understood dollars and cents. Publishers will see that a good deal of fax money comes in from a relatively few authors or labs, whose print production costs amounted to very little, while very little fax money will come in from hundreds of articles whose print production costs are great. Publishers who might have found citation data too complicated to comprehend, can certainly comprehend what amounts to individual article sales statistics. Publishers can then direct editors to give priority to authors who are demonstrably succeeding in rousing interest and whose works will sustain subscription demand for the journal. While publishers and editors will necessarily take some chances on papers from some new authors affiliated with some new labs, they will not give previously published authors, whose work has rarely generated either citations or fax requests, seemingly endless opportunities to come up with star papers eventually. New stars will displace old stars when those stars begin to dim in terms of citations and fax royalties. Fax-based royalty accounting may well speak to publishers and editors where citation data points alone might have been foolishly ignored. Journals will tend to be composed of papers that editors, who can be held accountable to their publishers as never before, are betting their jobs on as representing the hottest topics in science, a much smaller and ironically less expensive world for journal subscribers than the one we face today.

In closing, we offer Figure 13. It is an admittedly rough but hopefully convenient summary guide to our predictions.

## FIGURE 13: SUMMARY FINDINGS, 1979 - 1989
## INCLUDING PROMISING NEWCOMERS

| SUBSCRIPTIONS HIGHLY SECURE | SUBSCRIPTIONS SOMEWHAT SECURE | SOME FAX MIGRATION | FREQUENT FAX MIGRATION |
|---|---|---|---|
| Biochemistry | Am. J. Physiol. | Arch. Biochem. Biophys. | BBA |
| Brit. J. Pharmacol. | Arch. Microbiol. | Biochem. J. | Brain Res. |
| Cell | BBRC | Canad. J. Micro. | Chromosoma |
| Genes & Develop. | Develop. Biol. | Canad. J. of Physiol | Differentiation |
| J. Bacteriol. | Development | Exp. Cell. Res. | Exp. Brain Res. |
| J. Biol. Chem. | DNA | Eur. J. Cell. Biol. | Eur. J. Pharmacol. |
| J. Cell. Biol. | EMBO J. | FEBS Lett. | Gene |
| J. Gen. Physiol. | Eur. J. Biochem. | FEMS Lett. | J. Comp. Neurol. |
| J. Immunol. | Eur. J. Immunol. | Gen. Res. | Scan. J. Immunol. |
| J. Neurosci. | Eur. J. Neurosci. | Heredity | |
| J. Pharm. Exp. Therap. | Genome | Immunology | |
| Mol. Cell. Biol. | Infect. Immun. | J. Mol. Biol. | |
| Mol. Gen. Genet. | J. Cell Sci. | Neuroscience | |
| Neuron | J. Gen. Microbiol. | Neurosci. Lett. | |
| | J. Physiol. London | Nucleic Acids Res. | |
| | Naunyn-Schmied. | Roux Archives | |
| | Pflugers Arch. | | |

## REFERENCE NOTES

1. Eugene Garfield, Editor in Chief. *Journal Citation Reports* Philadelphia: Institute for Scientific Information, print vols. for 1979-1988, fiche edition for 1989. The key source for monitoring the relative standings and interactions of the world's most significant scientific journals.

2. We wish to thank FAXON for the use of their historical collection of catalogs.

3. Tony Stankus and Kevin Rosseel. "The Rise of Eurojournals: Their Success Can Be Ours." *Library Resources and Technical Services* 31(3):215-224, 1987.

4. Tony Stankus, Kevin Rosseel, and William C. Littlefield. "Is the Best Japanese Science in Western Journals?" *The Serials Librarian* 14(1/2):95-107, 1988.

5. Tony Stankus. "Asia's Other Sci-Tech Dragons: The International Publishing Patterns of Hong Kong, the People's Republic of China, Singapore, South Korea, and Taiwan." *Scientific Journals: Improving Library Collections Through Analysis of Publishing Trends.* New York: The Haworth Press Inc., 1990. pages 105-127.

# A Comparison of Science Related Document Delivery Services

Robert T. McFarland

**SUMMARY.** This paper describes a pilot project in the Chemistry Library at Washington University in St. Louis using the Chemical Abstracts Document Delivery Service. In addition, results from a comparative analysis of nine commercial document delivery vendors are included. Vendors were compared according to cost, turnaround time, cost efficiency, fill rate, reliability and vendor responsiveness with respect to delivery of individual documents. Recommendations are made with respect to vendor appropriateness in five science disciplines; Biology, Chemistry, Earth Sciences, Math and Engineering. The overall aim is to assist science librarians, wishing to implement such a service, in selecting document delivery vendors which would best meet their needs.

## INTRODUCTION

As library allocations begin to tighten and journal costs continue to rise, access versus ownership of the literature is taking on greater significance. For access to be successful, it must involve delivery

---

Robert T. McFarland is Chemistry Librarian at Washington University, 1 Brookings Drive, St. Louis, MO 63130, ROBMCF@WULIBS.BITNET. He received a BA in Biology from the University of Kansas, an MA in Biology at the University of Missouri-Kansas City and a MA in Library and Information Science at the University of Missouri-Columbia where he is currently a PhD candidate in Higher Education Administration. The author gratefully acknowledges the cooperation and assistance from the following individuals: Karen Croneis for her insightful comments; Shirley K. Baker, Dean of Washington University Libraries for funding the project; and a special thanks to Chris Barkeshli for collecting data and compiling vendor comparison information.

© 1992 by The Haworth Press, Inc. All rights reserved.

of not only bibliographic information but primary materials as well. Due to the exorbitant costs associated with owning chemistry related information, the chemistry library over the past eighteen months has gradually moved away from ownership of materials. Two primary means of access are utilized, online and FAX. Utilizing these sources allows the library to pay only for information needed instead of paying up-front costs for large amounts of information that is rarely used, i.e., paying only for one journal article instead of the entire journal. This paper first describes a pilot project involving the Chemical Abstracts Document Delivery Service and then a comparative analysis of other science related document delivery vendors on a number of service related parameters. The aim is to assist science librarians, wishing to implement such a service, in selecting vendors which would best meet their needs.

## PILOT PROJECT

In response to the pressures mentioned above, as well as an increased demand for timely access to the chemical literature not in the holdings of the Washington University Libraries, the Chemistry Library, in March 1991, initiated a document delivery service through the Chemical Abstracts Document Delivery Service.

Ardis and Croneis (1987) have shown that purchase of articles from commercial delivery services might be more cost effective than ownership of infrequently used titles. The Chemistry Library was an appropriate test site in that the scope of the subject areas are fairly well defined. Also, it was estimated that over 90% of requested documents would be available from a single source, the Chemical Abstracts Document Delivery Service. This service subscribes to over 10,000 journals covering all branches of chemistry as well as the core journals from a broad range of science related disciplines.

The first six months was a period of trial and error during which several "bugs" had to be overcome. Accounts had to be established; articles were inadvertently sent to units other than the Chemistry Library. Articles were sent first class mail instead of by FAX and vice versa, and frequently charges for a given request did not coincide with published fee schedules. There are many variations in the ways to submit and receive requested documents, and charges for each variation are different.

Despite these initial frustrations, the reliability of the CA Document Delivery Service greatly improved. We gradually gained familiarity with the proper ways of submitting requests, learning just what information the vendor could and could not provide. At the same time they became increasingly more responsive and familiar to our needs. After this six month trial period, full implementation of a document delivery service was initiated including vigorous promotion among faculty and students. The guidelines within which we originally operated are listed below.

## *Initial Guidelines*

1. Requested documents had to be available from Chemical Abstracts Document Delivery Service.
2. Requests had to be made in person at the Chemistry Library.
3. Requests were not accepted for articles from titles in the holdings of the Washington University Libraries unless it was at the bindery, book repair, pages were missing, volume was lost, etc.
4. Access to the service was available to all Washington University faculty and graduate students. Initially undergraduates were included, but were soon excluded because of their failure to pick up documents in a timely manner.
5. Requests were submitted online over STN. Initially, all documents were delivered by FAX.
6. Document ordering, receipt, record keeping and accounting were maintained by the Chemistry Library. All charges for documents were subsidized by the Olin Library System.

The Chemistry Library was now positioned to provide fast and reliable access to a much broader scope of the chemical literature than the library could ever hope to have in-house. Reactions to the service were immediate. Responses from faculty and students were overwhelmingly positive. During the trial period, over 130 different titles, not in the holdings of the University Libraries, were accessed. Requests for documents, while primarily from chemistry faculty and students, were received from over 13 different science related departments, including both the Hilltop campus and the Medical School campus. These data are shown in Table 1.

## *VENDOR ANALYSIS*

The success of the document delivery service in the Chemistry Library, prompted us to investigate the feasibility of expanding the service to the other science libraries within the university library system. To facilitate decentralization of document delivery services, we concluded that it would be beneficial to do a comparative analysis of document delivery vendors whose scope of coverage most closely matched that of the Olin Library System's science libraries including Biology, Chemistry, Earth Sciences, Math, and Engineering.

## *METHODOLOGY*

### *Vendor Selection*

Document delivery vendors were chosen on the basis of subject strengths that most closely matched the subject specialty of the different Washington University science libraries. Document delivery vendors chosen for specific science libraries are listed below.

| FULL NAME | ABBREVIATION |
|---|---|
| University of Chicago, John Crerar Library Photoduplication Service | CRERAR |
| Chemical Abstracts Document Delivery Service | CAS |
| Linda Hall Library | LHL |

TABLE 1

CHEMISTRY LIBRARY

DOCUMENT DELIVERY PILOT PROJECT

MARCH 1991 - OCTOBER 1991

Departments from which requests were received:

| | | |
|---|---|---|
| Anthropology | Earth & Planetary | Mechanical Engineering |
| Biology | Sciences | Pharmacology |
| Chemical Engineering | Immunology | Physics |
| Chemistry | Math | Radiation Sciences |

Total Number of Requests by all Departments - 192

| Faculty | Post-Doc | Graduate | Undergraduate | Misc |
|---|---|---|---|---|
| 54 | 34 | 90 | 10 | 4 |

Average number of requests/month - during pilot period    21.3
Average expenditure/month                                 $310.00
Average cost/request                                      $ 14.50

Total spent during pilot period                           $2,789.50

Mode of Document Delivery

| | | | | |
|---|---|---|---|---|
| FAX | 45% | Average time-to-delivery | 24 hours |
| FCM | 43% | Average time-to-delivery | 6 days |
| Express | 12% | Average time-to-delivery | 2 days |

FCM = First Class Mail
Express = Express Mail

Institute for Scientific
Information                                ISI
Genuine Article Service

University Microfilms
International                              UMI
Article Clearinghouse Service

Engineering Information, Inc.              Ei

Engineering Societies Library              ESL

American Mathematical Society              MATHDOC
MathDoc Service

American Geological Institute              GEOREF
GeoRef Service

To facilitate the vendor selection process tables were drawn up comparing the published or stated policies of selected vendors. Included were such basics as method and hours documents can be requested, basic services and charges, special services, coverage, and delivery times. Information for each vendor is shown in Appendices I-IX.

Four documents each were ordered from each of five vendors within a given subject area except for Math in which five documents were requested from three different vendors. Two documents each were requested to be delivered "regular" or first class mail (FCM) and two to be delivered "rush" or express mail/FAX. The total number of articles requested by vendor and subject area is shown in Table 2.

## Document Selection

Each subject specialty librarian submitted between 10 and 15 citations to the journal literature from their respective areas. Citations were either actual ILL requests submitted by faculty and graduate students or were chosen by the librarians.

TABLE 2

TOTAL NUMBER OF ARTICLES REQUESTED BY VENDOR AND SUBJECT AREA

|  | JOHN CRERAR | CAS | LHL | ISI | UMI | EI | ESL | MATHDOC | GEOREF | TOTAL NO. DOCUMENTS FROM EACH SUBJECT AREA |
|---|---|---|---|---|---|---|---|---|---|---|
| CHEMISTRY | 4 | 4 | 4 | 4 | 4 | | | | | 20 |
| EARTH & PLANETARY SCIENCE | 4 | 4 | 4 | 4 | | | | | 4 | 20 |
| MATHEMATICS | 5 | | 5 | | | | | 5 | | 15 |
| BIOLOGY | 4 | 4 | 4 | 4 | 4 | | | | | 20 |
| ENGINEERING | 4 | 4 | 4 | 4 | | 4 | 4 | | | 20 |
| TOTAL NO. DOCUMENTS FROM EACH VENDOR | 17 | 16 | 21 | 16 | 8 | 4 | 4 | 5 | 4 | 95 |

## Vendor Comparison of Service Related Parameters

Documents from each vendor were then compared on the following parameters:

Cost: Represents the actual cost of the requested document as stated on the vendor's invoice.
Expected Time: Refers to a vendor's published or stated time to deliver a requested document.
Actual Time: Represents the actual elapsed time, in working days, before receipt of a document.
Reliability: Refers to whether or not the vendor supplied a document within their published or stated time limits. Did they do what they say they can do?
Efficiency: Represents the ratio of actual cost to actual time-to-delivery. Which vendors could supply documents in the least amount of time at the lowest cost.
Vendor Responsiveness: Represented by the following scale:

    1 = Poor    Cooperation poor.
                      Did not notify if there were problems. Took several phone calls to work out problems.
    3 = Satisfactory    Cooperation OK.
                      No problems.
    5 = Excellent    Cooperation excellent.
                      Timely notification when there were problems.

## RESULTS

The total number of documents ordered from each vendor and for each subject library is shown in Table 2. An indication of the scope or comprehensiveness of a vendor's collection is also shown. Linda Hall appears to have the broadest scope supplying documents for all five subject areas examined. The collections of Chemical Abstracts, John Crerar and ISI were appropriate for 4 out of 5 subject areas. GeoRef, MathDoc, the Engineering Societies Library and

Engineering Information, having more specialized collections, were appropriate for one subject area each.

Comparison of rush versus regular documents for price, turn-around time, efficiency, fill rate, reliability, and vendor responsiveness are displayed in Tables 3-8.

## Price

Table 3 shows the average price for both regular and rush documents. Documents sent (Regular) first class mail across all vendors averaged $14.00 compared to $23.00 for documents sent (Rush) by express mail or FAX. Regular and rush documents, on the average, were the least costly from Linda Hall and John Crerar; $9.00 and

TABLE 3

COMPARISON OF SERVICE RELATED PARAMETERS

RUSH VERSUS REGULAR

PRICE

| Vendor | Regular | Rush | Rush-Regular Difference |
|---|---|---|---|
| Crerar | $9.50 | $14.00 | $4.50 |
| CAS | $10.00 | $18.00 | $8.00 |
| LHL | $9.00 | $14.00 | $5.00 |
| ISI | $12.00 | $18.00 | $6.00 |
| UMI | $12.00 | $21.00 | $9.00 |
| Ei | $21.00 | $31.00 | $10.00 |
| ESL | $23.00 | $47.00 | $24.00 |
| Mathdoc | $15.00 | NA | - |
| GeoRef | $16.00 | $31.00 | $15.00 |
| $\bar{X}$ | $14.00 | $23.00 | |

$14.00 respectively for both vendors. The Engineering Societies Library was the most expensive, having an average cost of $23.00 and $47.00 for regular and rush documents. Vendors having the lowest cost differential between regular and rush documents were John Crerar and Linda Hall in which rush documents for both averaged about $5.00 or 50% over that of a first class document. The Engineering Societies Library showed the largest difference with rush documents costing $24.00 above that of regular service.

## Vendor Turnaround Time

Vendor turnaround times are displayed in Table 4. Average time of delivery across all vendors for documents sent first class mail was

TABLE 4

COMPARISON OF SERVICE RELATED PARAMETERS

RUSH VERSUS REGULAR

VENDOR TURNAROUND

| Vendor | Regular | Rush | Rush-Regular Difference |
|---|---|---|---|
| Crerar | 9 days | 1 day | 8 days |
| CAS | 6 days | 1 day | 5 days |
| LHL | 11 days | 1 day | 10 days |
| ISI | 10 days | 3 days | 7 days |
| UMI | 2 days | 1 day | 1 day |
| Ei | 12 days | 7 days | 5 days |
| ESL | 5 days | 1 day | 4 days |
| Mathdoc | 2 days | 1 day | 1 day |
| GeoRef | 5 days | 2 days | 3 days |
| $\bar{x}$ | 7 days | 2 days | |

7 days whereas documents sent by express mail/FAX had a mean delivery time of 2 days. MathDoc and UMI, each having delivery times of 2 days, were fastest for documents sent first class mail. Linda Hall and Engineering Information were slowest showing significantly slower times of 11 and 12 days respectively.

Engineering Information's performance for rush requested documents was the slowest, taking an average of 7 days for delivery. The average time of delivery, as noted above, for all documents sent first class mail was 7 days.

Overall, delivery times of vendors were more consistent with respect to rush requested documents with 6 out of 9 vendors supplying information materials within 24 hours or less.

Linda Hall had the largest difference in time-of-delivery between regular and rush requested documents at 10 days while UMI showed a regular/rush difference of only 1 day.

*Cost-Efficiency*

Measures for cost efficiency are shown in Table 5. Efficiency measures were determined to assess which vendors could supply documents in the least amount of time at the lowest cost. More efficient vendors are represented by higher scores.

Scores for efficiency within the regular document data vary from lows of 1 for John Crerar, Linda Hall and GeoRef to highs of 3 for MathDoc and Engineering Societies Library and 4 for UMI. UMI was able to supply regular documents within 2 days at an average cost of $12.00 per document. Scores for efficiency in the rush document column show wider variations among vendors. John Crerar, Linda Hall and MathDoc all supplied documents within 24 hours and more often than not within the same day with charges around $15.00 per document. Particularly cost-ineffective were Engineering Information and the Engineering Societies Library. Ei's rush documents took an average of 7 days for delivery at about $31.00 per document. The Engineering Societies Library's faster delivery was offset by an average $47.00 per document charge for rush documents. Vendors were more consistent in the efficiency with which regular documents were delivered as reflected in a narrower range of scores. Overall, rush documents across all vendors were more

TABLE 5

COMPARISON OF SERVICE RELATED PARAMETERS

RUSH VERSUS REGULAR

COST-EFFICIENCY*

| Vendor | Regular | Rush | Rush-Regular Difference |
|---|---|---|---|
| Crerar | 1 | 8 | 7 |
| CAS | 2 | 5 | 3 |
| LHL | 1 | 7 | 6 |
| ISI | 2 | 4 | 2 |
| UMI | 4 | 5 | 1 |
| Ei | 0 | 1 | 1 |
| ESL | 3 | 1 | - 2 |
| Mathdoc | 3 | 7 | 4 |
| GeoRef | 1 | 2 | 1 |
| $\bar{X}$ | 2.0 | 4.5 | |

*Represents the ratio of actual cost to actual time-to-delivery. Higher scores represent more efficient vendors; i.e., those supplying documents in the least amount of time at the lowest cost.

cost-effective as demonstrated by a mean efficiency score of 4.5 compared to 2.0 for regular documents.

## *Fill Rate*

Fill rates across all vendors are shown in Table 6. Overall fill rates were excellent for all vendors within both regular and rush data; at 90% or above. The only exception was for a rush document in a subscription that was recently cancelled by the Engineering

TABLE 6

COMPARISON OF SERVICE RELATED PARAMETERS

RUSH VERSUS REGULAR

FILL RATE

| Vendor | Regular | Rush |
|---|---|---|
| Crerar | 100% | 100% |
| CAS | 100% | 100% |
| LHL | 95% | 90% |
| ISI | 100% | 100% |
| UMI | 100% | 100% |
| Ei | 100% | 100% |
| ESL | 100% | 50% |
| Mathdoc | 100% | 100% |
| GeoRef | 100% | 100% |

Societies Library. The excellent fill rate was to be expected and confirmed the appropriateness with which vendors were matched with subject specialty libraries.

## *Reliability*

Data for vendor reliability are shown in Table 7. Vendors were more consistent with respect to reliability within regular document data with 8 out of 9 vendors having scores of 80% or greater. UMI was the least reliable, supplying documents within their published or stated time limits only 50% of the time.

Vendors were even less reliable in delivering rush documents within specified time limits; only 5 out of 9 had scores of 80% or better. UMI supplied documents within their specified time limits

TABLE 7

COMPARISON OF SERVICE RELATED PARAMETERS

RUSH VERSUS REGULAR

RELIABILITY

| Vendor | Regular | Rush |
|---|---|---|
| Crerar | 100% | 100% |
| CAS | 100% | 100% |
| LHL | 80% | 91% |
| ISI | 88% | 63% |
| UMI | 50% | 25% |
| Ei | 100% | 50% |
| ESL | 100% | 50% |
| Mathdoc | 100% | 100% |
| GeoRef | 100% | 100% |

only 25% of the time and Engineering Information and the Engineering Societies Library at a 50% rate.

## Vendor Responsiveness

An established document delivery service tends to raise the expectations of library users and hence the sensitivity and responsiveness of vendors to local needs was tracked. The results are shown in Table 8. Noted was the timeliness of notification if there was a problem on the part of the vendor in filling a request and the cooperativeness with which they would resend a document if the quality was poor.

John Crerar and the Chemical Abstracts Document Delivery Service were exceptional in providing timely notification of prob-

TABLE 8

COMPARISON OF SERVICE RELATED PARAMETERS

RUSH VERSUS REGULAR

VENDOR RESPONSIVENESS*

| Vendor  | Regular | Rush |
|---------|---------|------|
| Crerar  | 3       | 5    |
| CAS     | 3       | 4    |
| LHL     | 1       | 2    |
| ISI     | 3       | 3    |
| UMI     | 2       | 2    |
| Ei      | 2       | 3    |
| ESL     | 3       | 2    |
| Mathdoc | 3       | 4    |
| GeoRef  | 3       | 4    |

*1= Poor;   3= Satisfactory;   5= Excellent

See text for details

lems. Crerar called when they could not transmit a FAX request—our FAX machine was unplugged; often, rush requests were received within 4 hours from the time they were sent. When requesting from Chemical Abstracts, documents older than 10 years must often be retrieved from remote storage. The CA Document Delivery Service consistently notified us that such a request might take a few days longer.

Other vendors were not quite as responsive, often taking several days before notifying us of problems in filling a request. A typical practice among many vendors was to send notification of problems by the same mode in which a document was requested to be delivered. Hence, if the document was to be delivered by first class mail, several days could pass before receiving notification that a particular request was not going to be delivered within their stated times.

## *DISCUSSION*

Decisions surrounding the selection of one vendor over another, within given subject areas, centered around four factors: reliability, ease with which documents could be ordered, primary subject strengths and cost in no specific order, since priorities were different depending upon the nature of the request, i.e., regular versus a rush.

Document delivery vendors deemed most appropriate for specific subject areas are presented below, in priority order, followed by a rationale for specific selections.

| | |
|---|---|
| Biology | 1. John Crerar |
| | 2. ISI |
| Chemistry | 1. John Crerar |
| | 2. Chemical Abstracts |
| Earth Sciences | 1. John Crerar |
| | 2. GeoRef |
| Math | 1. MathDoc |
| | 2. John Crerar |
| Engineering | 1. Ei |
| | 2. Linda Hall Library |

In light of the four factors mentioned above, John Crerar consistently supplied both regular and rush documents within published or stated delivery times. Their service accepts requests by phone or FAX at no additional charge. When a FAX request is submitted in the morning, more often than not, the document is delivered the same day. Basic rush requests priced at $14.00 were the cheapest among the vendors studied. A major advantage in using John Crerar was minimal "extra" or "add-on" charges for documents. Most document delivery vendors charge a base price for a document, then add on extra charges in a bewildering number of combinations depending on the method by which the document is ordered and delivered. Crerar charges one flat rate for first class mail or FAX requests. The personnel at their service center were consistently cooperative and sensitive to the local needs of our users. These factors in combination with the comprehensiveness of their collections makes John Crerar the vendor of choice for Biology, Chemistry and Earth Sciences.

ISI's Genuine Article service is an appropriate secondary source for Biology considering their scope which includes most documents from the literature indexed in Current Contents (all sections) and Science and Social Science Citation Indexes. ISI could not be included as a primary source due to limitations on availability of the retrospective literature, numerous add-on charges complicating the ordering process, above average pricing, and inconsistent reliability.

The Chemical Abstracts Document Delivery Service proved to be cost-effective for both regular and rush requests. Reliability was consistently excellent as was their cooperation and sensitivity to local needs. They will even cut and ship the original document (it must be returned) if there are copyright restrictions. However, Chemical Abstracts is not recommended as the primary source for Chemistry due to the difficulty in placing orders. The best rates are obtained when documents are ordered online over STN. For academic institutions having an academic account this means that orders cannot be submitted until after 5:00 p.m. local time. Furthermore, the CA accession number must be used instead of citation information which forces one to go online or have ready access to the printed CA and reference support materials such as CASSI.

The Chemical Abstracts Document Delivery Service also has a number of combinations by which documents can be ordered, with each one having a different charge. This, in addition to the restrictions mentioned above, discourages the use of Chemical Abstracts as a primary delivery source.

The American Geological Institute's GeoRef service demonstrated excellent reliability and cooperation by staff, and the ease by which documents could be requested was above average. These were offset, however, by extraordinarily high document charges particularly for rush requests which ran about $31.00 per document. In all likelihood, the Crerar Library would probably be able to fill a very high percentage of Earth Science requests leaving GeoRef to fill requests that are more specialized and/or esoteric.

The American Mathematical Society's MathDoc service does not distinguish between regular or rush service. They will send documents by either means and charge a flat rate regardless of whether sent FCM or FAX. MathDoc repeatedly displayed superb reliability in delivery of documents and staff responsiveness and cooperation was excellent. MathDoc, like the Crerar Library has minimal add-on charges which greatly simplifies the ordering process. For these reasons MathDoc is an excellent primary source for mathematical information.

Engineering Information (Ei) is recommended as a primary source for engineering only because they have a very comprehensive collection of engineering specifications, standards and related information. However, their price per document was well above average with numerous combinations of add-on charges. Their delivery time was slow for rush requests, taking 7 days at $31.00 per document. Reliability was excellent, but sensitivity to local concerns was marginal.

In charging $23.00 for regular and $47.00 for rush documents, coupled with inconsistent reliability, the Engineering Societies Library is not recommended as a secondary vendor for Engineering.

The one vendor conspicuously absent as a primary resource is Linda Hall Library. Linda Hall's collection compares favorably with that of the Crerar Library and is much stronger in holdings relevant to engineering. The primary disadvantage in using Linda Hall is that document delivery, as defined in this study, is a service which they have not completely adopted. Linda Hall was the only vendor who placed the burden of copyright responsibilities onto the requesting institution. They will supply documents beyond what is normally considered fair-use if they have written verification from the requesting library agreeing to accept responsibility for payment of copyright royalties. This may or may not be a problem for some libraries. If it is not, then Linda Hall should be recommended as a primary source for engineering as well as other subject areas. If it does present a problem for the requesting library, then Linda Hall should be considered as a secondary source for engineering and considered a last resort for other subject areas.

Finally, UMI is not recommended as a primary or secondary document delivery vendor for science libraries. Overall, their collection is too general, crossing many science and non-science related disciplines. For science and technology libraries there are other vendors who cover the same information as UMI but have more comprehensive collections in relevant subject areas. In fairness, UMI was probably the least-matched vendor for research level science and technology libraries.

A final word of caution is in order with regards to making generalizations from cross comparisons of the document delivery vendors selected for this study. Due to differences in their scope of coverage, not all vendors were able to provide appropriate information in all subject areas. Hence, the conclusions drawn are based on an unequal number of requests from the different vendors. The more specialized vendors such as ESL, MathDoc, GeoRef, and Ei were not as well represented with respect to the number of documents requested. Four documents each were ordered from Ei, the Engineering Societies Library and GeoRef. Experience has shown that a vendor's reliability and responsiveness greatly improves when they are used on a regular basis.

## *CONCLUSIONS*

The overall aim of this study was to compare science-related document delivery vendors on a number of service-related parameters. The intent is to assist science librarians, wishing to implement such a service, in selecting the vendors which would best meet their needs. There are two primary implications from the adoption of a document delivery service:

a. Fast and reliable access to a broader scope of the literature than a library could ever hope to have in-house, and
b. A means by which to supplement ownership by providing alternative means of access.

The emphasis has been on identifying primary and secondary vendors which together would satisfy a high percentage of requests. It is unrealistic to assume such vendors will be able to satisfy all requests and hence reliance on conventional ILL services will still be necessary.

To facilitate implementing a document delivery service, vendors should handle copyright royalties, either by including it in the price of a document or charging separately. Services that do not include copyright royalties as part of their fee structure should not be seriously considered unless special arrangements have been established.

All vendors provide several options for ordering documents, online, phone, and FAX. Several vendors charge differently depending upon the method by which a request was placed. Combine this with different charges for different methods by which a document is sent, and it becomes clear that most vendors invoke a bewildering number of combinations and variations by which documents are charged. This is a daunting, and to say the least, frustrating experience for librarians wanting to use these services. See Appendices I-IX.

The John Crerar Photoduplication Service and MathDoc, a service of the American Mathematical Society, are models by which other vendors should follow. Both charge reasonable rates, will accept requests in any format, are extremely cooperative and sensitive to the needs of local users, and most importantly have minimal or non-existent add-on charges. The result is basically a very simple fee structure similar to a flat rate per document which greatly eases the effort on the part of librarians in gaining familiarity with these services.

In the final analysis, selection of a commercial document delivery vendor should consider foremost the appropriateness of the information they are able to provide to the relevant subject area. Vendor selection should then be based upon the degree of reliability; the number and combinations of add-on charges–which affect the ease with which documents can be requested; vendor cooperativeness and sensitivity to local needs; and document cost.

## *Cautionary Note*

A primary advantage in using commercial document delivery services is their handling of copyright compliance and payments to publishers. Most of the services in this study included publisher copyright royalities as part of their fee structure. It is imperative that librarians using these services fully understand what a vendor will or will not do with respect to payment of publisher copyright royalities. While document delivery has been around for a number of years in one form or another, the advent of the plain paper fax machine has dramatically facilitated the ease with which documents can be transferred. As a result, librarians must exercise greater caution than ever before regarding copyright compliance. Neither I nor my employer advocate violating current copyright laws under any circumstances let alone for the sake of speedy access. Publishers must receive appropriate recompense; if abuses become evident, fax access and document delivery by any mode will be denied.

## REFERENCE

Ardis, Susan B.; Croneis, Karen S. Document delivery, cost containment, and serial ownership. *College and Research Libraries News.* 48:624-627; November 1987.

APPENDIX I

PUBLISHED OR STATED POLICIES OF SELECTED VENDORS

CHEMICAL ABSTRACTS DOCUMENT DELIVERY SERVICE

| | |
|---|---|
| Method of Request | Mail - 24 hours<br>Phone - 6:30a - 11p (M-F)<br>Fax - 24 hours<br>Online - 24 hours (DIALOG, OCLC, STN, ESA-IRS) |
| Basic Services | --Basic document through STN (up to 25 pages).....................$10.00<br>--Basic document with CA or CIN Accession No. using any method of request other than STN......... $14.00<br>--Basic document requested with information other than above...... $18.00<br>--Each document over 25 pages*....... $3.00<br>--Facsimile documents*............... $8.00<br>--Special Delivery*.................. $8.00<br>--Same day service ordered between 1:00p-3:00p EST*........... $5.00 |
| Additional Charges and Special Services | --Loan of an available item+*........ $3.00<br>--Loan of item not immediately available* (loan queue)............ $5.00<br>--Return call on status of an order.. $3.00<br>--Cancellation of an order in process.............................. $3.00<br><br>+*CAS will cut and loan those documents that cannot be photocopied because of copyright restrictions. |
| Coverage | --Covers almost anything that can be found in Chemical Abstracts (CA) since 1975.<br>--Covers Soviet journals in CA since the 1970's<br>--Covers American Chemical Society journals back to the 1800's. |
| Turnaround Time, Billing, Problems, and Limitations | Turnaround: Rush or Regular - 24 hours and Same Day before 3:00pm EST (Additional 2-3 days for documents older than 10 years)<br>Billing: Monthly invoices<br>Problems: Call 1-800-848-6538 |

\* This charge is in addition to the "basic document" cost.

## APPENDIX II

## PUBLISHED OR STATED POLICIES OF SELECTED VENDORS

### GENUINE ARTICLE

| | |
|---|---|
| Method of Request | Mail - 24 hours<br>Phone - 24 hours<br>Fax - 24 hours<br>Online - 24 hours (DIALOG, ORBIT, BRS, DIMDI, CLASS, OCLC) |
| Basic Services | --Basic document (up to 10 pages)....$10.70<br><br>--Each additional 10 pages........... $2.60<br><br>--30-Minute Facsimile documents<br>(up to 10 pages)*................. $10.50<br><br>--24 Hour*........................ $4.00<br><br>--48 Hour Facsimile documents<br>(up to 10 pages)*................. $6.75<br><br>--Special Delivery* (overnight),<br>per order......$11.00 |
| Additional Charges and Special Services | --Publisher copyright royalties..... Varies by item<br>--Extended Service (3-5 Days)<br>(Items older than 5 Years)*........ $7.75<br><br>--Hotline Telephone Service*......... $4.00<br><br>--Discounts for Account Customers |
| Coverage | --Can access almost 7,000 journals from hundreds of subject areas.<br><br>--Covers almost anything that can be found in Current Contents, Social Science Index, Science Citation Index, or the ISI Database. |
| Turnaround Time, Billing, Problems, and Limitations | Turnaround: Rush - 30 min., 24-48 Hours<br>Regular - 48 Hours<br>(Additional 3-5 Days for items older than 5 years)<br>Billing: Prepay for mail order items<br>Prepay through credit<br>Monthly invoices<br>Deposit accounts<br>Problems: Call 1-800-523-1850 |

\* This charge is in addition to the "basic document" cost.

APPENDIX III

PUBLISHED OR STATED POLICIES OF SELECTED VENDORS

ENGINEERING INFORMATION

| | |
|---|---|
| Method of Request | Mail - 24 hours<br>Phone - 8:30a - 4:30p (M-F)<br>Fax - 24 hours<br>Online - 24 hours (STN, DIALOG, ORBIT, ESA/IRS, RLIN) |
| Basic Services | --Basic document (up to 20 pages).....$16.00<br><br>--Each additional page over 20........$ .40<br><br>--Facsimile documents up to 10 pages*.$ 5.00<br><br>--Facsimile documents over 10 pages*. $ .50 per page<br><br>--Special Delivery*.......... Billed at cost<br><br>--Rush Service - Same Day*........... $15.00<br><br>--Rush Service - Next Day*........... $10.00 |
| Additional Charges and Special Services | --Publisher copyright royalties...Over $3.00 Billed at cost<br><br>--Orders through RLIN...... 40% discount on basic document |
| Coverage | --Covers almost anything that can be found in the Engineering Index and COMPENDEX*PLUS. |
| Turnaround Time, Billing, Problems, and Limitations | Turnaround: Rush - Same day, 24 Hours<br>Regular - 7 Days<br><br>Billing: Prepay all orders.<br>(RLIN orders billed on delivery)<br><br>Deposit Accounts<br><br>Problems: Call 1-800-221-1044 |

\* This charge is in addition to the "basic document" cost.

## APPENDIX IV

## PUBLISHED OR STATED POLICIES OF SELECTED VENDORS

### ARTICLE CLEARINGHOUSE

| | |
|---|---|
| Method of Request | Mail - 24 hours<br>Phone - 24 hours - 8:00a-5:00p EST<br>Fax - 24 hours<br>Online - 24 hours (DIALOG, OCLC, TYMENET) |
| Basic Services | --Basic document......................$11.75<br><br>--Facsimile documents up to 20 pages*..$9.00<br><br>--Each additional page over 20*.........$.30<br><br>--Rush 1st Class      per article*....$5.00<br><br>--Rush Overnight      per article*....$5.00<br>                              per package*...$10.00 |
| Additional Charges and Special Services | --Multiple copies......................$2.25<br>                   each, up to 49 copies<br>                 discount/over 50 copies<br><br>--Entire Journal issue............... $45.00<br><br>--American Society for Testing and<br>  Materials Standards............... $14.75<br><br>--Discounts for Account Customers. |
| Coverage | --Covers more than 12,000 titles - scholarly and technical journals, popular magazines, conference proceedings, and transactions, newspapers, and government documents dealing with a wide range of subjects. |
| Turnaround Time, Billing, Problems, and Limitations | Turnaround:   Standard - 48 Hours<br>                Does not apply to items older than 5 years which may take 4 days.<br><br>                Rush 1st Class - Same Day<br>                Rush Overnight - Same Day<br>                Fax Delivery - Same Day<br><br>Billing:      Monthly invoices<br><br>Problems:    Call 1-800-521-0600 |

* This charge is in addition to the "basic document" cost.

APPENDIX V

PUBLISHED OR STATED POLICIES OF SELECTED VENDORS

GEOREF

| | |
|---|---|
| Method of Request | Mail - 24 hours<br>Phone - 24 hours<br>Fax - 24 hours<br>Online - 24 hours (DIALOG, ORBIT, STN) |
| Basic Services | --Basic document up to 12 pages..... $14.00<br>--Each additional page over 12*..... $ .25<br>--Rush documents (Express charges not included)*..........$8.00<br>--Special Delivery*.................. At cost |
| Additional Charges and Special Services | --Publisher copyright royalties.... At cost<br>--Map copying..............per sq.ft. $1.30<br>--Unfilled order.................... $3.00 |
| Coverage | --Covers whatever can be found in the GeoRef database, Engineering Geology Abstracts, or the Bibliography and Index of Geology. |
| Turnaround Time, Billing, Problems, and Limitations | Turnaround: Rush - 24 Hours<br>            Regular - 2-3 Weeks<br>(Additional time for items over 10 years)<br><br>Billing: Billed upon delivery<br>        Monthly invoices<br>        Deposit Accounts<br><br>Problems: Call 1-800-336-4764<br><br>Limitations: Will not fax articles except in rare cases. |

\* This charge is in addition to the "basic document" cost.

## APPENDIX VI

## PUBLISHED OR STATED POLICIES OF SELECTED VENDORS

### MATHDOC

| | |
|---|---|
| Method of Request | Mail - 24 hours<br>Phone - 7:30a - 5:00p (M-F)<br>Fax - 24 hours<br>Online - 24 hours (DIALOG, E-MAIL) |
| Basic Services | --Basic document up to 10 pages...... $14.00<br>--Each additional 10 pages or less.... $2.50<br>--Facsimile document..........per page $ .50<br>--Special Delivery*................. At cost |
| Additional Charges and Special Services | --Publisher copyright royalties.....At cost |
| Coverage | --Covers whatever can be found in Current Mathematical Publications, Mathematical Reviews, and MathSci database. |
| Turnaround Time, Billing, Problems, and Limitations | Turnaround:  Rush - 24 Hours<br>      Regular - 3 days<br>Billing:   Billed upon delivery<br>      (5% discount on prepay through VISA/Mastercard)<br>Problems:  Call 1-313-996-5268 |

\* This charge is in addition to the "basic document" cost.

APPENDIX VII

PUBLISHED OR STATED POLICIES OF SELECTED VENDORS

ENGINEERING SOCIETIES LIBRARY

| | |
|---|---|
| Method of Request | Mail - 24 hours<br>Phone - 9:00a - 4:30p (M-F)<br>Fax - 24 hours<br>Online - 24 hours (OCLC, DIALORDER, MCI) |
| Basic Services | --Basic document up to 15 pages...... $15.00<br>--Each additional page*............... $ .40<br>--Rush service (next day)*........... $10.00<br>--Drop everything service (3 hours)* $100.00<br>--Fax Delivery (first 10 pages)*..... $20.00<br>--Each additional set of 10 faxed pages*.... $ 5.00<br>--Special Delivery*................. At cost |
| Additional Charges and Special Services | --Publisher copyright royalties at cost<br>--Discounts for members and account customers. |
| Coverage | --Covers almost anything that can be found in the Engineering Index. ESL is a depository for the publications of many engineering societies and collects heavily in standards, conference proceedings and other hard-to-find materials. |
| Turnaround Time, Billing, Problems, and Limitations | Turnaround: Rush - 3-24 Hours<br>Regular - 3 to 5 Days<br>Billing: Billed upon delivery<br>Deposit accounts<br>Problems: Call 1-212-705-7606 |

\* This charge is in addition to the "basic document" cost.

## APPENDIX VIII

### PUBLISHED OR STATED POLICIES OF SELECTED VENDORS

#### JOHN CRERAR LIBRARY

| | |
|---|---|
| Method of Request | Mail - 24 hours<br>Phone - 8:30a - 5:00p (M-F)<br>Fax - 24 hours<br>Online - 24 hours (OCLC, DOCLINE) |
| Basic Services | --Basic document up to 25 pages..... $ 7.50<br><br>--Each additional 25 pages........... $2.00<br><br>--Facsimile documents*............... $4.50<br><br>--Rush 1st Class*........per article..$3.00<br><br>--Special Delivery*.................At cost |
| Additional Charges and Special Services | --Publisher copyright royalties.......$2.00<br>  Special service to handle surcharge on all documents.<br><br>--They will handle copyright royalties for a customer. A service account must be established that is applied across the board to all documents ordered.<br><br>--Discounts for members |
| Coverage | --Contains over one million volumes covering a broad range of scientific, technical and medical interests.<br><br>--Can access over 48,000 currently received journals of the entire University of Chicago Libraries. |
| Turnaround Time, Billing, Problems, and Limitations | Turnaround:   Rush FCM - 24-36 Hours<br>               Rush Fax - 4-24 Hours<br>               Regular - 5-7 Days<br><br>Billing:     Billed upon delivery<br>           Deposit accounts<br><br>Problems:   Call 1-312-702-7031 |

\* This charge is in addition to the "basic document" cost.

## APPENDIX IX

## PUBLISHED OR STATED POLICIES OF SELECTED VENDORS

### LINDA HALL LIBRARY

| | |
|---|---|
| Method of Request | Mail - 24 hours<br>Phone - 9:00a - 5:00p (M-F)<br>Fax - 24 hours<br>Online - 24 hours (OCLC) |
| Basic Services | --Basic document-postage and handling..$4.00<br><br>--Hard copy item, per page*........... $ .50<br><br>--Microform item, per page*.......... $ .60<br><br>--Facsimile documents*................$10.00<br>          per item each page*..... $1.00<br><br>--Rush Mail sent within 24 hours (FCM) $9.00<br>  per article. Includes base price. |
| Additional Charges and Special Services | --Telephone Orders (Rush) per item.... $5.00<br><br>--Estimates, per item..................$3.00<br><br>--Fold-out maps, charts, oversize prints,<br>  etc., each........................ $2.00<br><br>--Minimum charge, per item............ $6.00<br><br>--Minimum charge for fax item........ $15.00 |
| Coverage | --Covers much of the literature related to Science and Technology except for medical, clinical, dental, nursing, and psychology.<br><br>--Covers back to the beginning of most journals that they cover. |
| Turnaround Time, Billing, Problems, and Limitations | Turnaround: Rush - 24 Hours<br>            Regular - 3-5 working days<br><br>Billing: Billed upon delivery<br>       Fax order invoices-next day<br><br>Problems: Call 1-816-363-4600<br><br>Limitations: Do not handle copyright royalites |

\* This charge is in addition to the "basic document" cost.

For Product Safety Concerns and Information please contact our EU
representative GPSR@taylorandfrancis.com
Taylor & Francis Verlag GmbH, Kaufingerstraße 24, 80331 München, Germany

www.ingramcontent.com/pod-product-compliance
Lightning Source LLC
Chambersburg PA
CBHW071822300426
44116CB00009B/1398